MR CHARLOTTE BRONTË

Mr Charlotte Brontë

The Life of Arthur Bell Nicholls

ALAN H. ADAMSON

McGill-Queen's University Press
Montreal & Kingston · London · Ithaca

ISBN 978-0-7735-3365-3

Legal deposit first quarter 2008
Bibliothèque nationale du Québec

Printed in Canada on acid-free paper that is 100% ancient forest free (100% post-consumer recycled), processed chlorine free.

This book has been published with the help of a grant from the Canadian Federation fo the Humanities and Social Sciences, through the Aid to Scholarly Publications Programme, using funds provided by the Social Sciences and Humanities Research Council of Canada.

McGill-Queen's University Press acknowledges the support of the Canada Council for the Arts for our publishing program. We also acknowledge the financial support of the Government of Canada through the Book Publishing Industry Development Program (BPIDP) for our publishing activities.

Library and Archives Canada Cataloguing in Publication

Adamson, Alan H

Mr. Charlotte Brontë: the life of Arthur Bell Nicholls / Alan H. Adamson.

Includes bibliographical references and index.
ISBN 978-0-7735-3365-3

1. Nicholls, Arthur Bell, 1819-1906. 2. Brontë, Charlotte, 1816-1855 – Marriage. 3. Authors' spouses – England – Biography. 4. Executors and administrators – England – Biography. I. Title.

PR4168.A62 2008 823'.8 C2007-907025-6

Typeset in Adobe Garamond 11/13.5
by Infoscan Collette, Quebec City

For Nicholas,
in response to his many questions

Contents

Abbreviations

NAMES

ABN	Arthur Bell Nicholls
CB	Charlotte Brontë
CKS	Clement K. Shorter
ECG	Elizabeth Cleghorn Gaskell (Mrs Gaskell)
EN	Ellen Nussey
GS	George Smith
HM	Harriet Martineau
MW	Margaret Wooler
PB	Patrick Brontë

BOOKS, JOURNALS, ETC.

ABN/MARTHA	Letters of Arthur Bell Nicholls to Martha Brown.
BST	Brontë Society, *Transactions* –. Haworth, 1895. Citations are given by volume, part, and page number, e.g., BST, 14:83:100.
BPM	Brontë Parsonage Museum.
Bell, F.E.	*A Hundred Years of Life* (n.p., n.d.)
Bell, H.K.	"Charlotte Brontë's Husband: His Later Life and Surroundings," *The Cornhill Magazine*, January 1927.

C and P	Chapple, J.A.V. and Arthur Pollard, eds. *The Letters of Mrs Gaskell.* Manchester, 1966.
Cochrane	Cochrane, Margaret and Robert, *My Dear Boy.* Beverley, 1999.
Edgerley	C. Mabel Edgerley, "The Rev. Arthur Bell Nicholls," BST 10:52.
Gérin	Winifred Gérin, *Charlotte Brontë: the Evolution of Genius.* Oxford, 1967.
JB	Juliet Barker. *The Brontës.* London, 1995.
L and D	John Lock and W.T. Dixon. *A Man of Sorrow: the Life, Letters and Times of the Rev Patrick Brontë.* London, 1965.
LCB	*The Letters of Charlotte Brontë,* ed. Margaret Smith, 3 vols. Oxford, 1995, 2000 and 2004.
LG	Lyndall Gordon. *Charlotte Brontë: a Passionate Life.* London, 1994.
Life	Elizabeth Cleghorn Gaskell. *The Life of Charlotte Brontë.* London, 1971. This edition follows the text of the unexpurgated first and second editions of 1857.
P.P.	Great Britain: Parliamentary Papers.
Quane	Michael Quane. "Banagher Royal School," *North Munster Antiquarian Journal.* 10:2, 1967.
Shorter	Clement K. Shorter. *Charlotte Brontë & Her Circle.* London, 1896.
Smith	Margaret Smith. Introduction to *The Letters of Charlotte Brontë,* vol. 1, 1829–1847. Oxford, 1995.
TCD	Trinity College, Dublin
Wilks	Brian Wilks. *Charlotte in Love: The Courtship and Marriage of Charlotte Brontë.* London, 1998.
W and S	T.J. Wise and J.A. Symington, eds. *The Lives, Friendships and Correspondence of the Bronte Family,* 4 vols. Oxford, 1933.

Acknowledgments

This book could not have been written without the nourishment of previous Brontë scholarship. I have been particularly indebted to the following writers: Juliet Barker, Margaret and Robert Cochrane, Rebecca Fraser, Winifred Gérin, Lyndall Gordon, Margaret Smith, Brian Wilks, and Tom Winnifrith. These authors are all contemporary; it would be churlish not to pay homage as well to Mrs Gaskell, whose work, despite its inaccuracies and distortions, was the initial source of my interest in the Brontës and in Arthur Bell Nicholls.

I am grateful to the Brontë Parsonage Museum for making available several photographs, for permission to quote from the letters of Arthur Bell Nicholls to Martha Brown, and for their unfailing cooperation in response to my many queries. For permission to quote from manuscript material in their possession, I gratefully acknowledge the following: John Murray, publishers (Ellen Nussey's and Arthur Bell Nicholls' letters to George Smith in the Smith Elder archive); Leeds University Library, Brotherton Collection (Arthur Bell Nicholls' letters to C.K. Shorter); and the University of Birmingham Library (the Arthur Bell Nicholls/ Patrick Brontë/Harriet Martineau correspondence in the Harriet Martineau collection). I am also grateful for the help of the British Library and the libraries of Concordia and McGill Universities, Montreal.

I have called on the help of many individuals, especially the following: David Adamson, Nigel Gallop, and Joyce Hart, who gave me access to their material on the Bell, Nicholls and Adamson families in Ireland; Christine Alexander, for her critical comments on an early draft; and Judith Adamson, for her encouragement, careful reading, and valuable suggestions.

Preface

Few people seeking to avoid the glare of notoriety have had more of it thrust upon them than Arthur Bell Nicholls. This can hardly be ascribed to any notable achievements on his part except one: he married Charlotte Brontë. "Reader," he might have crowed, "I married her!" But being always a retiring, private person, he would have murmured it only to himself. Partly on this account he has been treated in the voluminous Brontë literature often with condescension, sometimes with ill-disguised contempt. More than one critic has implied that Charlotte's decision to marry Arthur Nicholls doomed her writing career. There have even been suggestions that by dragging her out for a long walk which ended in a cold, drenching rain he may – albeit inadvertently – have caused her death. It is only in the comparatively recent work of scholars such as Juliet Barker, Margaret and Robert Cochrane, Rebecca Fraser, Winifred Gérin, Lyndall Gordon, Margaret Smith, and Tom Winnifrith that a more balanced view of his role in the Brontë saga has been established. Thanks largely to them, his life has now acquired an independent interest aside from its subaltern role in literary history. Still, with the exception of *My Dear Boy* by Margaret and Robert Cochrane, mine is the only account of Arthur's life with the focus on him, rather than on Charlotte or Patrick Brontë, Mrs Gaskell or George Smith. Although I have inevitably covered the same material as the Cochranes, there are significant differences of content and emphasis which distinguish my work from theirs, and although I have made extensive use of material already in print, readers familiar with the Brontë story will find much that is new in this book.

Martha Brown, daughter of Arthur's landlord, John Brown, and a domestic servant in the Brontë household, once told Charlotte she hated Arthur, yet when he returned to Ireland in 1861 she spent many years there and even put her finances in his hands. Charlotte herself, who was cool and often hostile to him in the early period of his curacy at Haworth, gradually came to respect, marry, and finally to love him. What kind of man could produce these radical changes of opinion and feeling?

This book will argue that a good part of the answer to that question lies in Arthur's early development in Ireland. There is fresh information here concerning the Bells of Banagher, Arthur's adoptive family, and the Banagher Royal School where he received his pre-university education. I have tried to show how certain traumatic experiences in these early Irish years influenced Arthur's psychological and intellectual formation and how these in turn affected his religious outlook. The second phase of his life, the critical sixteen years of his curacy at Haworth, is an oft-told story in which Arthur usually plays an important but secondary part. In presenting him as the central rather than as a subordinate figure, I have reinterpreted as well his relations with all the other major players in the Brontë drama – Charlotte and Patrick of course, but also Ellen Nussey, Mrs Gaskell, George Smith, Harriet Martineau, Thomas Wemyss Reid, Clement Shorter, and T.J. Wise. Finally, using family material in my own possession, I have described the third period of his life from 1861 to 1906 more fully than has previously been done. With the benefit of this new material, I trust the reader will be able to construct a fair portrait of someone who struck those who knew him intimately as a naturally loveable man, one whom Charlotte Brontë came to think of as "my dear boy."

Arthur Bell Nicholl's adoptive mother,
Harriette Lucinda Bell

Cuba House as Arthur knew it. The school building is on the right.
(Courtesy the Brontë Society)

The remains of Cuba House

Arthur as Charlotte knew him
(Courtesy the Brontë Society)

Haworth parsonage in Arthur's time (Courtesy the Brontë Society)

Patrick Brontë (Courtesy the Brontë Society)

Charlotte Brontë, from the oil painting
by J.H. Thompson (Courtesy the Brontë Society)

Mary Anna Bell Nicholls, Arthur's second wife
(Courtesy the Brontë Society)

Martha Brown (Courtesy the Brontë Society)

Clement Shorter (Courtesy the Brontë Society)

Ellen Nussey (Courtesy the Brontë Society)

Arthur talking to a friend in Banagher, c. 1904
(Courtesy the Brontë Society)

Arthur in old age (Courtesy the Brontë Society)

The Hill House, Banagher: Arthur's extension is on the left (Courtesy the Brontë Society)

Kill House, near Clifden in Connemara. Arthur's cousin, Harriette Bell, who turned down his proposal in 1851, with her husband, John Evans Adamson, and six of their seven children, c. 1868

Arthur's grave, St Paul's Churchyard, Banagher

Alan Adamson and son, Nicholas, on the steps of Cuba House

William Nichol = Margaret Bell

Anna Maria (1809)
Eliza (1812)
William (1813)
George (1814)
Alan (1816)
Arthur Bell (6 January 1818 or 1819) → Arthur Bell Nicholls (widower of Charlotte Brontë) 1818–1906) = Mary Anna (1830–1915)
Jane (b. ?)
Margaret (1821)
Susan (1822)
Richard (1827)

Arthur Christopher (1856–1917) = Edith Moore

10 children

2 sons (died in infancy)
William Alan (1882–1885)
John Evans (1884–1961)
Robert (1885–1905)

Rev. Dr. Alan Clerke Bell = Harriette Lucinda Adamson
(1789–1839) (1801–1902)

Harriette = John Evans Adamson
(1833–1911) (1822–1869)

Alan (1821–1868)
Susan (1823–184[illegible])
James (1826–1891)
Arthur (1828–1891)
Joseph (1831–1891)
Frances (1835–1850)
William (1839–1870)

Alan Joseph = Julia McAllister Turriff
(1857–1928) (1857–1925)

5 other children

Christopher Arthur (1887–1940)

Alan Bell (1885–1965)

James Douglas (1890–1965)

Lily Jane (1891–1967)

Herbert (1894–1984)

Hariette Bell (1898–1967)

Gilbert Logie (1901–1985)

MR CHARLOTTE BRONTË

CHAPTER ONE

The Irish Background

One summer evening in 1825, three people were holding a family conference in a farmstead kitchen in Killead, County Antrim. The matter was painful, though not uncommon in an era of high birth rates. The farmer William Nichol[1] and his wife, Margaret, had been notably prolific. In sixteen years Margaret had given birth to nine children, and she would have one more in 1827.[2] Their farm, Tully, kept the family in food and clothing, but beyond that William's resources were limited. Hence the matter under discussion: what was to become of that numerous family brood?

The future of the five daughters was quickly disposed of: they would marry or go into some kind of service. As well, Margaret and William had determined that the oldest boy, William, Jr, would inherit Tully and perhaps share it with George, the next in line, if he could find some way of adding to his acreage. And indeed, that was what occurred. William and George spent the rest of their lives as Tully farmers. But that still left the two younger boys, Alan, then aged nine, and Arthur, seven. What was to become of them?

The third member of that conference was Margaret Nicholls' brother, the Rev. Alan Clerke Bell (1789–1839). The Bells had roots in Glenavy, on the edge of Lough Neagh west of Belfast, where a tombstone marks the grave of an Alan Bell who died in 1722 at the age of one hundred.[3] Both families had come to Ireland from Scotland in the seventeenth century, but while William Nicholls was Presbyterian, the Bells belonged to the Established church. Alan Bell's father was also a farmer but he must have been more prosperous than his son-in-law, for he was able to send young Alan to Trinity College Dublin where he earned a BA in 1814. Later, in 1832, Glasgow University awarded him an LLD. Having taken holy orders, Bell began his clerical career as rector of Glenavy, his home parish, but he soon moved from the cure of souls to the more rigorous enterprise of disciplining the minds and bodies of young boys. By 1819 he was master of a classical school at Downpatrick on Strangford Lough, and at the time of the family conference, he was master of the Royal Free School at Banagher, King's County (present-day County Offaly).

Bell proposed a solution to the Nicholls' problem. He offered to take Alan and Arthur to Banagher, where he would bring them up as part of his own family and where they would receive an education in his own school. It was a generous offer, though surely a painful one for Margaret, softened perhaps by the company of her seven remaining children – an eighth would follow in 1827. Before the night was out an agreement was reached, and the next morning the two little boys set off with their uncle. They never saw their parents again. Their mother ("poor animal," Jane Austen would have called her) died in 1830, worn out by hard domestic and biological labour. Their father died in 1849 at the age of eighty.[4]

Banagher stands on the east bank of the Shannon just as the river turns south-west to flow into the Atlantic. It is an ancient settlement whose strategic location commands the crossing to and from Connaught. The MacCoghlan clan maintained a stronghold at Garry Castle, one and a half miles south-east. The remains of the twelfth-century Cloghan Castle lie two miles south, while four miles to the east are those of Clonony Castle, associated with the Boleyn family. In those days it was a pleasant market and post-town (Anthony Trollope was stationed there as deputy postal surveyor between 1841 and 1845), with a population that had grown from 1,800 at the beginning of the century to some 2,700 in 1825. It would reach its peak of 3,000 in 1846, only to sink back after the famine, to around 1,200 in 1871.

Its principal street, running from the river up a steep hill, was lined with "good and tolerable dwellings," while "several villas, some wood and much cultivation in the environs … produce a sense of cheerfulness in a stranger." Its rapidly rising pre-famine population reflected a thriving economy with two tan-yards, a distillery, a brewery and a corn-mill, but its main claim to fame was the annual Banagher "Great Fair," a four-day festival beginning September fifteenth. It was the largest fair of its kind in the Irish Midlands, one "at which everything from cattle and sheep to boots and basket chairs was on sale."[5] There was a more genteel market in human flesh as well. According to H.K. Bell, a child watching the proceedings from the top of the hill heard one farmer exclaim to another: "Banagher's the greatest place for match-making ever ye saw! Ladies comes to the best hotel and brings their daughters or their nieces, and when they meet a man with a fine place, *don't* they cock him up!" In the midst of this press of men, women, and children, a poor but enterprizing old lady took advantage of the lack of toilet facilities, plying "the thronged streets with a billy-can, shouting 'Cack in me can – cack in me can, young man!'"[6]

Bell and his nephews arrived in the middle of July when the town was still asleep. No old woman invited them to "cack in her can" as a servant drove them through the centre of town. Just on the outskirts they drove up a steep hill then, almost at the top, they passed through a set of imposing iron gates and up a long avenue of ancient limes, at the end of which stood Cuba House, their new home. Standing on the front steps to welcome them was Alan Bell's wife, Harriette Lucinda (1801–1902), the young woman who was to be the two boys' adoptive mother.

Bell had met her in 1818 when, still a lowly cleric in Glenavy, he had been invited by her father James Adamson (1774–1824), to take his summer holidays in Bray, County Wicklow. Adamson was to play an important role in the young clergyman's career. He was secretary of The Incorporated Society for Promoting English Protestant Schools in Ireland. Usually known as "The Charter Society," a charitable organization founded in 1733 whose aim was to rescue lower-class Irish children from the ideological grip of the Catholic Church, it has been described by a modern historian as a "Taj Mahal built on quicksand, the elaborate central administration swallowed up by incompetence and abuse."[7] One of its most dubious practices was transplanting children to localities distant from their families so that they would not relapse into Catholicism when they left the Protestant schools. However ineffective, the society disposed of considerable sums of money, its grants averaging about £20,000 in the first years of the nineteenth century, reaching a peak of £38,000 in 1818. As secretary during this period, James Adamson was in a position to wield some influence in the Irish educational world.[8]

Harriette was the apple of her father's eye. He enjoyed a comfortable private income so, when she was fourteen and he decided that she needed to be properly finished, he took her across St George's Channel to a boarding school in London. But finding life "quite insupportable without his little daughter," after three weeks he made the long trip back to London to bring her home. London left a deep impression on young Harriette. The Battle of Waterloo had just taken place and she remembered seeing the city illuminated in celebration of the victory. She remembered too an unannounced visit of Queen Charlotte. Perhaps because of her Dublin accent Harriette was regarded as something of an exotic specimen, and the queen asked especially to see "the little Irish girl." In later years, Harriette would always complete the account of her London experience by observing that, in three short weeks, she had "learned to speak High English": a strange remark in our day, when Dublin's Trinity College accent is argued by many to be the purest English in the world.

Whatever Harriette's accent, she impressed Charlotte Brontë in 1854 as just like "an English or Scotch Matron quiet, kind and well-bred." Although it was said of her "that she had never struck a match in her life and had never put coals upon the fire," she managed to rear eleven children, nine of her own plus the two adopted Nichol nephews, and to run Cuba House once Alan Bell became headmaster of the Royal Free School situated there. As capable women often did, she also managed to find time to be "a great reader, an expert needlewoman, a pianist, and a keen gardener."

When Alan Bell first met her in 1818, however, she was not yet this formidable matron. Young, "vivacious and captivating," her vivacity quickly captivated the young clergyman, who wasted no time in proposing to her. They were married in 1820 and according to family legend, when they returned from their honeymoon Harriette's favourite dog, Fairy, proved that she was as attractive to animals as to man by expiring "in a fit of absolute joy." Harriette was subsequently accused of marrying an old man for his money, although the age difference would not then have been considered that great, nor was Bell a wealthy man.[9]

Although James Adamson did not oppose the marriage, he missed his daughter when she went off with her husband to his school in distant Downpatrick. The pain of her absence was sharpened by the death of his own wife while Harriette and Alan were on their honeymoon. And he found himself physically isolated as well, because Harriette's marriage and his wife's death had coincided with his retirement not only from his profession, but also from the excitement of Dublin's social and intellectual life, of which his York Street house had been an established part. He had bought an estate, Belle Vue, in the environs of Banagher and while Banagher may have been a pretty village, it was, after all, just a village. It offered little of what was then referred to as "society". In 1823, the town and its neighborhood boasted the following individuals listed as "Gentry and Clergy": eight army officers (a colonel, five captains, two lieutenants and one ensign); fifteen esquires; four clergymen; and a "Mrs Taylor". There were also John Fahy and Francis Molloy, owners of the celebrated passage boat known as "The Speed of Molloy."[10] After Dublin, this made for pretty thin pickings.

Finally, there was the Banagher Royal Free School just outside the village. This institution had a curious history or, more accurately, non-history.[11] Established by Charles I in 1628, it never had a pupil until 1806, when the newly established commissioners of Education appointed the Rev. Thomas Morris as master. Morris took a lease on two adjoining buildings in Banagher but the rent alone, just under £157, ate up virtually the entire profit from the lands with which the school had been endowed. There was simply nothing left over to cover stipends for Morris and any assistants he might wish to hire, not to mention the provision of *free* schooling that the charter had specified.

Since his only other income was a £50 curacy, Morris was left no choice but to charge fees. His rates were not cheap: the total for a boarder whose parents opted for all the extras (washing and mending, writing, arithmetic, stationery, French, and dancing) came to £62.4.0. Originally Morris planned to accept only boarders, but pressure from the town forced him to take in day boys as well. In his first year there were only seventeen boarders and fifteen day boys, but enrollment rose quickly. The average number of boarders between 1807 and 1817 was forty-five, the Shannon's cheap and convenient navigation providing the school with a catchment area which included north Kerry, Clare, Limerick, and north Tipperary. The pupils were sons of the gentry, almost all of them destined for Trinity College Dublin, Oxford or Cambridge. In fact, by 1814 the school's reputation was so high that most of his day scholars were not of local origin, but instead were the "sons of gentlemen of moderate means who have come to reside in Banagher for the convenience of being near the school."

Two problems threatened the school's future. Although Morris was not a young man he insisted, despite having four assistants, on reserving the upper class exclusively to himself, a teaching load "seriously detrimental to a constitution naturally delicate." Then the owner of the school buildings gave notice to terminate the lease. Morris had to search for alternative space. He found what he was looking for in Cuba House (or Court), overlooking Banagher and the Shannon below. Described by a modern architectural historian as "perhaps the most splendidly masculine house in the whole country," Cuba House might be said on that count alone to be ideal as the site of an institution designed to produce young Anglo-Irish gentlemen. It was a classic example of the double-pile plan already common in seventeenth-century England and introduced to Ireland by Sir Edward Lovett Pearce. "In its simplest form the plan is an arrangement of six rooms, with two ranges (or piles), each of three rooms, placed back to back."[12]

A triangular pediment above the central triple windows of the south front with its seven bays, and a matching pediment on the west front with its five bays, eased the building's otherwise uncompromising square-shouldered aspect. It was built around 1734 by a man called Fraser, who had made his fortune growing sugar in Cuba. Fraser having exhausted his wealth in the construction of the house, it fell into the hands of the Daly family, prominent members of the local ascendancy. In 1804, Dennis Bowes Daly rented Cuba House to the army medical board for use as a hospital, but since it was under-utilized, the board was happy to assign the building to the commissioners of Education. Morris took over in July 1817 and, after the commissioners had provided a loan of just under £300 to put the house in order, had every reason to feel the school had been given a new lease of life.

By then Morris was close to seventy, and his delicate health impelled him to find a new situation less demanding of his energy and financially more secure. Through influential connections he procured a rectory. That was a normal procedure at the time. What was not so normal was the way the next master succeeded him. Having first resigned, Morris sold the mastership and the school to Alan Bell for £1,000 in 1822. Apparently "it was the Secretary of the Commissioners who suggested it, and it was through him the arrangement was carried out."[13] But behind this questionable arrangement can be seen the influence of Arthur Bell's father-in-law, James Adamson. Though retired, he was still *au courant* with everything and everybody in Dublin who had anything to do with education, and must have seen Morris's difficulties as a heaven-sent means of solving some personal problems. His wife had just died, his sons were all fledged, and his beloved daughter was exiled to distant Downpatrick. Were his son-in-law to be installed as master of Cuba House, Harriette would be close by, and he could finally begin to enjoy his retirement. Unfortunately, his pleasure was to be short-lived; he died in 1824.

When the Nicholls boys arrived that sleepy July morning in 1825, there were only two young children in the Bell family: another Alan, four years old, and Susan, just two. A third baby was due the next year and six more would arrive before Alan Bell senior's death in 1839.[14] Unlike their own mother, Aunt Harriette appeared to thrive on the strenuous challenge of uninterrupted child bearing. Arthur and his brother had thus joined a family that grew to be even larger than the one they had left. Nonetheless the psychological effect of such a sudden and, it must have seemed to them, inexplicable separation from their own family, could only have been traumatic, although its impact appears to have been milder on the older boy. For Arthur, the consequences were deep, complex, and permanent: in adult life he was careful about exposing himself to strong personal attachments, but once having committed himself he tended to become deeply, even demandingly, attached to the object of his affection. This apparent contradiction in his personality between reserve and passion helps to account for the contradictory impressions he made on those with whom he came in contact, some reacting negatively to what they took to be his rigidity, others valuing the depth of his feelings, still others, such as Mrs Gaskell, Patrick Brontë, and Charlotte herself, responding at different periods to one side or the other of his character.

Their new school must have been another shock. They would enjoy – or more appropriately be subjected to – the Anglo-Irish equivalent of an English public school education. Both boys were entered as scholars in the fall term at the Royal Free School. Since much was later to be made by Charlotte of Arthur's limited intellectual horizon, the precise content of the Banagher curriculum is worth examining. In 1836, the Rev. Bell (also Dr after receiving an LLD from Glasgow University in 1832) told a select committee that it included Latin and Greek, French and English, Algebra, Euclid, Arithmetic, Geography, and English History. The idea of teaching Irish History would have been regarded as bizarre.

However, to get a fuller picture of the sort of education Arthur received we must turn to the Rev. Morris's "System of Education" as he described it in 1814, since this was basically the same course of study still followed in 1825. It was assumed that at the usual age of entry (eight to ten years old) a boy would be sufficiently "well taught in Reading and Spelling as to admit his being put immediately to the study of Latin Grammar" and he would be kept at this discipline "until an accurate knowledge of the principles is attained."

From 6 to 9 a.m. a pupil in the first class was taught reading and spelling by the English assistant; from 10 to 11 and again until 2 in the afternoon, parsing by the classical assistants; after that arithmetic and Latin writing, in which the rules of syntax were illustrated "by constantly repeated exercises (which are never wholly discontinued during the course of school education)." The second class continued with grammar exercises, including verb formations through all their inflections. In the third, the students read Ovid, Burrowe's *Schola*, and Nepos, and began to study Greek grammar and prosody. "In the course of this year they read the Gospels of John and Luke and write exercises from long sentences of Clarke's *Introduction to Latin Grammar*, accompanied by Latin Verses, Hexameter and Pentameter, but at first constructed with regard only to the rules of Prosody." In the fourth class "they read Virgil, Caesar, the Acts of the Apostles and *Lucian's Short Dialogues* and their morning exercises are taken partly from Clarke's Greek and Roman History and latterly from Goldsmith's Roman History, which they translate into Latin … They now also begin the study of the astronomical part of *Sharman's Geography* … In the Fifth Class they read the odes, satires and epistles of Horace, Sallust, the Long Dialogues of Lucian and Epictetus. They also write themes on Monday in English, which they translate on the following day into Latin … During Vacations they are required to translate certain portions of Psalms into Latin Verse." Finally, in the sixth class the boys read Homer, Juvenal and Terence, were introduced to Hebrew Grammar, and went through Elrington's *Euclid* and Murray's *Logic*.[15]

On paper the curriculum appears rigorous, even daunting, to modern eyes. But it was not all parsing, conjugating, and construing Latin and Greek texts. Oscar Wilde's father William, who was at the school in the 1820s, spent more of his schooldays betting on cockfights and fly-fishing with Paddy Walsh than at his studies.[16] Arthur himself might now and again have gone absent without leave, for it was in the countryside around Banagher that he developed his love of long walks, usually accompanied by one of the Bell dogs that he trained to point grouse and pheasant without himself becoming a huntsman; and it was in the streams running into the Shannon that he learned to catch trout always by hand, never angling. But one can only suppose that he was an infrequent truant, for once he crossed the invisible border between Cuba House and the adjacent school building the fact that he was part of the master's family would have subjected him, *a fortiori*, to school discipline.

In any case, for the next ten years Arthur worked his way through his uncle's scholastic obstacle course successfully enough to be admitted as a pensioner to Trinity College Dublin on 4 July 1836, still styling himself "Nichols" rather than "Nicholls." The entrance exam provides a good idea of what had been instilled into him under his uncle's tutelage: candidates were required to display their knowledge of eight books of Homer's *Iliad*, as well as works by Virgil, Sallust, Livy, Terence, and Lucian, plus the four Gospels and Acts.[17] Less interested in scholarly matters, his brother Alan had already completed his schooling in Banagher and had gone straight into commerce, where he had a successful career. He was the manager of the Grand Canal Company linking Dublin with the Shannon when Charlotte Brontë met him in Dublin on her honeymoon in 1854. She found him "a sagacious, well-informed and courteous man." He later became a successful shipping agent; so successful that when he died on holiday in Paris in 1890, he left a considerable estate for his two daughters, Ellen and Charlotte Brontë Nicholls.[18]

Arthur's road would not be so smooth. He had barely completed his first year at Trinity College Dublin when his uncle called him back to Cuba House as classical master at an annual salary of £50. This would seem to indicate that in Dr Bell's eyes, Arthur was a competent scholar, but it might just as well argue his uncle's parsimony. From a financial point of view the affairs of the school had not been going well. Bell had invested £1,000 in the school when he took it over and he expected a decent return on his investment. An outbreak of cholera in 1834–35, followed by typhus, had devastated Banagher and seriously affected enrollment at the school. He himself had nearly died although no one else in the family seems to have been infected. In a fit of cost-cutting, or profit maximization, or both, Bell had then reduced the number of assistant masters from four to two. Arthur was an inexpensive replacement, and from 1837 to 1839 he labored faithfully in his uncle's vineyard.

It was a rigorous training for a young man involving the multiple tasks of course preparation, classroom teaching, grading, and the never-ending problem of imposing order on boys ranging in age from eight to eighteen years old. Bell himself tried to govern the school like a Scottish *dominie*; one ex-pupil, in the only direct reference that has survived, described him as "of ugly aspect," but whether this refers to his face or his manner is not clear.[19] Whatever his aspect, he was no longer a well man. A chronic asthmatic, he had been greatly weakened in the cholera-typhus epidemic and he was not fully recovered even three years later when a second disaster occurred. On the night of 6 January 1839 Banagher, along with several other parts of Ireland, was struck by what was later known as "The Big Wind." Bell left the following account of its effect on Cuba House.

> This house suffered great damage from the storm last night. About nine o'clock the wind commenced and it continued to increase till about twelve o'clock, when it ceased for about twenty minutes … then it began more furiously carrying everything with it – slates, glass, &c. from windows in the house, and one in the school-room has [sic] been driven in totally and the wood broken. In the front of the School-room one hundred and thirty-one panes broken; in the house between sixty and seventy. Part of the wall between the schoolyard and the playground with the door and door frame were blown into the schoolyard. Two doors and their frames of the offices were blown out and broken into pieces. The coal house door was also broken as also the doors of the offices. Altogether the place has a most dilapidated appearance – to add to our discomfort I understand a foot of glass is not to be gotten in Banagher … The storm has left thirty-three families in Banagher without a home … The appearance of the town and neighbourhood is most melancholy, and I fear the news from sea will be bitter. There is scarcely a room in this house habitable.[20]

The "Big Wind" was a natural metaphor, its violence and disorder prefiguring the tragedy that was to grip Ireland in the 1840s. It also removed the last of the wind from Alan Bell's sails. His already delicate health was made even more precarious by his exertions on that night. He became seriously ill and had to go for medical treatment to Dublin, where he was advised to try to recover his strength in the south of France. But on 3 June 1839, while waiting in Kingstown to board ship at the house of Harriette's brother, Captain Joseph Adamson, he died from an asthma attack. Four days later the commissioners of Education reduced his stipend from £200 to £100 on the grounds that, since the endowed school masters were charging fees, they had other means of supplementing their income. Not only did they feel that the master's salary was excessive; they also implied that Bell had not run a proper school. This was made quite clear in their 1840 report: "The Mastership of Banagher Royal School having become vacant, we have made such regulations as have enabled us to expend in repairs of the schoolhouse such sums as the nature of our tenure thereof seems to warrant; and we trust that under the management of the master lately appointed by your Excellency a good school will soon be established at Banagher."[21] In other words, now that Bell is out of the way, we may be able to clean this mess up.

For the Bell family, 1839 was an *annus horribilis*. First came the "Big Wind," then Alan Bell's death. Harriette had just given birth to her ninth child and her oldest son was only eighteen years old. Now this large, fatherless brood had to move out of Cuba House; cold, damp, and drafty as it was, it had still been the centre of a lively life. With Harriette herself at the piano there had always been dancing, and singing, and parties with the local gentry. Now all that was suddenly changed.

Still, things could have been worse. All around them the peasantry were eking out a marginal existence on a diet of milk, potatoes and the odd piece of meat from the pigs and chickens who lived with them cheek, jowl, and wattle. One remembers the often related story of Sir Jonah Barrington knocking on the door of a west-country cabin, curious to see what lay within, and being greeted by the head of the house who shouted to his wife: "Kathleen! Let the pigs out and let the gentleman in!" At least the widow Bell, with a jointure from her father and the land and shares of her husband's estate, was able to keep the family together and ensure the university education of her sons, three ending up in the church, one in the army, and one in medicine.

For Arthur, 1839 was a traumatic year in another way as well. After the initial shock of separation from his biological family in early childhood, he had become deeply – perhaps neurotically – attached to his adoptive family, especially to Harriette. In the aftermath of his uncle's death, his future was uncertain, his attachment to his aunt and cousins threatened, and his position as classical master at Cuba House in jeopardy. In July 1839 the Rev. James Hamilton was appointed the new master, but he resigned as soon as he arrived in Banagher, having found the school buildings in such bad repair that boarders could not be accommodated. The post was next offered to the Rev. John Brown, LLD, then master of the Bandon Endowed School some fifteen miles south-west of Cork. He too was shocked to find Cuba House "uninhabitable and in such a bad state that parents could not be induced to send their children to it." So as Arthur's family resettled themselves in Banagher, Rev. Brown scuttled back to Bandon where he had built up a going concern with eighty pupils, taking Arthur Nicholls with him as his classical master. Arthur must have impressed him as an effective teacher, for Brown offered him a salary somewhat higher than the £50 his uncle had paid him, Arthur taught there for a year, but without a university degree his prospects were limited. So, with his aunt's help, he resumed his studies at Trinity College.[22]

In the 1840s, Trinity College Dublin (TCD) was among the more distinguished educational institutions in the United Kingdom, ranking in reputation just behind Oxford and Cambridge. In addition to the regular undergraduate degree in Arts, it offered degrees in Law, Engineering, and Science. Most students, being the sons of gentlemen, tended to go into Law or read for the BA degree but before the Church of Ireland was disestablished in 1869, about one third of those who chose the latter path, as Arthur did, took holy orders.

When Arthur first entered TCD in 1836, the College was strongly affected by the emotional power, "the ferment, the earnestness and the bigoted but sincere sectarianism" of the evangelical movement. Emerging first in England, where the twin forces of the industrial and French revolutions had destabilized the surface equilibrium of the eighteenth century, Evangelicalism had proved a powerful force for moral reform. Described in one formulation as Methodists who had refused to leave the Church of England, Evangelicals were behind the movement for the abolition of slavery and the slave trade, for the building of churches in newly industrialized cities, and for Sunday schools for the young. The Evangelical movement affected the Church of Ireland somewhat later than the English church, but it was in full spate by the 1830s and was particularly strong at TCD, where many students spent their extra-curricular time organizing Bible classes and teaching in Sunday schools. Arthur must have been deeply influenced by their example during his first year at Trinity, and it is a safe assumption that before he became the high-church Puseyite who so irritated and amused Charlotte Brontë, he was an Evangelical.[23]

In addition to the impact of Evangelicalism, TCD had also experienced an academic revolution led by Bartholomew Lloyd, provost between 1831 and 1837. In 1833, Lloyd reconstituted the undergraduate course structure: honours courses, term exams and exam prizes were introduced. The teaching of Divinity was transformed from a one-year to a two-year course, the first year of which could be taken while a student was still in his senior sophister or fourth year. A degree in Divinity thus required five years, so that when Arthur resumed his undergraduate education he still had four more years of study. When he received a second-class degree in Divinity in 1844, Arthur was twenty-six and of the canonical age to be ordained. This is worth emphasizing because some Brontë scholars, apparently unaware of his interrupted studies between 1837 and 1840, assume that the reason he spent seven years as a TCD undergraduate was that he was a slow, lazy, or intellectually under-endowed scholar.[24]

Upon completing his degree, Arthur's expectation would have been to find an assistant curacy under an older clergyman who would pay him a stipend for taking over the daily drudgery of parish duties. But even such underpaid positions were becoming harder and harder to find in the Ireland of the 1840s. While the number of Church of Ireland communicants was decreasing (from 853,160 in 1834 to 693,357 in 1861), the number of benefices was increasing. The result was that many parishes simply let their assistant curates go.[25] Thus demography and economics combined to narrow Arthur's prospects in Ireland. Politics played a role too because the two influential men who might have helped him, his uncle Alan and James Adamson, were both dead.

In addition, there was an ideological element that blighted his hopes of preferment in the Church of Ireland. At some point in his university career, Arthur had become involved in Tractarianism and the related Oxford Movement. What attracted him was undoubtedly what drew many other concerned individuals to the extreme wing of the high church: it provided a framework of ritual and tradition which offered to confront the bewildering and socially destabilizing changes of early industrialization with a vision looking back to the days of a powerful medieval church with final authority to pronounce on all matters of doctrine. Arthur's own childhood experiences, especially the trauma of separation from his siblings and parents, surely contributed to his fear of chaos and disorder, and reinforced his attraction to the aesthetic security of the high church. But the Tractarians' stress on issues such as the apostolic succession of bishops, the vital significance of sacraments in church life, and their emphasis on the Church of England as part of the universal catholic church, found little resonance in the Church of Ireland. The Irish church remained a minority institution in a sea of Roman Catholics who, having achieved political emancipation in 1828, saw the tithes they were compelled to pay to a religious institution in which they did not believe as unjust and oppressive.

Then there was the spiritual torpor that the Church of Ireland had inherited from the eighteenth century and which was to continue well into the Victorian period, so that even in the 1860s a young Scottish clergyman on a visit to Westmeath could be shocked by what he saw in the local parish church.

> A more melancholy sight I never beheld. The congregation consisted of five county families who spend the season in London; so that the congregation must consist in the summer of the incumbent's family. There were no poor and I never saw so undevotional a congregation. During the prayers no one knelt. Some stood with their backs to the altar and the officiating clergyman, and one knee resting on the seat, some sat and others reclined in the half empty pews nursing one leg stretched out full length on the cushioned seat. During the singing no more than half the congregation stood up and the same during the reading of the gospel.[26]

For those Irish churchmen who felt that this combination of sloth and inequity put them under threat of a guillotine, the Evangelical movement provided a greater hope of salvation than Tractarianism, the Oxford Movement, or Edward Bouverie Pusey. By the time Arthur reached TCD the Evangelicals had begun a steady penetration of the Church; they would be the predominant force by mid-century. The tone was set by Richard Whately, Archbishop of Dublin, who although not himself an Evangelical, was so violently opposed to Tractarianism that he supervised the publication of *Cautions for the Times* (a response to *Tracts for the Times*), refused to receive Newman, his old Oxford colleague, and denied Pusey permission to preach in his archdiocese.

When Arthur returned to Trinity, the Divinity School was not only strongly Protestant in outlook but even more heavily "tinctured with evangelicalism" than during his first year there. Its most influential chair, Archbishop King's Lectureship, was held until 1842 by the Rt. Rev. J.T. O'Brien, well known as an ardent anti-ritualist and anti-tractarian. His successor, Thomas McNeece, although "restrained … gave short shrift to those who obfuscated the plain truth of the Gospels with the verbal subtleties of Tractarian metaphysics."[27] Thus it is unlikely that Arthur's Puseyite views, which Charlotte Brontë would later gently satirize in *Shirley*, were formed by anyone on the Trinity faculty.

However, there were other possible sources of influence on Arthur outside the Divinity School. One of these was The Theological Society, a student organization established in 1823 to provide an opportunity for students to discuss important doctrinal issues without the direct influence of their mentors. In the 1840s, the society was very much under the influence of J.H. Singer, an earnest Evangelical, but its discussions were under the control of no particular outlook. Since the students invited "prominent controversialists" from outside, anything and everything, including the ideas of Newman, Keble, and Pusey, were examined and debated. That the direction of these discussions was not always along evangelical lines is suggested by the fact that the society was later placed under the supervision of the divinity school faculty.[28]

During his years at TCD, Arthur frequently attended St Paul's Church, Grange Gorman, where Harriette's uncle was curate. Arthur Smyth Adamson (1793–1843) was far from being an Evangelical, or a high churchman, much less a Tractarian. Indeed, his infrequent attendance on Sundays, and a bitter legal battle with the householders of Grange Gorman, a suburb of Dublin, over the payment of "Minister's Money" – a kind of ecclesiastical house tax levied in suburban areas where new housing had made the payment of tithes impractical – suggest he was simply an old-fashioned eighteenth-century cleric and could hardly have been a role model for the young divinity student. But his successor William Maturin was cut from a different cloth. He took his daily parochial duties seriously and was a regular and powerful preacher. One acquaintance described how "his simple and burning words reflected the zeal of his spirit. ... I saw him crush by his fiery words a mob of young men, who came to disturb his service ... and drive them cowed and shrinking from his church." His refusal to modify his Tractarian views made him unpopular with the church hierarchy, with the result that he spent his career as the humble incumbent of Grange Gorman. Although in England "he would have been considered a moderate churchman ... to the Irish evangelicals he always appeared as little removed from a Roman Catholic."[29] To Arthur he must have seemed a shining example on which to model himself.

There was one further influence much closer to home: the Rev. Alexander Ross, rector of Banagher during Arthur's youth. When he was home in Banagher on vacations from Trinity, Arthur, already thinking of a clerical career, had long discussions with his pastor. Ross, who was known as a "high-minded episcopalian" had begun to read Tractarian literature in 1839 and had found "much in the tone and character of some of their early works to attract and captivate him. Their profession of zeal for the Church, for primitive order, and for exact conformity to the doctrine and discipline of the Book of Common Prayer were in harmony with that portion of his views in which he had most rarely met with perfect sympathy." In the Tractarians Ross hoped to have found a "perfect union of Christian principles with evangelical doctrine." His emphasis on order and conformity even before he had read the Tractarians points to a doctrinal scrupulosity which would have had a powerful influence on Arthur, although Ross later rejected the Tractarians as "hollow and fallacious" and was one of ninety-three of the ninety-five clergymen in his diocese who signed a petition attacking them in 1844.[30] That Arthur did not follow his mentor suggests a certain intellectual independence. Perhaps, as well, he stayed the Tractarian course because it satisfied his need for a set of beliefs that could not be altered by the unpredictable whims of individual conscience.

The paucity of documentary data such as letters and memoirs concerning Arthur Bell Nicholls before he left Ireland condemns one to conjecture: to "might," "could," "would," or "probably" in place of the simple indicative, a common but dangerous procedure in biography.

Still, in Arthur's case, there is enough circumstantial evidence to suggest what went into his psychological and intellectual formation. Without putting too strong a Freudian emphasis on it, there can be little doubt that early separation from his parents and siblings left a permanent imprint on his personality. Some psychologists argue that a trauma of this sort can lead in later life to a condition known as "anxious attachment": that is, to the formation of relationships whose strength is a function more of insecurity than of genuine affection. What "genuine" might mean in this context is a moot point: all bonds of affection carry a certain charge of insecurity. Nevertheless, the concept does possess utility in helping to understand the mature Arthur Bell Nicholls, a man always wary of committing himself but who, once having done so, would prove a fast friend and a constant lover. There is also an element of anxious attachment in his Puseyite religious view in the sense that it is consonant with a psyche that fears the sudden eruption of personal, social or political disorder. Early childhood trauma, the disruption of the Bell family in 1839, chronic violence in rural Irish society, and the rapidly changing culture of early industrial Britain would all reinforce this outlook. Fear of chaos and sudden change helped produce that rigidity in doctrine which Charlotte Brontë would find so distasteful, as well as that surface austerity and brusqueness which some of his West Riding parishioners would later mistake for arrogance and pride.

This was the student who received a degree in Divinity in February 1844. Between then and May 1845 Arthur's whereabouts are unknown; all that is clear is that, at some point, he gave up the search for a curacy in Ireland and decided that England offered a more hopeful field for a young, unordained BA in divinity. But having crossed St George's Channel, that Rubicon in his career, he was to find that the procedure required of a young man in search of clerical preferment was quite bureaucratic, according to Margaret and Robert Cochrane. "The candidate had to send with his request for Ordination: a certificate of baptism; a testimonial from three beneficed clergymen, which in addition had to confirm that he had not at any time 'held, written or taught anything contrary to the doctrine or discipline of the United Church of England and Ireland;' a letter from the Incumbent and a Churchwarden of his Parish Church confirming that his request for Ordination had been read out … his College references and, in the case of graduates from Trinity, his Divinity Testimonium; and, lastly, his proposed appointment."[31]

For Arthur, having no English connections, the most difficult of these requirements was to find an incumbent who would give him a "Title for Orders," or right to ordination based on a proposed appointment. Along with scores of other young divinity graduates, he may have advertised for such a title in *The Ecclesiastical Gazette*, a monthly publication devoted to the affairs of the church.[32] Just as aspiring graduates advertised in the *Ecclesiastical Gazette*, so did incumbents looking for curates. One of these was the Rev. Patrick Brontë, the perpetual curate of St Michael's and All Angels in Haworth, a village in the West Riding of Yorkshire. In the summer of 1844 Brontë had lost his curate, the Rev. James W. Smith. Although he had been unhappy with Smith, who was later to be used by his daughter Charlotte as the model for the ill-mannered and self-satisfied priest, Peter Augustus Malone, in her novel *Shirley*, he was desperately in need of a replacement. In his seventieth year, his eyesight failing, and unable to afford a horse and carriage, Patrick Brontë was no longer able to carry out all the strenuous duties that an extensive parish entailed. He began to look for a new man in July, but without success. In November he placed an advertisement in *The Ecclesiastical Gazette*, and it was almost certainly this which caught Arthur's eye and which led, after a visit to Haworth, to Patrick accepting him. On 18 May 1845, Arthur was ordained deacon by the Bishop of Lichfield and he was licensed to the Haworth curacy on 5 June. His £90 stipend may have been meager, but it was almost twice what his uncle had been willing to pay him to teach unruly boys Latin and Greek in Banagher.[33]

CHAPTER TWO

Mr Macarthey

Within a few days of his ordination, Arthur Bell Nicholls climbed Haworth's steep Kirkgate to the little square at its top, trudged on to Parsonage Lane running along the north wall of St Michael's and All Angels Church, and stopped at Sexton House. This cottage, beside the National School and a few yards from the church, was inhabited by the sexton John Brown, his wife, and their large family of daughters. It was where Arthur was to lodge. When he entered John Brown's house, he entered in all innocence a world different from anything he had known before. Although the language he heard was English, it was spoken with an accent and in a dialect that would take him some time to comprehend, and which immediately lent an alien cast to the place.

The culture of Haworth was foreign to him in other more important ways as well. Despite its physical isolation, perched high up on the West Riding moors, the little town of about 2,000 was deeply involved in the most significant social, economic, and political developments of the time. For centuries it had been at the centre of the West Riding woolen industry, in 1810 ranking next to Bradford, and ahead of Leeds and Halifax, in the amount of wool consumed in the worsted trade. In Arthur's day, the steep valleys that surrounded Haworth were still dotted with water-driven mills, although by the time he arrived the old domestic economy had been undermined by power-driven machinery, a painful process that produced some of the bitterest class confrontations in

English history. In 1812, Patrick Brontë had held an incumbency only a few miles from the scene of a Luddite attack by desperate weavers at Rawfold's Mill, where the owner had introduced new machinery. It was an incident his daughter Charlotte was to use as the centrepiece of *Shirley*. In the 1840s, memories of Luddism were still alive but Chartism had taken its place: radical and democratic, it was the first truly national working-class movement in British history. These events made the people of Haworth a sturdy, stubborn, independent-minded citizenry. The evolution of the town's religious life was molded by the same characteristics. William Grimshaw, curate of St Michael's between 1742 and 1763, was a major figure in the Evangelical revival that had "swept like a moorland wind over Britain, and turned a small Pennine valley church into a living of the first importance … He was a mixture of brutality and compassion, of coarseness and sensitivity," a man who would walk "over thirty miles across the moors to Lancashire and back if he could bring comfort. He would preach as many as twenty sermons a week … But he could be ruthless too. He would raid the inns, driving the unwilling hearers to the church at his whip's end." The intense heat of his religious practice, sometimes rising to hysteria, is caught in a recollection of Selina, Countess of Huntingdon. She came to Haworth in September 1749 to hear the famous Evangelical preacher, George Whitefield. In the midst of Whitefield's sermon "a man shrieked and fell dead. Grimshaw jumped to his feet and shouted: 'Brother Whitefield, you stand amongst the dead and the dying – an immortal soul has been called into eternity – the destroying angel is passing over the congregation, cry aloud and spare not.' Whereupon the person standing next to Selina fell dead also."[1]

Although Patrick Brontë professed all the Evangelical pieties, he was less harsh than his fervid predecessor. Even those villagers who were not members of his church appreciated his relatively easy-going approach; they respected him most perhaps because, unlike Grimshaw, he left them alone. In a village that in addition to his own church boasted two thriving Baptist churches and a large Wesleyan chapel, this was good practical politics. Patrick's real opinion of his parishioners was reserved for private correspondence. "I have resided in Yorkshire above thirty years," he told the secretary of the National Society, "and have preached and visited in different parishes … the populace in general are either ignorant or wicked, and in most cases where they have a little learning it is of a schismatical, vainly philosophical or treacherously political nature."[2]

If this town seemed foreign to Arthur, the parsonage and its inhabitants must have struck him as verging on the exotic. On his first morning in the sexton's house he was awakened by a sharp report. It was the parson standing at his bedroom window with a pistol in his hand. Ever since the days of the Luddites, Patrick had gone to bed with a loaded weapon near him and his first duty on rising was to discharge it, usually taking aim at the church tower. Even Patrick thought of himself as eccentric. That, at least, was how he characterized himself to Mrs Gaskell. And at seventy, his eyesight and general health failing, the old man was becoming increasingly reclusive. Except for breakfast, he had his meals served to him alone in his study, apart from the rest of his family. In his younger days he had covered the moors on foot in the Grimshaw tradition, but now he was forced to rely more and more on the youthful energies of his curates.

Nor did his children fit the conventional image of a parson's family. His wife, Maria Branwell, had had six offspring in just over six years between 1814 and 1820, and had died the following year from a combination of excessive childbearing and ovarian cancer. The four surviving children – Charlotte, Branwell, Emily, and Anne – had led a secret creative life from early childhood, living in the imaginary worlds of Glasstown, Angria and Gondal. On reaching adulthood they had all gone into the world, the girls in the tradition of frayed gentility as teachers and governesses, Branwell as a painter (failed), tutor (twice dismissed), and railway clerk (dismissed). All had found the great world harsh, pitiless, dull, humiliating, or a combination of all four, and one by one they had returned to the parsonage.

In the spring and early summer of 1845 they were together again, but although they delighted in each other's company, their reunion was not joyous. Emily was perhaps the only one who felt without reservation that she was where she wanted to be. The gentle Anne returned from Thorp Green glad to be free after five thankless years as a governess, but although she was attached to Haworth almost as deeply as Emily, she found herself in a state of wretched depression. The reason was Branwell. Beginning in January 1843, he had joined her at Thorp Green as a tutor at the home of the Rev. Edmund Robinson, a semi-invalid who died a couple of years later. While he languished, Branwell and Mrs Robinson had developed a relationship that went beyond the ordinary intimacies of tutor and mistress; according to Juliet Barker, it is now generally accepted that they had an affair.[3] On 17 July 1845, in Haworth for a brief vacation, Branwell received a letter from his employer dismissing him, and "charging him on pain of exposure to break off instantly and for ever all communication with every member of his family." Coming after his failure as a painter and his previous dismissal as a railway clerk because of "a discrepancy in the accounts," this dismissal threw Branwell into despair. His abuse of drugs and alcohol, addictions that hitherto had been intermittent, now became habitual. "We must all," reflected Charlotte, "prepare for a season of distress and disquietude."[4]

Charlotte had been undergoing her own season of self-torment and humiliation. For most of 1842, she and Emily had been pupils at the Pensionnat Heger in Brussels, returning in November when the death of their aunt Branwell left Patrick alone. Emily stayed on in Haworth but Charlotte, drawn by her attraction to Constantin Heger, professor of rhetoric and husband of the school's head, returned to Brussels. She spent a miserable year there; Heger was polite but unresponsive to her infatuation while Madame grew increasingly hostile. "I returned to Brussels," she confessed later, "against my conscience, prompted by what then seemed an irresistible impulse. I was punished for my selfish folly by a total withdrawal for more than two years of happiness and peace of mind." The exquisite pain to which she subjected herself, enhanced by Heger's gentle rejection, is captured in the letters she wrote to him after her return to Haworth.

> I will tell you candidly [she confessed] that … I have tried to forget you, for the memory of a person one believes one is never to see again, and whom one nevertheless greatly respects, torments the mind exceedingly and when one has suffered this kind of anxiety for one or two years, one is ready to do anything to regain peace of mind. I have done everything. I have sought occupations, I have absolutely forbidden myself the pleasure of speaking about you – even to Emily, but I have not been able to overcome either my regrets or my impatience – and that is truly humiliating – not to know how to get the mastery over one's own thoughts, to be the slave of a regret, a memory, the slave of a dominant and fixed idea which has become a tyrant over one's mind. Why cannot I have for you exactly as much friendship as you have for me – neither more nor less?[5]

These words were written six months after Arthur had taken up his duties in Haworth. No wonder her announcement of his arrival was laconic. "Papa has got a new Curate lately," she informed a friend, "a Mr Nicholls from Ireland. He did his duty for the first time on Sunday [25 May 1845] – he appears a respectable young man, reads well, and I hope will give satisfaction."[6] Even this patronizing assessment was more encouraging than might have been expected from someone who had as low an opinion of curates – particularly Irish curates – as Charlotte did. Arthur would have been shocked to know what she was saying about them to her friend Ellen Nussey only a few weeks after his arrival. "Curates," she wrote,

> seem to me a self-seeking, vain empty race. At this blessed moment we have no less than three of them in Haworth Parish & God knows there is not one to mend another.
>
> The other day they all three ... dropped or rather rushed in unexpectedly to tea. It was Monday & I was hot & tired – still if they had behaved quietly and decently – I wd. have served them out their tea in peace – but they began glorifying themselves & abusing dissenters in such a manner – that my temper lost its balance & I pronounced a few sentences sharply & rapidly wh. struck them all dumb – Papa was greatly horrified also – I don't regret it.[7]

In this non-fictional incident the three curates, all high church, were Arthur, the Rev. J.B. Grant of neighboring Oxenhope, and the Rev. James Chesterton Bradley, perpetual curate of Oakworth, some two miles from Haworth. Four years later, Charlotte would make use of this incident in Chapter VII of *Shirley*, in which Mr Helstone's three curates are mercilessly satirized as insensitive, ill-mannered, ill-bred louts. There is one significant difference: fictionalized more gently elsewhere in the book as Mr Macarthey, Arthur is not among them.

Lynne Reid Banks has imagined that day with Arthur pontificating against Christian Socialism: "Dr. Pusey has declared war on this whole pack of so-called Christian Socialists, who are no more than Dissenters in a new guise."[8] For Puseyites, a belief in the regenerative efficacy of baptism and the real presence of Christ in the Eucharist were matters of vital import, but they meant little or nothing to the people of

Haworth. Even its small Church of England congregation preferred Patrick Brontë's morally fervent but less doctrinally rigid Evangelical outlook. Haworth itself was much more of Charlotte's *Shirley* than of Emily's *Wuthering Heights.* These were not the kind of people to ignore a slight, whether social or religious, but the new young curate, assertive and brusque in the certainty of his religious convictions, made a poor beginning in trying to win their respect. On 20 July 1846, a benefit oratorio was organized in Haworth church for a local man, Thomas Parker, a well-known north-country tenor. Because Parker was a Baptist, Arthur and other Puseyite clergymen in the district boycotted the concert. By contrast Patrick, whose long residence in the area had taught him to be more tolerant of non-Anglican townspeople, made a point of "sitting prominently in the vestry gallery with his like-minded clerical friends." It was a sensible political act on his part: the Haworth Baptists had two chapels and a school, while the Wesleyan Methodists, who had been in Haworth since 1842, were about to open a new chapel with seating for 650.[9]

Arthur also made a poor start with Charlotte, and not only because she lumped him together with his intrusive brother curates. When her close friend Ellen Nussey mentioned a rumor that "Miss Brontë was going to be married to her Papa's Curate," all Charlotte's bile (and perhaps injured *amour propre*) burst forth: "It puzzles me to think how it could possibly have originated – A cold, far-away sort of civility are the only sort of terms on which I have ever been with Mr Nicholls – I could by no means think of mentioning such a rumour to him even as a joke – It would make me the laughing stock of himself and his fellow – curates for half a year to come – They regard me as an old maid, and I regard them, one and all, as highly uninteresting, narrow and unattractive specimens of the 'coarser sex'."[10]

If, a few years later, Charlotte had remembered this letter, her use of the term "coarse" would have struck her with bitter irony. Following the publication of *Jane Eyre* and *Shirley* it was she, not Arthur and his fellow curates, who would be widely accused of coarseness. The letter is characteristic of Charlotte's irritability whenever there was gossip about her and marriageable men. She had said almost the same thing in 1840 about one of Arthur's predecessors, the flirtatious William Weightman, or "Celia Amelia," as the sisters dubbed him: "You are not to suppose from this, that Mr. W[eightman] and I are on very amiable terms; we are not at all. We are distant, cold, and reserved. We seldom speak; and when we do, it is only to exchange the most trivial and commonplace remarks." And Weightman, who died of cholera in 1842, was the one curate whom the three sisters could tolerate. In a lighter (but characteristically acerbic) portrait, Charlotte described him as "bonny pleasant – light-hearted – good-tempered – generous, careless, crafty, fickle & unclerical."[11] With the exception of M. Heger, Charlotte used contempt protectively whenever an eligible male crossed her path.

There is no evidence to indicate whether Arthur was aware of Charlotte's disdain or, indeed, what his own feelings were towards her at this time. Inevitably, he was thrown together a good deal with her and her sisters. He lived just down Parsonage Lane and, as Patrick's curate, had to consult with him frequently. Since Patrick was suffering from deteriorating health and eyesight, Arthur had to take over most of his clerical duties. When he took his first vacation in November 1846 to visit his relatives in Banagher, Charlotte was concerned about her father's ability to carry on: "Next Sunday he will have to take the whole duty of the three services himself." If Arthur should get a parish of his own "then Papa will be left without assistance. This rather troubles me – the whole duty is too much for him at his age."[12] Recognition of Arthur's value to her father, however, did not improve her assessment of him as a human being. If anything, it deteriorated. In September 1847, Arthur begged a second vacation in Banagher. "Mr Nicholls is not yet returned," Charlotte told Ellen on 7 October, "but is expected next week. I am sorry to say that many of the parishioners express a desire that he should not trouble himself to re-cross the channel, but should remain quietly where he is – This is not the feeling that ought to exist between shepherd and flock." A week later she declared that "Mr Nicholls is returned just the same – I cannot for the life of me see those interesting germs of goodness in him you discovered, his narrowness of mind always strikes me chiefly – I fear he is indebted to your imagination for his hidden treasures."[13] How radically the views of these women would later be reversed!

Charlotte's disdain may have contained an element of self-protection, since so far as one can see Arthur had shown no interest in her during these early years. As for the other two sisters, Emily treated him with "uncompromising contempt. She had no time for the unimaginative, and would dive past him without a word." Even Anne thought of him as "no news at all."[14] He had a more profound effect upon other women in the community, however. It was an ancient custom among the women of Haworth to lay their washing out to dry on the tombstones in the graveyard. Arthur regarded this practice with horror as dishonoring the dead, and he determined to stop it. Arthur's war against female profanation was protracted, dragging on through the summer of 1847, and though he eventually won, it was a pyrrhic victory that further damaged his reputation. Patrick watched the struggle from the sidelines with amused detachment, mixed perhaps with a pinch of *schadenfreude*. He even commemorated his curate's battle in verse.

In Haworth, a parish of ancient renown,
Some preach in their surplice, and others their gown,
And some with due hatred of tower and steeple,
Without surplice or gown, hold forth to the people;
And High Church and Low Church, and *No Church at all* –
Would puzzle the brains of St Peter and Paul –
The Parson, an old man, but hotter than cold,
Of late in reforming has grown very bold,
And in his fierce zeal, as report loudly tells,
Through legal resort, has reformed the bells –
His Curate, who follows – with all due regard –
Though Foild by the Church, has reform'd the Churchyard.
The females all routed have fled with their clothes
To stackyards and backyards, and where no one knows,
And loudly have sworn by the suds that they swim in,
They'll wring off his head, for his warring *with women*.
Whilst their husbands combine and roar out in their fury,
They'll *Lynch* him at once, without trial by Jury.
But saddest of all, the fair maidens declare,
Of marriage or love he must ever despair.

Patrick may have had his own daughters as well as the fair maidens of Haworth in mind when he penned the final couplet. That Arthur preserved a copy of it in Patrick's hand suggests that he was capable of seeing the humor of the situation, and even of laughing at himself. [15]

The battle over the Haworth laundry might have been won, but the war over the churchyard was far from finished. Arthur was not the only clergyman to be appalled by the parishioners' determination to treat it as common land rather than as holy ground. Nearly twenty years later, Patrick's successor, the Rev. John Wade, sent the ecclesiastical commissioners a description of the "fearful nuisances" he had to contend with. "I can bear personal testimony to the following, that horses have been turned into the churchyard at night; that pigs and hens are turned in even in the daytime; that the inside of the gateway, being contiguous with an Inn is hardly better than a public urinal, and that the steeple of the church, standing close to one of the paths is defiled in the same way… Lastly, within the past few weeks fragments of a coffin and human bones have been found unearthed and scattered about.[16]

While Arthur was preoccupied with laundry in the churchyard, Patrick's three daughters were quietly and anonymously making literary history. 1846 and 1847 were for them years of extraordinary productivity. In May 1846 there appeared *Poems* by Currer (Charlotte), Ellis (Emily) and Acton (Anne) Bell. (More than one Brontë biographer has speculated that the choice of "Bell" as a *nom de plume* referred elliptically to Arthur's middle name, and may have been a gentle way of teasing him for his family pride.) In the same year Charlotte completed, but could not find a publisher for, *The Professor*. Then came 1847, the sisters' *annus mirabilis*. *Jane Eyre* was published in October, followed by *Wuthering Heights* and *Agnes Grey* in December.

In three short months the sisters had laid the foundation for their literary celebrity, although they were to have little time to savor their triumph. In September 1848 Branwell, the gifted but dissolute only son in whom Patrick had invested so much hope, succumbed to what the attending physician described as "chronic bronchitis and marasmus,"[17] likely a combination of tuberculosis and delirium tremens. Just before Christmas Emily died of tuberculosis, to be followed in May of 1849 by Anne, who succumbed to the same disease. Of his six children only Charlotte now survived to look after her aged, ailing, virtually blind father. The physical remoteness of Haworth reinforced Charlotte's feelings of loneliness and isolation and may have inclined her insensibly toward the reserved Arthur, whom she saw almost daily when he came to the parsonage to discuss parish affairs. Writing about *Villette* a few years later, Thackeray suggested that "rather than have fame, rather than any other earthly good or mayhap heavenly ones she wants some Tomkins or another to love her and be in love with. But you see she is a little bit of a creature without a penny worth of good looks, thirty years old I should think, buried in the country and eating up her own heart there, and no Tomkins will come … [H]ere is one a genius, a noble heart longing to mate itself and destined to wither away into old maidenhood with no chance to fulfil the burning desire."[18]

Thackeray could not have known that that Tomkins would be Arthur Bell Nicholls, but not quite yet. From December 1847 until January 1850, there is not a single mention of his name in Charlotte's voluminous correspondence. All we know about Arthur during this period is that he officiated and gave the funeral oration at Branwell's memorial service, and less than three months later buried Emily. What he said about Branwell has not survived. It would have been a difficult duty to fulfil; although Arthur never knew him in his better days, he was nonetheless intimately acquainted with Branwell's alcohol and drug-sodden decline. His duty to Emily would have been easier, and whatever she thought of Arthur, she would have been grateful to know that he assumed the responsibility for her dog, Keeper, after her death. The poor creature "walked along side of the mourners, and into the church, and stayed quietly there all the time the burial service was being read. When he came home he lay down at Emily's chamber door, and howled pitifully for many days."[19] Only Arthur seemed to be able to console him, taking the dog for long walks on the moor. Perhaps his care of Keeper made him and Charlotte a little more intimate, or at least showed her a different side of the brusque curate.

The true identity of Currer Bell did not become known until after the publication of *Shirley* on 26 October 1849. Arthur first heard a rumor in Keighley that Charlotte was Currer Bell, the famous author of *Jane Eyre* and *Shirley*. It is a measure of his stiff, unimaginative outlook that, far from being delighted, "he came cold and disapproving one day, to ask her if the report he had heard at Keighley was true." Two months later he became president of the Haworth Mechanics' Institute (of which Charlotte herself was a life member) and "counseled the members to abstain from novel reading and to enjoy more solid works." His disapproval was characteristic of that high-minded element of the Victorian middle class who looked upon novel-reading as a terrible crime. One fervent Evangelical had even constructed a "spiritual barometer" according to which novel-reading stood at 40°F. This is not as surprising as it may sound, since Britain had just lived through a decade of extraordinary social tension, two major economic crises, the repeal of the Corn Laws, soaring unemployment, strikes, and the rise of Chartism. Sir Robert Peel told a friend in 1847 "the ground is mined beneath our feet." He spoke just months before revolution exploded in the major cities of continental Europe. In such a world Arthur, like much of English middle-class society, felt that anything threatening to excite the lower orders ought to be kept out of their hands. Writing novels was bad enough. The daughter of a clergyman writing novels was doubly reprehensible.[20]

But a month later, a different man reacted to Charlotte's novels. "Mr Nicholls," Charlotte announced, "having finished 'Jane Eyre' is now crying out for the 'other book' – he is to have it next week – much good may it do him." Nine days later she reported that "Mr Nicholls has finished reading 'Shirley,' he is delighted with it – John Brown's wife seriously thought he had gone wrong in the head as she heard him giving vent to roars of laughter as he sat alone – clapping his hands and stamping on the floor. He would read all the scenes about the curates aloud to papa – he triumphed in his own character."[21]

When Charlotte spoke of Arthur triumphing in his own character she was referring to the curates in Chapter VII. Arthur cold not possibly have seen any of his own traits in Messrs. Donne, Malone or Sweeting. It was rather in Mr Macarthey, the curate who replaced Mr Malone, and who was described only in the last chapter of the book, that he recognized himself. Despite her satirical tone, Charlotte presents the character of Macarthey with tolerance and generosity.

> Perhaps I ought to remark, that on the premature and sudden vanishing of Mr. Malone from the stage of Briarfield parish … there came as his successor another Irish curate, Mr. Macarthey. I am happy to be able to inform you, *with truth*, that this gentleman did as much credit to his country as Malone had done it discredit: he proved himself as decent, decorous, and conscientious, as Peter [Malone] was rampant, boisterous, and – (this last epithet I choose to suppress, because it would let the cat out of the bag). He laboured faithfully in the parish: the schools, both Sunday and day-schools, flourished under his sway like green bay-trees. Being human, of course he had his faults; these, however, were proper, steady-going, clerical faults; what many would call virtues: the circumstance of finding himself invited to tea with a Dissenter would unhinge him for a week; the spectacle of a Quaker

> wearing his hat in the church – the thought of an unbaptised fellow-creature being interred with Christian rites – these things could make strange havoc in Mr. Macarthey's physical and mental economy; otherwise, he was sane and rational, diligent and charitable.[22]

After he had read *Shirley*, Arthur presented Charlotte with a Book of Common Prayer: a sign of respect, if not affection, on his part. Apparently his exposure to *Jane Eyre* and *Shirley* broadened his reading, for in the 1850s, his meager clerical library expanded to include some works by Thackeray and Mrs Gaskell.

Does Charlotte's gentle treatment of Macarthey signal a serious change in her feelings? Certainly the contempt she expressed in 1845–46 had eased. In May and June of 1850 she visited London, and while she was there her publisher, George Smith, commissioned George Richmond to paint the portrait of her that now hangs in the National Portrait Gallery. Nearly half a century later, Richmond's son said his father had told him that on the last day of the sittings, Charlotte had come with a Mr Nicholls. This recollection of a recollection, recorded long after the event, is highly improbable. Still, Lyndall Gordon appears to accept Arthur's presence and even wonders whether, in London, Charlotte "felt safe from the ridicule for chasing a curate which she feared in Haworth." She speculates further that Charlotte had "warmed toward Mr Nicholls" while writing *Shirley* (i.e. in 1848 and 1849) "at a time when she had lost two sisters in six months … when she herself was in great need of kindness as she returned from Scarborough [where Anne had died] to an empty Parsonage, to lonely evenings in the dining-room with Papa still immured in his study across the hall."[23]

But even though he had been a close and compassionate witness of the tragic events of 1848 and 1849, there is no evidence, aside from his unlikely presence in Richmond's studio, that Arthur's relations with Charlotte had altered in any significant way. Even as late as the summer of 1851 when he had invited himself to tea prior to leaving for a vacation in Banagher, Charlotte could not resist remarking that he had "comported himself somewhat peculiarly for him – being extremely good – mild and uncontentious."[24] Her old irritation with what she regarded as his religious bigotry was far from dead, but she had learned to appreciate his reliability through those years when he had taken the burden from

Patrick's shoulders. And for a responsible curate the burden was indeed heavy. As Brian Wilks notes, he spent most of his time "burying those younger than himself, burying the children of those he married as well as the parents of those children." In that part of Yorkshire, the infant mortality rate was "one of the highest in the country, 45 per cent of children never achieving six years of age, while the average life span of a villager was a mere twenty-five years."[25]

It was about this time, in letters to her father, that Charlotte first began to include Arthur in the greetings she sent to the circle around the parsonage along with the old housekeeper, Tabby Aykroyd, Martha Brown, who was taking over from Tabby, and Keeper and Flossy, the family dogs. In late May 1852, after a prolonged but undiagnosed illness, Charlotte took a month's recuperative holiday at Filey, an East Riding seashore resort. One Sunday she attended a bizarre service at the local church and reported to Patrick: "At one end there is a little gallery for the singers – and when these personages stood up to perform – they all turned their backs upon the congregation – and the congregation turned *their* backs upon the pulpit and the parson – the … effect of this manœuvre was so ludicrous – I could hardly help laughing – had Mr Nicholls been there – he certainly would have laughed out."[26]

As long as Branwell, Emily, and Anne were alive, Charlotte had been part of an exclusive family circle. Arthur was foreign to that world: he was an Irishman, in their view (despite their father's Irish roots) well below them socially; his religious views were unsympathetic; and unlike the flirtatious, gregarious William Weightman, who sent the sisters valentines and was not averse to the odd drink with Branwell at the Black Bull, Arthur seemed cold. When the Brontë siblings were together, they shut him out and did not really get to know him. But that self-sufficient world was gone and Charlotte, despite having become a major literary figure, found herself physically isolated and intensely lonely. In these circumstances, she could hardly fail to pay more attention to Mr Nicholls and even to begin to think of him as virtually one of the family. Nonetheless, it was a far cry from acceptance, or even friendship, to love.

Other developments in Charlotte's life during this period may also have disposed her to look on Arthur in a more generous way. In 1850 and 1851 she and James Taylor, a senior manager in the firm of her publisher, Smith Elder & Co., had been conducting a curious, indeterminate courtship, circling about each other like a couple of flyweights looking for an opening. When Taylor visited Haworth, and when they wrote to each other, Charlotte enjoyed his quick mind and wide reading. They spoke the same cultural language. But she found the "little man" physically repelling: "each moment he came near me – and that I could see his eyes fastened on me – my veins ran ice." This collision of physical repulsion and intellectual companionship was characteristic in its violence of much of Charlotte's emotional life. Still, in the extremity of her isolation she could not help herself wondering if she could "ever feel for him enough love to accept of him as a husband." Matters suddenly came to an end with Taylor's announcement that he was to be stationed in India for five years as Smith Elder's representative. Margaret Smith speculates that he proposed to Charlotte and was turned down. In any case, the relationship ended decisively and after his departure for India in May of 1851, Charlotte found that "his absence and the exclusion of his idea from my mind – leave me certainly with less support and in deeper solitude than before." Meanwhile, there was her father's curate, narrow and bigoted perhaps, but responsible, loyal, dependable, and – unlike James Taylor – almost Rochesterian in his physical proportions, tall, with austere good looks and hair "black as a coil."[27]

CHAPTER THREE

Macarthey in Love

Charlotte's letters give us an extraordinarily detailed picture of her life. Through them we can trace her activities and feelings from season to season, even from day to day, and since we have nothing comparable with which to follow Arthur, we are dependent on what she chooses to tell us when we try to reconstruct the development of his feelings for her.

She told George Smith that Arthur had been in love with her for several years before he finally summoned up the courage to propose. Why had he been such a laggardly lover? His meager stipend was one obvious factor. How could he, living in one room in the sexton's house, hope to maintain a wife and family on £90 or £100 per annum? After 1847 she had become a national, even an international, celebrity. Moreover he knew, if only from reading *Shirley*, that she regarded his high-church views with, at best, tolerant amusement. How could he, a poor Irish curate, hope to win her love? Finally, there was the simple fact that she had never given him the slightest intimation that she might return his love. Aware of these obstacles, a man of Arthur's diffident nature was not likely to act aggressively.

So what was he to do? Almost every summer since coming to Haworth he had taken his holidays with his family in Banagher. On one of those occasions, most probably in the summer of 1851, he proposed to his cousin Harriette who was then nineteen and a "strikingly pretty" girl, as Charlotte was later to describe her.[1] Rather than indicating a fickle nature, this apparently sudden transfer of affection is best construed as the act of a man desperate to find emotional compensation for the love he sought in Charlotte but which he sensed she could not give. He felt secure with Harriette: he had known her all her life and into the bargain, she had become a beautiful young woman. Those living in a permissive age should pause before dismissing Arthur's behaviour with derision or contempt. In a society which laid a heavy injunction against extra-marital sex, rapid serial proposals – desperate, business-like, or both – were not uncommon. Mr Gladstone is an example of the former: he made love to and was rejected by two young women before Catherine Glynne accepted him. The Rev. Henry Nussey, Ellen's brother, typified the latter. Having been rejected by his former vicar's sister, he noted in his diary: "All right, but God knows best what is good for us. Write to a Yorkshire friend, C[harlotte] B[rontë]." Charlotte's polite but unfavourable response was calmly put down to "the will of the Lord." Five years later this plodding but determined suitor finally found a mate. In times like these, it is not surprising that Arthur proposed to his cousin. In fact, Margaret and Robert Cochrane state that there was a persistent rumour that he was also engaged at one time to another woman, Margaret Eggleston, the sister of one of his clerical friends.[2]

In the event, Harriette Bell turned her cousin down. Her rebuff sent him back to Haworth in the fall of 1852 in an acutely depressed mood, constantly complaining about his health and threatening to return to Ireland. Patrick responded "with little sympathy and much indirect sarcasm," Charlotte with "dim misgivings." For some time she had noticed "a long series of indications whose meaning I scarce ventured hitherto to interpret to myself." She discovered their precise meaning in mid-December.

> On Monday evening Mr Nicholls was here to tea. I vaguely felt without clearly seeing, as without seeing, I have felt for some time, the meaning of his constant looks, and strange, feverish restraint. After tea I withdrew to the dining-room as usual. As usual, Mr Nicholls sat with papa till between eight and nine o'clock, I then heard him open the parlour door as if going. I expected the clash of the front-door. He stopped in the passage: he tapped: like lightning it flashed on me what was coming. He entered – he stood before me. What his words were you can guess; his manner –

> you can hardly realise – never can I forget it. Shaking from head to foot, looking deadly pale, speaking low, vehemently yet with difficulty – he made me for the first time feel what it costs a man to declare affection where he doubts response.
>
> The spectacle of one ordinarily so statue-like, thus trembling, stirred, and overcome, gave me a kind of strange shock. He spoke of sufferings he had borne for months, of sufferings he could endure no longer, and craved leave for some hope. I could only entreat him to leave me then and promise a reply on the morrow. I asked him if he had spoken to papa. He said, he dared not. I think I half led, half put him out of the room. When he was gone I immediately went to papa, and told him what had taken place. Agitation and anger disproportionate to the occasion ensued; if I had *loved* Mr Nicholls and had heard such epithets applied to him as were used, it would have transported me past my patience; as it was, my blood boiled with a sense of injustice, but papa worked himself into a state not to be trifled with, the veins on his temples started up like whipcord, and his eyes became suddenly bloodshot. I made haste to promise that Mr Nicholls should on the morrow have a distinct refusal.[3]

Charlotte dutifully sent off her letter of refusal the following day. "Attachment to Mr N I never entertained," she told Ellen, "but the poignant pity inspired by his state on Monday evening, by the hurried revelation of his sufferings for many months, is something galling and irksome. That he cared something for me, and wanted me to care for him, I have long suspected, but I did not know the degree or strength of his feelings."[4] Pity, and the sudden perception that here was a man who, despite his outward reserve and lack of imagination, was capable of passions as deep and powerful as her own, initiated the process that would eventually carry Charlotte from indifference and contempt through acceptance and respect, and finally, to love.

The atmosphere in and around the parsonage was oppressive. "You ask how papa demeans himself to Mr Nicholls," Charlotte wrote three days after his proposal:

> I only wish you were here to see papa in his present mood: you would know something of him. He just treats him with a hardness

> not to be bent, and a contempt not to be propitiated. The two have had no interview as yet: all has been done by letter. Papa wrote, I must say, a most cruel note to Mr Nicholls on Wednesday. In his state of mind and health (for the poor man is horrifying his landlady, Martha's mother, by entirely rejecting his meals) I felt that the blow must be parried, and I thought it right to accompany the pitiless despatch by a line to the effect that, while Mr N must never expect me to reciprocate the feelings he had expressed, yet at the same time I wished to disclaim participation in sentiments calculated to give him pain; and I exhorted him to maintain his courage and spirits.[5]

Charlotte, tiny in stature but great in emotional courage, was caught between two men, each in his own way quite out of control. Patrick's fury was an amalgam of several emotions. One was pure and simple patriarchal possessiveness. Mary Taylor, the sturdy, independent rationalist on whom Rose Yorke in *Shirley* was based, wrote from New Zealand after Charlotte's death that she "could never think without gloomy anger of Charlotte's sacrifices to the selfish old man." Virginia Woolf was equally caustic. "Thus protected [by patriarchy] it was perfectly possible for the Rev. Patrick Brontë to cause acute pain to his daughter Charlotte for several months, and to steal several months of her short married happiness without incurring any censure from the society in which he practiced the profession of a priest of the Church of England; though had he tortured a dog, or stolen a watch, that same society would have unfrocked him and cast him forth."[6]

In addition to the self-indulgent if understandable desire of an old man to retain the last of his children, Patrick advanced other objections to Arthur's proposal. He was angry (and Charlotte thought this anger "not altogether groundless") "that Mr. N has behaved with disingenuousness in so long concealing his aims – forging that Irish fiction, etc." It is not clear what that "Irish fiction" was, but probably Arthur had been boasting of the grandeur of Cuba House and of the Bell pedigree. His commonplace book contains a genealogy that includes a Sir Michael Bell, colonel in the army of William III, who was created a knight banneret at the Battle of the Boyne, and subsequently became the governor of Athlone. Patrick and Charlotte believed this to be nothing more than Irish blarney, and perhaps they were right.

Arthur's meager stipend was another cause for concern. "I am afraid also," Charlotte continued, "that papa thinks a little too much about his want of money; he says that the match would be a degradation – that I should be throwing myself away – that he expects me, if I marry at all – to do very differently." This was doubly ironic, coming as it did from the son of Hugh Brunty, an illiterate Irish peasant. Patrick had himself been rebuffed on the same ground when he was a young curate in 1808, and proposed to Mary Burder of Finchingfield Park, Essex. Mary would probably have accepted him had her guardian not "spirited" her out of the neighborhood. Curiously, Patrick accepted the guardian's judgment. "All along," he told a fellow clergyman, "I violated my conscience. 'Be not unequally yoked,' says the Apostle." Charlotte herself was not free of class pretension. Patrick had been "out of patience" with her in the spring of 1851 when she had objected to the suit of James Taylor on the ground that he was "no gentleman." But her rejection of Arthur had nothing to do with class or income. It arose "from a sense of incongruity and uncongeniality in feelings, tastes – principles."[7]

Lyndall Gordon has conjectured that behind her pity and her strong sense that her father was treating Arthur unjustly lay deeper feelings that had begun to germinate long before Arthur's proposal. She suggests that as early as the summer of 1851, when "hope had frozen" that something might develop between herself and her publisher, George Smith, Charlotte "may have turned spontaneously to faithful Mr Nicholls."[8] Others have even imputed a certain cunning on Arthur's part in sensing that the loneliness that overwhelmed her in the summer of 1852, as she worked with such difficulty toward the completion of *Villette*, would make her vulnerable to his advances. I can find no evidence to support either of these suggestions. But she did pity him, and doubtless that pity deepened her sense of his isolation.

When Arthur's proposal and her rejection of him became common knowledge – as it always must in a small village – everyone turned against him. Everyone but Charlotte herself. "I am sorry for one other person whom nobody pities but me. Martha is bitter against him, John Brown [the sexton and Martha's father] says *he should like to shoot him*. They don't understand the nature of his feelings – but I see what they are. Mr. N is one of those who attach themselves to very few, whose sensations are close and deep – like an underground stream, running strong but in a narrow channel. He continues restless and ill – he carefully performs the occasional duty – but does not come near the Church, procuring a substitute every Sunday."[9] This letter is the first evidence we have that something beyond pity for Arthur was beginning to stir, though perhaps only sub-consciously, in Charlotte's heart. The powerful feelings he had exposed during his proposal had shown her that his surface demeanor was protecting a passionate inner man.

Arthur's situation was impossibly painful. Not only had Charlotte rejected him, but his landlord wanted to shoot him, Martha was hostile, and Patrick was like cold steel against him. Small wonder that he broke down, took to his room, stopped eating, and found substitutes in order to avoid Sunday services. He even resigned his position following Patrick's "cruel note" two days after the proposal, but soon thought better of that decision, realizing no doubt that it would cut him off forever from any contact with Charlotte. The two men ceased to speak to each other and communicated only by letter. Sometime after Christmas Arthur wrote again to withdraw his resignation, but Patrick would only agree if Arthur for his part agreed "never again to broach the obnoxious subject either to him or to" Charlotte. "This he has evaded doing, so the matter remains unsettled."[10]

If the strain had left Arthur dysfunctional and Charlotte distraught, Patrick's anger appeared to do him a world of good. He had suffered a stroke during the previous summer, but by the end of December he had recovered so well that Charlotte was able to use his improved health as sufficient grounds to escape the tense atmosphere at the parsonage and take a short holiday in London. There she had a few weeks' respite, although two letters from Patrick reminded her that the war of wills in Haworth continued unabated. One of these purported to come from Flossy, Anne Brontë's favourite King Charles spaniel. After Anne's death, Arthur had exercised Flossy during his walks on the moor, as he had done with Keeper after Emily's death.

> "Having only paws," says Flossy, "I cannot write, but I can dictate – I see a good deal of human nature, that is hid from those who have the gift of language … One thing I have lately seen, which I wish to mention – No one takes me out to walk now, the weather is too cold or too wet for my master [Patrick] to walk in, and my former traveling companion [Arthur], has lost all his

> apparent kindness, scolds me, and looks black upon me … Ah! my dear Mistress, trust dogs rather than men – They are very selfish, and when they have the power … very tyrannical."[11]

The other letter provides a more chilling picture of Patrick's implacable hostility.

> You may wish to know how we have been getting on here especially in respect to *Master*, and *Man*, On yesterday, I preached twice, but my man, was every way, very queer – He shun'd me as if I had been a Cobra de Capello – turning his head from the quarter, where I was, and hustling away amongst the crowd, to avoid contact. – It required no Lavater to see, that his countenance was strongly indicative of Mortified pride, and malevolent resentment – people have begun to notice these things, and various conjectures, are afloat – You thought me too severe – but I was not candid enough – His conduct might have been excus'd by the world, in a confirmed rake – or unprincipled army officer, but in a *Clergyman*, it is justly chargeable, with base design and inconsistency, – I earnestly wish that he had another and better situation – As I can never trust him any more, in things of importance – I wish him no ill – but rather good, and wish that every woman may avoid him, forever, unless she should be determined on her own misery – All the produce of the Australian *Diggins* would not make him and any wife he might have, happy.[12]

What Patrick refers to here is Arthur's threat, even before his proposal, to go to Australia as a missionary. When he applied to the Society for the Propagation of the Gospel on 28 January 1853, the very day *Villette* was published, Charlotte herself was convinced that such an undertaking would be the best way to end his "suffering in solitude." He gave as his reason "a strong inclination to assist in ministering to the thousands of of [sic] our fellow Countrymen, who by Emigration have been in great measure deprived of the means of grace."[13] It turned out to be a weak decision; Arthur was no St John Rivers. A month later he informed the selection committee that he had begun to have doubts owing to the solicitation of friends, and on 1 April he withdrew his application on the feeble excuse of rheumatism.

The letters of recommendation that accompanied his application nonetheless provide ample evidence that Arthur was not held in such low esteem in the neighborhood as Charlotte indicated to Ellen Nussey. Even Patrick provided a just, if understandably restrained, assessment of his incumbency, noting that in his seven years of service, Arthur had "behaved wisely, soberly, and piously – He has greatly promoted the interest of the National, and Sunday Schools; he is a man of good abilities, and strong constitution – He is very discreet, is under no pecuniary embarrassment, that I am aware of, nor is he, I think, likely to be so, since, in all pecuniary and other matters, as far as I have been able to discover, he is wary, and prudent – In principles, he is sound and orthodox."[14]

Arthur's fellow clerics were unreservedly enthusiastic in their praise. Sutcliffe Sowden, the vicar of Hebden Bridge, pointed out that because of Patrick's age, Arthur had taken over most of the responsibilities of the parish. Joseph Grant of Oxenhope described his achievements in terms that were, indirectly, a criticism of Patrick's own incumbency.

> When he [Arthur] first came to Haworth the Church was in a very sad condition … the National School which at *that period* did not number above 60 scholars now numbers between two & three hundred, while the service in the Church especially of an Evening has increased six-fold. In the neighbouring hamlet of Stanbury he has also been the means of building a Schoolroom: of a weekday & Sunday School & service there on Sundays … he had much to contend against both in the want of rich men to aid as well as in the strenuous opposition of Dissenters. But in all things he acted so discreetly and wisely that I am sure he will be much regretted both by Churchmen and Dissenters.[15]

But it was left to William Cartman, headmaster of the grammar school at Skipton, to provide the most impressive evaluation of Arthur's work. He declared that "for uprightness & steadiness of Conduct, Activity in the prosecution of his pastoral labours, Zeal & devotion to his ministrations, and … successful management of the Parochial Schools in his Parish, there is not to [be] found his equal. In the whole Course of my ministerial Career for the last 30 years (& I do indeed speak advisedly) I never met with a young man whom in every respect as to his general demeanour & personal Qualities I so much admired."

Juliet Barker observes that Cartman, perhaps "fearing that Patrick might do his curate less than justice in his reference ... made a point of informing the Society that Patrick had often told him how invaluable Arthur's services had been "and has frequently said that shd he leave him, he should not know how to supply his place." The vicar of Bradford saw him as a successful warrior in the Church of England's battle for souls: "in a very wild & rough part of this extensive Parish for several years ... amongst a rude and dissenting population by his exertions the Church has gain'd ground."[16] Even when allowances are made for the fact that most of these assessments came from friends, they make an impressive comment on the value of Arthur's work in the previous seven years.

After returning from London at the beginning of February, Charlotte was diverted for a short time by the success of *Villette* and the flood of reviews that poured in, most of them full of praise. But she could hardly fail to notice that Arthur continued in his misery since he was unable to control his feelings even in public. John Robinson, a young boy who used to visit Arthur's lodgings every Saturday morning for special lessons, recalled, "it was Mr. Nicolls who taught me what love sickness means. I have heard him moan with anguish when things did not run smoothly."[17] In early March, Dr Charles Longley, Bishop of Ripon (later to become Archbishop of Canterbury), visited the parish. Arthur was necessarily involved in arranging this visit, and was therefore constantly present in the Brontë house. Charlotte thought Longley "a most charming little Bishop; the most benignant little gentleman that ever put on lawn sleeves." When the local parsons came to supper and tea, she observed that "Mr Nicholls demeaned himself not quite pleasantly – I thought he made no effort to struggle with his dejection, but gave way to it in a manner to draw notice; the Bishop was obviously puzzled by it." Far from being puzzled by Arthur's distress, the "benignant little gentleman" appears to have sensed its cause. Over a year later, Charlotte told her old teacher, Margaret Wooler, that the bishop's "penetration discovered the state of things when he was here in Jany. 1853 – while his benevolence sympathized with Mr N – *then* in sorrow and dejection. I saw him press his hand and speak to him very kindly at parting."[18] But his sympathy came after the party was over. At the time Charlotte was not amused:

> Mr N – also showed temper once or twice in speaking to papa. Martha was beginning to tell me of certain 'flaysome' [terrifying] looks also – but I desired not to hear of them. The fact is I shall be most thankful when he is well away – I pity him – but I don't like that dark gloom of his – He dogged me up the lane after the evening service in no pleasant manner – he stopped also in the passage after the Bishop and the other clergy were gone into the room – and it was because I drew away and went upstairs that he gave that look which filled Martha's soul with horror. She – it seems – meantime, was making it her business to watch him from the kitchen door – If Mr. N – be a good man at bottom – it is a sad thing that Nature has not given him the faculty to put goodness into a more attractive form – Into the bargain of all the rest he managed to get up a most pertinacious and needless dispute with the Inspector [of National Schools] – in listening to which all my old unfavourable impressions revived so strongly – I fear my countenance could not but shew them.[19]

This hardly bears out the notion entertained by some Brontë scholars that Charlotte's pity for Arthur was already beginning to turn to affection. Nevertheless something was beginning to ferment in her complex psyche, always so much in need of strong attachments. In April a rumor began to circulate that Arthur had got himself another curacy, and Charlotte hoped that it was so. Her letters to Ellen show that she was observing him carefully, watching his every move from a secure distance, trying to understand what was really going on behind that frozen manner and overcast countenance.

> You ask about Mr. N I hear he has got a curacy – but do not yet know where – I trust the news is true. He & Papa never speak. He seems to pass a desolate life. He has allowed late circumstances so to act on him as to freeze up his manner and overcast his countenance not only to those immediately concerned but to everyone. He sits drearily in his rooms – If Mr Cartman or Mr Grant or any other clergyman calls to see and as they think,

> to cheer him – he scarcely speaks – I find he tells them nothing – seeks no confidant – rebuffs all attempts to penetrate his mind – I own I respect him for this – He still lets Flossy go to his rooms and takes him to walk [Patrick's Flossy-letter appears to have been inaccurate and unfair] – He still goes over to see Mr Sowden sometimes – and poor fellow – that is all. He looks ill and miserable. I think and trust in Heaven that he will be better as soon as he gets away from Haworth. I pity him inexpressibly. We never meet nor speak – nor dare I look at him – silent pity is just all I can give him … He is now grown so gloomy and reserved – that nobody seems to like him – his fellow-curates shun trouble in that shape – the lower orders dislike it – Papa has a perfect antipathy to him… Martha hates him – I think he might almost be *dying* and they would not speak a friendly word to or of him. How much of all this he deserves I can't tell – certainly he never was agreeable or amiable … and alas! I do not know him well enough to be sure there is truth and true affection – or only rancour and corroding disappointment at the bottom of his chagrin. In this state of things I must be and I am – *entirely passive.*

Externally passive she might have been, but without a break in the paragraph she suddenly lets drop a thought that contradicts everything she has previously said about Arthur and shows her considering him seriously as a possible mate. "I may be losing the purest gem – and to me far the most precious – life can give – genuine attachment – or I may be escaping the yoke of a morose temper – In this doubt conscience will not suffer me to take one step in opposition to Papas will – blended as that will is with the most bitter and unreasonable prejudices."[20]

So matters continued through April. The rumor that Arthur had found another curacy turned out to be true. It was at Kirk Smeaton, six miles from Pontefract, held by a pluralist vicar, the Rev. Thomas Cator.[21] He arranged to leave Haworth at the end of May, by which time Patrick had found a replacement. But before his departure two more emotional scenes took place. On Whit-Sunday, 15 May, Arthur, who had by this time managed to drag himself back to his clerical duties, took his last communion service. It was a "strange sort of day at church," Charlotte reported to Ellen:

> It seems as if I were to be punished for my doubts about the nature and truth of poor Mr N[icholls'] regard. Having ventured on Whitsunday to stay to the sacrament – I got a lesson not to be repeated. He struggled – faltered – then lost command over himself – stood before my eyes and in the sight of all the communicants, white, shaking, voiceless – Papa was not there – thank God! Joseph Redman [the Parish clerk] spoke some words to him – he made a great effort – but could only with difficulty whisper and falter through the service. I suppose he thought; this would be the last time; he goes this week or the next. I heard the women sobbing round – and I could not quite check my own tears.
>
> What had happened was reported to Papa either by Joseph Redman or John Brown – it excited only anger – and such expressions as "unmanly driveller." Compassion or relenting is no more to be looked for [from Papa] than sap from firewood.
>
> I never saw a battle more sternly fought with the feelings than Mr. N – fights with his – and when he yields momentarily – you are almost sickened by the sense of the strain upon him. However he is to go – and I cannot speak to him or look at him or comfort him a whit – and I must submit.[22]

When the news of Arthur's impending departure spread through the town it became apparent that, despite what Charlotte had said about "the lower orders" disliking him, there was considerable esteem and, as the sobbing women at the Whitsun service attested, a good deal of sympathy for their curate. A subscription was raised and Arthur was given the usual gold watch, inscribed "Presented to the Revd A.B. Nicholls B.A. by the teachers, scholars, and congregation of St. Michael's Haworth Yorkshire May 25 1853." The presentation was made at a public meeting, which Charlotte advised Patrick to use ill health as an excuse *not* to attend. Michael Merrall, the son of a local mill owner and a good friend of Branwell Brontë, spoke of Arthur's kindness and feeling. "His zeal and energy in behalf of the church and schools, as well as his kind and judicious conduct to all have won him the respect and esteem of the parishioners: so it is with sincere regret that they are parting with him." Even Arthur's war with the washerwomen would appear to have been forgotten. It must have been a bittersweet moment for him. Forty years later, as he walked Clement Shorter over his farm at Banagher he produced the watch "with actual pride."[23]

The churchwardens were concerned about Arthur's real motives for leaving and, as Charlotte related, "put the question to him plainly Why was he going? Was it Mr Brontë's fault or his own? His own – he answered. Did he blame Mr Brontë? 'No: he did not: if anybody was wrong it was himself.' Was he willing to go? 'No: it gave him great pain.'" Arthur's chivalrous refusal to allow publicly that there was bad feeling between him and Patrick was maintained even forty-two years later. Having read Augustine Birrell's book on the Brontës, he wrote Clement Shorter that he wished to disabuse Birrell's mind "of the impression that there ever was any quarrel between Mr. Brontë and myself – An unkind or angry word never passed between us – we parted as friends when I left Haworth – my leaving was solely my own act – I was not driven away by him – I always felt that he was perfectly justified in his objection to my union with his daughter." This bears an odd resemblance to what Patrick had said about his own rejection when he proposed to Mary Burder in 1808. Charlotte was impressed by Arthur's probity and sense of honour. But she continued to be irritated by his other, less attractive side.

> Yet he is not always right. I must be just. He shews a curious mixture of honour and obstinacy; feeling and sullenness. Papa addressed him at the school tea-drinking – with *constrained* civility, but still with *civility*. He did not reply civilly; he cut short further words. This sort of treatment offered in public is what Papa never will forget or forgive – it inspires him with a silent bitterness not to be expressed. I am afraid both are unchristian in their mutual feelings: Nor do I know which of them is least accessible to reason or least likely to forgive. It is a dismal state of things.

Although Arthur had by this time got sufficient control of himself to resume his clerical duties, the service on his final Sunday was "a cruel struggle" and one that Charlotte thought he ought not to have had to endure. His last duty, perhaps appropriately given the joyless atmosphere, was a burial.[24]

On the evening of 26 May, Arthur called at the parsonage to leave the deeds of the National School (which he had done so much to develop) and to make his final farewell. The servants were cleaning the dining room that served as Charlotte's study, so he did not see her there. Nor did she go into the parlor where she would have had to speak to him in her father's presence.

> He went out thinking he was not to see me – And indeed, till the very last moment – I thought it best not – But perceiving that he stayed long before going out at the gate – and remembering his long grief I took courage and went out trembling and miserable. I found him leaning against the garden-door in a paroxysm of anguish – sobbing as women never sob. Of course I went straight to him. Very few words were interchanged – those few barely articulate: several things I should have liked to ask him were swept entirely from my memory. Poor fellow! but he wanted such hope and such encouragement as I *could* not give him. Still I trust he must know now that I am not cruelly blind and indifferent to his constancy and grief. For a few weeks he goes to the south of England – afterwards he takes a curacy somewhere in Yorkshire but I don't know where.
>
> Papa has been far from strong lately – I dare not mention Mr. N's name to him – He speaks of him quietly and without opprobrium to others – but to me he is implacable on the matter. However he is gone – gone – and there's an end of it. I see no chance of hearing a word about him in future – unless some stray shred of intelligence comes through Mr. Grant or some other second hand source. In all this it is not I who am to be pitied at all and of course nobody pities me – they all think in Haworth that I have disdainfully refused him &c. if pity would do Mr. N – any good – he ought to have and I believe has it. They may abuse me, if they will – whether they do or not – I can't tell.[25]

There is a plaintiveness in "he is gone – gone" and in the forlorn realization that she has no means of getting in touch with him. Hardly had Arthur disappeared when Charlotte fell ill, first with influenza, then with headaches and what Patrick described as "frequent sharp attacks of [tic-] douloureux [trigeminal neuralgia] in the head," which forced her to put off a visit from Mrs Gaskell. Then just as she began to recover, Patrick had a second stroke, and was for some days totally blind. Her life at that period must have been infinitely dreary. When you "come to Haworth," she told Mrs Gaskell, "you must do it in the spirit which might sustain you in case you were setting out on a brief trip to the backwoods of America. Leaving behind your husband, children and civilisation, you must come out to barbarism, loneliness, and liberty."[26]

Arthur's new appointment did not begin until August. No one knows what he did in the interval. Charlotte thought he spent at least some of his time in the south, but it is more likely that he went back to Banagher to be consoled by his adoptive family. Wherever he was and whatever he was doing in June, we do know that sometime in July he came to stay with his friend the Rev. Joseph Grant at Marshlands, Oxenhope within easy walking distance of Haworth. He kept the visit secret from Patrick, but managed to see Charlotte, and succeeded in getting permission to write to her. According to Catherine Winkworth, who got it from Mrs. Gaskell, who got it from Charlotte herself, "he wrote to her very miserably; wrote to her six times and then she answered him – a letter exhorting him to heroic submission to his lot, etc. He sent word it had comforted him so much that he must have a little more, and so she came to write to him several times." These letters reverse the roles formerly enacted by Charlotte and Constantin Heger, where she played the passionate supplicant and Heger the gently aloof beloved. As Brian Wilks observes, "they must have struck a chord and aroused a bitter memory in Charlotte. She knew the cruelty of silence"[27]. None of these letters survive, but the account of them shows that even deep in despair Arthur was not without cunning in his pursuit of Charlotte Brontë.

In September he made a second visit to Oxenhope, and it too was kept secret from Patrick: something that must have put an additional strain on Charlotte, for she was not accustomed to dissimulation, least of all with her father: one remembers how she crossed the hall and spoke to him immediately after Arthur proposed. But the old man may have sensed that something was going on behind his back because Mrs Gaskell, who visited Haworth in September, caught the jealous, proprietary "glare of his stern eyes over his spectacles at Miss Brontë once or twice which made me know my man." The glance which Mrs Gaskell observed made her "sadly afraid of him in my inmost soul." (Her perception may have been better than she knew; when Charlotte was visiting Miss Wooler for a few days, prior to Mrs Gaskell's arrival, Patrick had opened a letter to her from Arthur.) While Mrs Gaskell may not have been aware that Arthur was nearby at Oxenhope when she was visiting Haworth, Charlotte did tell her all about his proposal and their secret correspondence. She said it was a "great anxiety" to her and not something from which she was expecting a happy outcome: "she was trying to school herself against ever anticipating any pleasure." Unlike the robust, no-nonsense Mary Taylor, Mrs Gaskell admired what she saw as Charlotte's "patient docility which she displayed in her conduct towards her father."[28]

This was not the case with Ellen Nussey, who was let into the secret as early as 12 August, when she wrote to Mary Taylor in New Zealand. Years before, when Ellen had encouraged the idea of marriage between Charlotte and Arthur she had been briskly rebuffed. Now she saw him as a potential rival who threatened to replace her in Charlotte's affections. Although Ellen's letter has not been preserved, it is clear from Mary's reply to it that Ellen had disguised her jealousy by arguing that Charlotte ought to be obedient to Patrick's wishes. Mary Taylor would have none of this disingenuous piety:

> You talk wonderful nonsense abt C. Brontë in yr letter. What do you mean about "bearing her position so long, & enduring to the end"? and still better – "bearing our lot whatever it is." If it's C's lot to be married, shd n't she bear that too? or does your strange morality mean that she shd refuse to ameliorate her lot when it lies in her power. How wd. she be inconsistent with herself in marrying? Because she considers her own pleasure? If this is so new for her to do, it is high time she began to make it more common. It is an outrageous exaction to expect her to give up her choice in a matter so important, & I think her to blame in having been hitherto so yielding that her friends can think of making such an impudent demand.[29]

For all her outward docility, Charlotte did not appreciate Ellen's attitude any more than Mary Taylor did. Their friendship, close for so many years grew colder during the summer, and their correspondence ceased between 6 October 1853 and sometime in February 1854.[30] After Mrs Gaskell's visit, Charlotte spent a week at Hornsea with her old schoolmistress, Margaret Wooler, to whom she unburdened herself concerning her rupture with Ellen and her continuing secret contact with

Arthur. Miss Wooler, another advocate of female passivity, urged her to re-establish relations with Ellen, but Charlotte was not to be moved. "Do not think that your kind wish respecting E. Nussey and myself does not touch or influence me; it does both; yet I hardly know how to take the step you recommend." Her more intimate feelings were revealed in the next sentence, which begins "My heart ..." and then breaks off. Either Miss Wooler, who assured Arthur on 30 April that she would retain no letter which might give him pain, had destroyed what followed, or Charlotte herself broke the letter off, overcome by her own feelings.

Charlotte started writing to Ellen again sometime in January or February 1854; by March they were corresponding regularly. Then a curious, perhaps Freudian, slip occurred. Charlotte mistakenly enclosed in an envelope addressed to Ellen a letter to Arthur, which she told Ellen "was intended to relieve him of great anxiety." Was this unconsciously designed to allow Ellen to see the extent to which Charlotte's relations with Arthur had changed and evolved into intimacy?[31]

There was one other emotional tie in Charlotte's life that had not been fully resolved, and perhaps the two were connected. For some time she and her publisher George Smith had been circling each curiously in what was not precisely courtship but was certainly more than friendship, a relationship not dissimilar in its tentativeness from the abortive one with James Taylor. Smith was attracted to Charlotte's ardent nature but was never serious about marriage; she was more strongly interested, but was afraid to expose her powerful feelings to the kind of abrasion they had suffered in her relations with M. Heger. She decided to go to London hoping perhaps to bring matters to a head. Juliet Barker suggests that in addition to discovering the reason for Smith's long silence, Charlotte may have wanted to establish the exact value of the investments that he had made on her behalf to see how far her income might supplement Arthur's meager stipend. But just before her departure a letter arrived from George Smith's mother – he hadn't the courage to tell her himself – announcing his engagement to the daughter of a wealthy wine merchant. Charlotte immediately cancelled her London trip. "Man *pro*poses but Another *dis*poses," she wrote to Emily Shaen. The bitterness which lay behind her short note to George Smith acknowledging the official announcement of the engagement – "In great happiness, as in great grief – words of sympathy should be few. Accept my meed of congratulation" – could not be disguised. Juliet Barker speaks of "the scorching intensity of Charlotte's pain … The relationship between Currer Bell and Smith, Elder & Co., Charlotte Brontë and George Smith, lay in smouldering ruins."[32]

If, in November 1853, Charlotte was still allowing herself to risk some hope that her relations with Smith would evolve into something more than friendship, what does this suggest about her feelings for Arthur at that time? Does her relationship with Smith invalidate the notion that pity was beginning to change to respect, and outright rejection to a genuine consideration of marriage? Hardly. In *Villette,* Thackeray had seen Charlotte's picture of Lucy Snowe in love with two men at the same time as the autobiographically naive confession of a noble heart longing to find a mate. But for all her passionate longing, Charlotte had always been – except perhaps in the case of Constantin Heger – cautious about investing all her emotional capital in one person. When the news of George Smith's engagement removed him from the running, Arthur moved to the forefront of her emotions.

Charlotte's isolation was now untempered. "I wonder how you are spending these long winter evenings," she wrote Miss Wooler. "Alone – probably – like me."[33] Meanwhile, Mrs Gaskell, who knew that one of Patrick's objections to Arthur as a potential son-in-law was his slender income, had been conducting a secret operation of her own. Remembering the poverty of the Haworth parsonage, she asked the philanthropist Richard Monckton Milnes (later Lord Houghton), to use his influence with the Royal Literary Fund to find Charlotte a small pension. Then she had another idea: "I have been thinking over little bits of the conversation we had relating to a pension. I do not think she would take it; and I am quite sure that *one* hundred a year given as acknowledgement of his [Arthur's] merits, as a good faithful clergyman would give her ten times the pleasure that *two* hundred a year would do, if bestowed upon her."[34]

Monckton Milnes arranged to see Arthur in Yorkshire, and duly reported back to Mrs Gaskell.

> He is a strong-built, somewhat hard-featured man, with a good deal of Celtic sentiment about his manner & voice – quite of the type of the northern Irishman.
>
> He seemed sadly broken in health & spirits and declined two cures, which Dr. Hook [Walter Farquhar Hook, vicar of Leeds]

> enabled me to offer him - one in Lancashire of considerable interest, but requiring much energy – another in Scotland, requiring none at all. He gave me the impression of a man whose ardour was burnt out. I was amused at his surprise over the interest I took in him and I carefully avoided any mention of you. He spoke with great respect of Mr Brontë's abilities and character and of her simply & unreservedly.[35]

Although nothing came of Monckton Milnes' intervention, Mrs Gaskell believed that "your kind words may have made him feel that he was not so friendless as he represented [himself] & believed himself to be at first – and might rouse his despondency up to a fresh effort."[36]

The incident is revealing. It shows that the strain of the last year on Arthur was visible even to a complete stranger like Monckton Milnes. It shows once again his proud sense of honour in refusing to speak poorly of Patrick, although with Patrick himself he was all stiff acrimony. It suggests that despite his appearance of being burnt out, Arthur was determined to win Charlotte's hand, since the two attractive livings Monckton Milnes offered would have removed him from striking distance of Haworth, and also indirectly, that Charlotte was seriously thinking of marriage with Arthur well before the news of George Smith's engagement arrived in late November. Why otherwise would Mrs Gaskell have been trying to mollify Patrick's objection to Arthur on the grounds of poverty? She had even approached the Anglican archbishop of Leeds in the hope that he could provide Arthur with a curacy.

After his secret visit to Oxenhope in September, Arthur saw little of Charlotte, but they continued to keep in touch by letter. "The correspondence pressed on my mind," Charlotte later told Ellen. "I grew very miserable in keeping it from Papa. At last sheer pain made me gather courage to break it – I told all. It was very hard and rough work at the time – but the issue after a few days was that I obtained leave to continue the communication."[37] Mrs Gaskell, to whom Charlotte gave a more detailed account, described how hard that work really was.

> To hear her description of her conversation with her father when she quietly insisted on her right to see something more of Mr Nicholls was really fine. Her father thought that she had a chance of some body higher or at least farther removed from

> poverty. She said "Father I am not a young girl, not a young woman even – I never was pretty. I now am ugly. At your death I shall have 300£ besides the little I have earned myself – do you think there are many men who would serve seven years for me?" And again when he renewed the conversation and asked her if she would marry a curate? – "Yes I must marry a curate if I marry at all; not merely a curate but *your* curate; not merely *your* curate but he must live in the house with you, for I cannot leave you." The sightless old man stood up & said solemnly "Never. I will never have another man in this house," and stalked out of the room. For a week he never spoke to her. She had not made up her mind to accept Mr Nicholls & the worry on both sides made her ill – Then the old servant [Tabby Aykroyd] interfered, and asked him, sitting blind and alone, "if he wished to kill his daughter?" and went up to her and abused Mr Nicholls for not having "more brass."[38]

In the end the frail daughter broke the will of the steely patriarch, partly because Charlotte's assertion that she could not leave him meant that if he accepted Arthur, she would stay with him for the rest of his life. It was a clever move on Charlotte's part, the outcome of which was that Patrick permitted her not only to correspond with Arthur but also to see him openly, so that she could know him better. So Arthur returned to the neighborhood in January for a ten-day visit, during which the couple took long walks together on the four-mile pathway between Oxenhope and Haworth. Brian Wilks thinks it "surely ridiculous that a grown man and woman, aged thirty-five and thirty-seven and both single, should have to resort to such measures merely in order to have a conversation,"[39] but to their contemporaries it would have appeared a prudent mode of courtship. "All I learnt inclined me to esteem and, if not love – at least affection," Charlotte reported to Ellen. "Still Papa was very, *very* hostile – bitterly unjust." She noted that though she had warned Arthur of "the great obstacles that lay in his way. He has persevered." And during a visit in early April, the perseverance bore fruit. "The result of this his last visit is – that Papa's consent is gained – that his respect, I believe, is won – for Mr Nicholls has in all things proved himself disinterested and forbearing. He has shewn too that while his feelings are exquisitely keen – he can freely forgive. Certainly I must respect him – nor can I withhold from him more than mere cool respect. In fact, dear Ellen, I am engaged."

She confessed to George Smith that "my own feelings have been much impressed and changed by the nature and strength of the qualities brought out in the course of his long attachment."[40]

These quiet, tentative announcements are a far cry from Jane Eyre's triumphant "Reader, I married him!" They resemble more closely the advice that Charlotte had given Ellen Nussey almost fourteen years earlier:

> no young lady should fall in love till the offer has been made, accepted – the marriage ceremony performed and the first half year of wedded life has passed away – a woman may then begin to love but with great precaution – very coolly – very moderately – and very rationally – If she ever loves so much that a harsh word or a cold look from her husband cuts her to the heart – she is a fool – if she ever loves so much that her husband's will is her law – and that she has got into a habit of watching his looks in order that she may anticipate his wishes she will soon be a neglected fool – Did I not once tell you ... of a Relative of mine who cared for a young lady till he began to suspect that she cared more for him and then instantly conceived a sort of contempt for her – ?[41]

For Arthur the engagement was a great victory though it carried with it certain conditions. Charlotte had agreed that she would never leave her father and she proposed an arrangement that would allow Patrick to "maintain his seclusion and convenience uninvaded," even with another man living in the house. The "seclusion" referred to Patrick's habit spending almost the entire day alone in his sitting room. Breakfast was the only meal he shared with Charlotte. "Fancy it!" exclaimed Mrs Gaskell, "and only they two left. What he does with himself through the day I cannot imagine!"[42] In compensation, Arthur was to be provided with a room of *his* own by converting a small pantry behind the dining room into a study.

Besides Charlotte's determination, Patrick might have been influenced to change his mind because Arthur's replacement as curate, the Rev. George de Renzy, had turned out badly, making more palatable the prospect of a son-in-law who was energetic and reliable. Charlotte was also acute enough to point out the financial advantage. Despite her father's initial declaration that he would never, never have another man in the house, he saw that a live-in curate would "bring him gain instead of loss." Slowly he began to shed his hostility and "really begins to take pleasure in the prospect." It was arranged that Arthur would return to his old position in Haworth as soon as another place could be found for the indolent de Renzy. In effect, he had become an ecclesiastical indentured servant for the balance of his father-in-law's life, but since he got the daughter in return, his servitude must have appeared an emancipation. As for Charlotte, she faced the prospect of matrimony without illusion, declaring: "I am still very calm – *very* – inexpectant. What I taste of happiness is of the soberest order. I trust to love my husband – I am grateful for his tender love to me – I believe him to be an affectionate – a conscientious – a high-principled man – and if with all this, I should yield to regrets – that fine talents, congenial tastes and thoughts are not added – it seems to me I should be most presumptuous and thankless. Providence offers me this destiny."[43]

The absence of congenial tastes is evident in the narrow scope of Arthur's reading. The core of the tiny library he brought with him to Haworth can be found in the Brontë Parsonage Museum: *Practical Sermons*, *The Churchman's Companion*, and *A Discourse on Church Government*, although he did add to it some popular fiction of the day. But it was not only his narrow intellectual horizon and limited taste which bothered Charlotte. Arthur was already beginning to manifest a proprietary attitude that threatened to limit her circle of friends, never very wide at the best of times. During his April visit she told him that she would like to have Ellen over while he was there – she was desperate to discuss with an intimate friend her "cares fears … mixed inextricably with hopes … [but] Arthur – as I now call him … said it was the only time and place when he could not have wished to see you."[44] Ellen Nussey's fear that Arthur might be a threat to her friendship with Charlotte, already evident in her letter to Mary Taylor, now began to deepen. And the groundwork for the bitter relations that developed between the two after Charlotte's death was laid.

Charlotte continued to express an equivocal attitude toward the prospect of marriage after Arthur returned to Kirk Smeaton for Easter. The wedding was planned for July: she would have preferred a later date, but the impatient Arthur insisted. "I find myself what people call 'engaged'," she told Mrs Gaskell. "My destiny will not be brilliant, certainly, but Mr Nicholls is conscientious, affectionate, pure in heart and life. He offers a most constant and tried attachment – I am very grateful to him. I mean to try and make him happy, and papa too." Mrs Gaskell seized on the passive, subservient note in Charlotte's letters. "I am sure that Miss Brontë could never have borne not to be well-ruled and ordered … she would never have been happy but with an exacting, rigid, law-giving, passionate man." But she feared that Arthur's narrow religious views would cut Charlotte off from "us heretics" as she styled herself and her husband (the Gaskells were Unitarians). Charlotte was worried about this too, and was undoubtedly relieved that Arthur's clerical duties at Kirk Smeaton prevented him from accompanying her on a visit to Mrs Gaskell at the beginning of May. Indeed, she did not tell him that he had been included in the invitation, thus avoiding "certain little awkwardnesses of feeling I would have tried to get over for the sake of introducing him to old friends." She thought it best

> not to be instrumental in unsettling him. Yet I trust the day will come when he will see both you and Mr Gaskell. I had a little talk with him about *my* "latitudinarianism" and *his* opposite quality. He did not bristle up at all – nor feel stiff and unmanageable – he only groaned a little over something in "Shirley" touching "baptismal regeneration and a wash-hand basin." Yet if he is indulgent to some points in me – I shall have to respect certain reverse points in him. I don't mean to trifle with matters deep-rooted and delicate of conscience and principle. I know that when once married I shall often have to hold my tongue on topics which heretofore have rarely failed to set that unruly member in tolerably facile motion. But I *will not* be a bigot – My heart will always turn to the good of every sect and class.[45]

During Charlotte's visit to Mrs Gaskell she took part in a revealing conversation with her hostess and their mutual friend Catherine [Katie] Winkworth. In this splendidly freewheeling exchange of ideas, three strong-minded, intelligent Victorian women can be observed intellectually uncorseted, exploring the world of marriage. Their discussion gives us the clearest account we have of Charlotte's inner turmoil during the period of her engagement. The account is by Catherine Winkworth in a letter to her sister, Emma Shaen.

I went in [to the Gaskell's] on Wednesday. Lily [Mrs Gaskell] drew me in directly to the room, whispering: "Say something about her marriage."… When she was summoned away I began: "I was very glad to hear something Mrs Gaskell told me about you." "What was it?" "That you are not going to be alone any more." She leant her head on her hand and said very quickly: "Yes, I am going to be married in June." "It will be a great happiness for you to have someone to care for, and make happy" "Yes; and it is a great thing to be the first object with any one." "And you must be very sure of that with Mr. Nicholls; he has known you and wished for this so long, I hear." "Yes, he has more than once refused preferment since he left my father, because he knew he never could marry me unless he could return to Haworth; he knew I could not leave my father." She stopped, and then went on: "But, Katie, it has cost me a good deal to come to this." "You will have to care for his things, instead of his caring for yours, is that it?" "Yes, I can see that beforehand." "But you have been together so long already that you know what his things are very well. He is very devoted to his duties, is he not? – and you can and would like to help him in those?" "I have always been used to those, and it is one great pleasure to me that he is so much beloved by all the people in the parish; there is quite a rejoicing over his return. But those are not everything, and I cannot conceal from myself that he is *not* intellectual; there are many places into which he could not follow me intellectually." "Well; of course everyone has their own tastes. For myself, if a man had a firm, constant, affectionate, reliable nature, with tolerable practical sense, I should be much better satisfied with him than if he had an intellect far beyond mine, and brilliant gifts without that trustworthiness. I care most for a calm, equable atmosphere at home." "I do believe Mr. Nicholls is as reliable as you say, or I wouldn't marry him." "And you have had time to prove it; you are not acting in a hurry." "That is true; and indeed, I am quite satisfied with my decision; still" – here Lily came in, and Miss Brontë repeated what I had been saying, ending with – "still such a character would be far less amusing and interesting than a more impulsive and fickle one; it might be dull!" "Yes, indeed," said Lily. "For a day's companion, yes," I said, "but not for a life's; one's home ought to be the one fixed point, the one untroubled region in one's lot; at home one wants peace and settled love and trust, not storm and change and excitement; besides such a character would have the advantage that one might do the fickleness required one's self, which would be a relief sometimes." "Oh, Katie, if *I* had ever said such a wicked thing," cried Lily; and then Miss Brontë: "Oh, Katie, I never thought to hear such a speech from *you*!" "You don't agree with it?" "Oh, there is truth in it; so much that I don't think *I* could ever have been so candid," Miss Brontë said; "and there is danger, too, one might be led on to go too far." "I think not," I said; "the steadiness and generosity on the other side would always keep one in check." But they made a great deal of fun and laughing about this, and then Lily was called away again, and Miss Brontë went on: "He is a Puseyite and very stiff; I fear it will stand in the way of my intercourse with some of my friends. But I shall always be the same in my heart towards them. I shall never let him make me a bigot. I don't think differences of opinion ought to interfere with friendship, do you?" "No." And we talked about this a little, and then I said: "Perhaps, too, you may do something to introduce him to goodness in sects where he has thought it would not be." "That is what I hope; he has a most sincere love of goodness wherever he sees it. I think if he could come to know Mr Gaskell it would change his feeling."[46]

These doubts, apprehensions, and misgivings continued to plague Charlotte as the wedding day, now set for 29 June, approached. Sometimes they broke out into a general irritation with the whole masculine sex. Towards the end of May, Charlotte discovered that Arthur had been suffering from the "rheumatic affliction" to which he had been frequently subject prior to his proposal, and which Patrick had used as yet another argument against their marriage. Now her vivid imagination cast her in the role of a permanent nursemaid to a cripple. "If he is doomed to suffer – it seems that so much the more will he need care and help – And yet the ultimate possibilities of such a case are appalling.". When Arthur arrived soon after for a visit he was

wasted and strange, and his whole manner nervous. My worst apprehensions – I thought were in the way of being realized. However – inquiry gradually relieved me. In the first place –

> he could give his ailment no name. He had not had one touch of rheumatism – that report was quite groundless – He was going to die, however, or something like it. I took heart on hearing this – which may seem paradoxical – but you know – dear Nell – when people are really going to die – they dont come a distance of some fifty miles to tell you so.
>
> Having drawn in the horns of my sympathy – I heard further that he had been to Mr Teale [a Leeds physician] – and was not surprised to receive the additional intelligence that that gentleman informed him that he had no manner of complaint whatever except an over-excited mind – In short I soon discovered that my business was – instead of sympathizing – to rate him soundly. He had wholesome treatment while he was at Haworth – and went away singularly better. Perfectly unreasonable however on some points – as his fallible sex are not ashamed to be – groaning over the prospect of a few more weeks of bachelorhood – as much as if it were an age of banishment or prison. It is probable he will fret himself thin again in the time – but I certainly shall not pity him if he does – there is not a woman in England but would have more sense – more courage – more sustaining hope than to behave so.
>
> Man is indeed an amazing piece of mechanism when you see – so to speak – the full weakness – of what he calls – his strength. There is not a female child above the age of eight but might rebuke him for the spoilt petulance of his wilful nonsense.[47]

During this visit Charlotte drew up a marriage settlement. Before the passage of the Married Women's Property Act, a wife's entire estate automatically became her husband's property. Whenever there was a desire to prevent this from happening it had become standard practice to place the prospective wife's property in a trust. This is what Charlotte now did, transferring her entire estate of £1,680 into a trust with Mary Taylor's brother Joe as sole trustee. The terms were explicit. Interest and dividends arising out of the trust were directed to be paid to Charlotte "for her sole and separate use independent of the said Arthur Bell Nicholls her intended husband who is not to intermeddle therewith neither shall the same [Charlotte] be subject or liable to his debts." If Charlotte should die before Arthur the trust would pass not to Arthur but to Patrick; if there were children, the estate would remain in trust for their benefit until they were of age, when it would be divided among them; and if Arthur should predecease his wife, the trust would be dissolved and the capital would revert to her.[48]

Why was Arthur excluded? Juliet Barker felt originally that this marriage settlement "reflected Charlotte's unease about Mr Nicholls' motives in marrying her;" but she later changed her mind and decided that Charlotte was concerned to secure the financial security of her father should she predecease him. Rebecca Fraser believes that it was Patrick who pressed for this clause in order to protect Charlotte. Certainly there is no evidence that Charlotte distrusted Arthur; quite the contrary. Before she developed any real affection for him, she had always emphasized his honesty, dependability, and lack of ulterior design: "Mr Nicholls only in his last letter refers touchingly to his earnest desire to prove his gratitude to Papa, by offering support and consolation to his declining age. This will not be mere *talk* with him; he is no talker, no dealer in professions." And Arthur apparently was fully in accord with the nature of the settlement. Along with Joe Taylor and Charlotte, he was a co-signatory. Still, his exclusion from any interest in Charlotte's estate indicates that he was not yet regarded as a full member of the family.[49]

Even before resuming his duties as curate officially, Arthur was taking parish problems on his shoulders, chief of which was the delicate question of what to do about Rev. George de Renzy. Understandably upset, de Renzy had "the deplorable weakness to go and pour out acrimonious complaints to John Brown, the National School-master [William Cartman] and other subordinates." Patrick had given him three weeks paid leave, but de Renzy asked for an additional two weeks holiday. "Mr de R's whole aim," Charlotte told Ellen, "is to throw Papa into the dilemma of being without a curate for some weeks. Papa has every legal right to frustrate this at once by telling him he must stay till his quarter is up – but this is just the harsh decided sort of measure which it goes against Papa's nature to adopt and which I *can* not and *will* not urge upon him while he is in delicate health. I feel compelled to throw the burden of the contest upon Mr Nicholls who is younger – more pugnacious and can bear it better." But since Arthur lacked the authority to do the hard things Patrick could not, "Mr de Renzy has succeeded in obtaining his holiday … Mr Nicholls with his usual trustworthiness – takes all the trouble of providing substitutes on his own shoulders."[50]

Gratitude notwithstanding, Charlotte found her fiancé's presence intrusive as she prepared for the wedding. In her letters to Ellen she had reverted from "Arthur" to "Mr Nicholls." "My worthy acquaintance at Kirk-Smeaton refuses to acknowledge himself better yet," she complained, "and I got thoroughly provoked yesterday by an announcement that he is coming again directly … I wrote immediately that he positively should not stay the whole week… I wish he would have kept away till July … I want to clear up my needle-work a little and have been sewing against time since I was at Brookroyd. – Mr. N – hindered me for a full week."[51]

When she visited Haworth in September 1853, Mrs Gaskell had been shocked by the way Patrick left his daughter to eat her meals and spend her long evenings alone. What she perhaps did not realize was the way that this enforced solitude provided the writer with a room of her own and the time to work at her profession. Now this large Irishman, hitherto so reserved and circumspect, was crowding her accustomed space. The standard image of the Rev. Arthur Bell Nicholls is that of the friendless recluse sitting alone at night in his little room at John Brown's. But he was far from a hermit. He had many close friends, including some local clergymen: Joseph Grant (Mr Donne in *Shirley*), and the brothers George and Sutcliffe Sowden. When Charlotte came to send out wedding announcements she limited her own list to eighteen individuals and families. She originally asked Ellen to order fifty cards, but had to increase the order, since "Mr. N – has such a string of clerical acquaintances to whom he wishes to send … There is no end to his string of [P]arson friends."[52]

No doubt Arthur would have wished that some of this numerous acquaintance should share in the joy at his wedding, but this was the last thing the preternaturally shy Charlotte wanted. He capitulated to his bride on this question. "Mr Nicholls is a kind considerate fellow with all his masculine faults in some points – he enters into my wishes about having the thing done quietly in a way which makes me grateful – and if nobody interferes and spoils his arrangements – he will manage so that not a soul in Haworth shall be aware of the day."[53] And so, on the morning of 29 June 1854, when Charlotte and Arthur were married in St Michaels by Sutcliffe Sowden, the only witnesses to the ceremony were Charlotte's bridesmaid Ellen Nussey, Margaret Wooler, Joseph Grant, John Brown the sexton, Joseph Redman the parish clerk, and young John Robinson, whose job was to warn the parsonage when the groom's party was approaching from Oxenhope. One of the few villagers who caught a glimpse of her that day said that Charlotte looked like a snowdrop in white muslin trimmed with green embroidery, her figure seeming more diminutive than usual by the presence at her side of the tall, dark groom. Martha and Tabby were also probably present although they are not mentioned anywhere, but one important figure was notably absent: the bride's father. On the evening before the wedding,

> when all was finished – the trunk packed, the morning's breakfast arranged, the wedding-dress laid out, – just at bedtime, Mr. Brontë announced his intention of stopping at home while the others went to church. What was to be done? Who was to give the bride away? There were only to be the officiating clergyman, the bride and the bridegroom, the bridesmaid, and Miss Wooler present. The Prayer-book was referred to; and there it was seen that the Rubric enjoins that the Minister shall receive "the woman from her father's or *friend's* hands," and that nothing is specified as to the sex of the "friend." So Miss Wooler, ever kind in emergency, volunteered to give her old pupil away.[54]

While it is true that Patrick's health had deteriorated as the wedding approached, he was not bedridden and this was his last child who was about to be married. Brian Wilks' suggestion that he stayed away because he could not trust himself to hold his tongue when the minister asked if any knew "cause or just impediment why these two persons should not be joined together" is quite at odds with the old man's nature. It is difficult not to conclude that Patrick was simply overcome at the last moment by a strong attack of jealousy. Ten days after Charlotte's wedding, he sent Ellen a characteristically orotund letter resembling the response to a death; in it he referred obscurely to the wedding of "my Daughters."[55]

CHAPTER FOUR

Tomkins' Brief Triumph

The honeymoon couple took the railway from Keighley to the ancient walled town of Conway in North Wales. Reliable as ever, Arthur "had arranged everything – the tickets, the time table, the luggage," the comfortable room at the Castle Hotel. The Cochranes suggest that Charlotte, used to doing everything for herself, enjoyed having other hands take responsibility for all the troublesome details of life. "All Charlotte had to do was relax." Before leaving Haworth she had caught cold as she often did when under stress, but she still managed to get off a short note to Ellen on her wedding night: "the evening is wet and wild, though the day was fair chiefly with some gleams of sunshine. However, we are sheltered in a comfortable inn." Charlotte was in her thirty-ninth year, Arthur almost two years younger; she was a virgin, he almost certainly one. As Juliet Barker observes, we can only guess what either made of their first sexual experience: "though she did not love Mr Nicholls when she married him, she had never found him physically repugnant like the unfortunate James Taylor, and her honeymoon letters, full of affectionate references to 'my dear husband,' suggest a growing and happy intimacy."[1]

From Conway the couple traveled by coastal railway to Bangor (Gwynedd), spending the next few days taking day trips into the countryside. Despite the unfavourable weather, Charlotte found that some of the scenery "surpassed anything I remember of the English lakes."[2] After six days, the Welsh part of the honeymoon came to an end. The couple crossed the Menai Straits to Anglesey and Holyhead, where on 4 July they took the Irish packet, a paddle steamer, to Kingstown (now Dun Laoghaire). From there they went to Dublin, where they were met by Arthur's brother, Alan, then manager of the Grand Canal, and two cousins. One, Joseph Bell (1835–1891), was a student at Trinity. He would go on to serve as vicar of St Paul's, Rynagh, Banagher, Canon of Kells and of St Patrick's Cathedral in Dublin, acquiring on the way a considerable reputation for his eloquence in the pulpit. The other cousin, Mary Anna Bell (1830–1915), was "a pretty lady-like girl with gentle English manners."[3] She walked with a pronounced limp, the result, depending on the source, either of rheumatic fever or a childhood riding accident. She was the older sister of Harriette, to whom Arthur had previously proposed. Ten years later, Mary would become his second wife. This pleasant young company took Charlotte on a tour of Dublin. Arthur was anxious that she should see the spendours of Trinity College – its chapel, its magnificent classical library housing the Book of Kells, and the neo-Gothic museum so highly praised by Ruskin – but because her cold persisted, they decided to cut the sight-seeing short and take the steamer to Banagher.

Charlotte's honeymoon letters describing Cuba House suggest that she was under the impression it was the property of the Bell family, and did not realize that the Bells lived there only so long as Arthur's cousin James retained the headmastership of the Banagher Royal Free School. Eager to reinforce the picture of easy gentility the great house conveyed, Arthur probably did nothing to disillusion her. In July this would not have been difficult since the school was on vacation. In any case she was duly impressed. She had come to Ireland with the standard set of English prejudices but among the Bells she was "greatly surprised to find so much of English order and repose in the family habits and arrangements. I had heard a great deal of Irish negligence."

> I cannot help feeling singularly interested in all about the place. In this house Mr Nicholls was brought up by his uncle Dr. Bell – It is very large and looks externally like a gentleman's country-seat – within most of the rooms are lofty and spacious and some – the drawing room – dining-room &c. handsomely and commodiously furnished – The passages look desolate and bare – our bed-room, a great room on the ground-floor would have looked gloomy when

> we were shewn into it but for the turf-fire that was burning in the wide old chimney -. The male members of this family – such as I have seen seem thoroughly educated gentlemen. Mrs Bell is like an English or Scotch Matron quiet, kind and well-bred – It seems she was brought up in London. [Thus had Harriette Lucinda or Arthur transformed three short weeks in a London finishing school.]
>
> Both her daughters are strikingly pretty in appearance – and their manners are very amiable and pleasing. [Charlotte would never know that Arthur had proposed to Harriette, who in that same year and perhaps stimulated by the sight of Arthur as the happy bridegroom, married John Evans Adamson, another cousin on her mother's side. Nor would she know that Mary had always harbored a special affection for Arthur and would become his second wife.] I must say I like my new relations. My dear husband too appears in a new light here in his own country. More than once I have had deep pleasure in hearing his praises on all sides. Some of the old servants and followers of the family tell me I am a most fortunate person for that I have got one of the best gentlemen in the country. His Aunt too speaks of him with a mixture of affection and respect most gratifying to hear. I was not well when I came here – fatigue and excitement had nearly knocked me up – and my cough was become very bad – but Mrs. Bell has nursed me both with kindness and skill, and I am greatly better now.[4]

As for the Bells, it was immensely exciting to have the internationally famous author as a guest in their house, and as a relation to boot. They were all Brontë enthusiasts. Even when they had known Charlotte only as Currer Bell, they had been "electrified" by *Jane Eyre.* Although the three-volume novel was published in England as a whole, in Ireland each volume appeared separately and the Bells "could hardly endure the suspense between one part and another, and used to drive to Birr to get them at the earliest possible moment." Mrs Bell found it difficult to identify the novelist with the shy, diminutive creature she had nursed back to health. "Sitting over the fire like this," she remarked after a long and intimate talk, "I quite forget that I am speaking to the celebrated authoress."[5]

After a week at Cuba House, the couple traveled through the south and west of Ireland. Charlotte's letters describing this trip show her far from sure that she had made the right decision, still struggling and failing to match the depth of Arthur's love for her. Her tortuous, qualified sentences betray the uncertain nature of her feelings: "I trust I feel thankful to God for having enabled me to make what seems a right choice – and I pray to be enabled to repay as I ought the affectionate devotion of a truthful, honourable, unboastful man;" a week later: "I believe my dear husband to be a good man, and trust I have done right in marrying him. I hope too I shall be enabled always to feel grateful for the kindness and affection he shews me." Still, their differing sensibilities continued to worry her. "My husband is not a poet or a poetical man – and one of my grand doubts about marriage was about 'congenial tastes'," she wrote to Katie Winkworth from Cork, resuming the discussion they and Mrs Gaskell had had before her marriage. But she was beginning to discover in Arthur an unsuspected degree of sensitivity to *her* poetical spirit. On their first morning at Kilkee, where the local inn provided her with more than enough of that Irish negligence she had failed to discover at Cuba House,

> we went out on to the cliffs and saw the Atlantic coming in all white foam, I did not know whether I should get leave or time to take the matter in my own way. I did not want to talk – but I *did* want to look and be silent. Having hinted a petition, licence was not refused – covered with a rug to keep off the spray I was allowed to sit where I chose – and he only interrupted me when he thought I crept too near the edge of the cliff. So far he is always good in this way – and this protection which does not interfere or pretend – is I believe a thousand times better than any half sort of pseudo sympathy. I will try with God's help to be as indulgent to him whenever indulgence is needed.

Arthur's reaction to the same scene, although enthusiastic was, predictably, more prosaic than his wife's: "the finest shore I ever saw," he told George Sowden, "completely girdled with stupendous cliffs – it was most refreshing to sit on a rock & look out on the broad Atlantic boiling & foaming at our feet."[6]

The curate and his wife returned to Haworth on 1 August. If the honeymoon was in many ways a revelation of Arthur's past, now the business of married life began in earnest. Arthur, conventional to the marrow, took it for granted that Charlotte would absorb herself in *his* life and interests. Though he had demonstrated his consideration for her need to absorb things by herself on the cliffs of Kilkee, back at Haworth, his possessiveness struck her with full force. She had to cut short a note to Catherine Wooler with the observation that: "my husband is just now sitting before me kindly stretching his patience to the utmost, but wishing me very much to have done writing, and put on my bonnet for a walk," and wrote to Ellen, "Since I came home I have not had an unemployed moment; my life is changed indeed – to be wanted continually – to be constantly called for and occupied seems so strange: yet it is a marvelously good thing. As yet I don't quite understand how some wives grow so selfish – As far as my experience of matrimony goes – I think it tends to draw you out of, and away from yourself." A cryptic paragraph followed:

> during the last 6 weeks – the colour of my thoughts is a good deal changed: I know more of the realities of life than I once did. I think many false ideas are propagated – perhaps unintentionally. I think those married women who indiscriminately urge their acquaintance to marry – much to blame. For my part – I can only say with deeper sincerity and fuller significance – what I always said in theory – Wait God's will. Indeed – indeed Nell – it is a solemn and strange and perilous thing for a woman to become a wife. Man's lot is far – far different.

Tom Winnifrith has suggested that this letter "possibly contains some veiled reference to the secrets of the marriage bed."[7]

There is another, more obvious meaning to these remarks. For all her shyness and self-sacrifice, Charlotte Brontë had been her own mistress, physically as well as intellectually, from an early age. Her father's habit of shutting himself up in his study had allowed her to make the dining room *her* study, especially after the deaths of her sisters. By disrupting that practical domestic arrangement, marriage had caused Charlotte to lose her balance. The phrase "solemn and strange and perilous" is charged with more than mere sexual overtones. It suggests that, confused by conflicting feelings, by the rich satisfaction of being needed every minute of the day balanced against losing the time and space for her writing, she found herself unsure of her new bearings. Hence all she could do was "Wait God's will."

Arthur, by contrast, had become "Tomkins Triumphant" and was reveling in marriage. All his pre-nuptial psychosomatic disorders had disappeared. "Have I told you how much better Mr Nicholls is?" Charlotte asked Ellen. "He looks quite strong and hale – he gained 12 lbs. during the 4 weeks we were in Ireland. To see this improvement in him has been a main source of happiness to me; and to speak truth – a subject of wonder too." To Margaret Wooler she wrote, "It makes me content and grateful to hear him from time to time avow his happiness in the brief plain phrase of sincerity." Charlotte too was in better health: "I think I am decent – better certainly than I was two months ago, but people don't compliment me as they do Arthur – excuse the name – it has grown natural to use it now." The cough that had bothered her at the beginning of the honeymoon had disappeared before she left Ireland "and since my return home I have scarcely had an ailment except occasional head-aches."[8]

Like most Victorian males – and many in our own day – Arthur took it for granted that his wife would submerge her interests in his. Charlotte even found it difficult to answer her correspondence, which she had thought to clear up immediately upon her return from Ireland, "but I reckoned without my host," she told Margaret Wooler.

> Marriage certainly makes a difference in some things and amongst others the disposition and consumption of time. I really seem to have had scarcely a spare moment since that dim quiet June Morning when you, E. Nussey and myself all walked down to Haworth Church -. Not that I have been hurried or oppressed – but the fact is my time is not my own now; Somebody else wants a good portion of it – and says we must do so and so. We *do* 'so and so' accordingly, and it generally seems the right thing – only I sometimes wish I could have written the letter as well as taken the walk.

To Ellen she was less restrained. "Take warning Ellen – the married woman can call but a very small portion of each day her own. Not that

I complain of this sort of Monopoly as yet – and I hope I never shall incline to regard it as a Misfortune, but it certainly exists."[9] Charlotte's correspondence throughout this early marriage period is filled with muffled statements of protest immediately balanced by counter-statements of contentment. The "as yet" and "it certainly exists" are signs that the creator of Jane Eyre, Shirley Keeldar and Lucy Snowe had not been wholly suffocated. Arthur, however, was not a blind Rochester to be led about by an ascendant Jane.

In addition to the walks, frequent and long, there was a string of Arthur's friends who had to be looked after, as well as the members of the local congregation.

> We have had … latterly some little occupation in the way of preparing for a small village entertainment. Both Mr. Nicholls and myself wished much to make some response for the hearty welcome and general good-will shewn by the parishioners on his return; accordingly the Sunday and day-Scholars and Teachers – the church ringers, singers, &c. to the number of 500 were asked to Tea and Supper in the schoolroom-. They seemed to enjoy it much, and it was very pleasant to see their happiness. One of the villagers in proposing my husband's health described him as "*a consistent Christian and a kind gentleman.*" I own the words touched me – and I thought … that to merit and win such a character was better than to earn either Wealth or Fame or Power. I am disposed to echo that high but simple eulogium *now.* If I can do so with sincerity and conviction *seven years – or even a year hence* – I shall esteem myself a happy woman. Faultless my husband is not – faultless no human being is; but as you well know – I did not expect perfection.[10]

Five hundred guests out of a village of 2,000, a large proportion of whom were Dissenters, is an impressive number. How many turned out to welcome back the newly-married couple, how many to honour their curate, how many to ogle the famous writer, how many just to enjoy the free food and drink?

While social obligations absorbed one part of Charlotte's day, she was also discovering that a curate who took his responsibilities as seriously as her husband did left little free time for himself or his wife. Arthur operated like a Swiss watch: "my dear Arthur is a very practical as well as a very punctual, methodical man." Every weekday morning between 9 and 10:30 he was in the National School giving religious instruction, and almost every afternoon he visited the poor: "Of course he often finds a little work for his wife to do, and I hope she is not sorry to help him." But even when he was not involved in clerical duties he absorbed her time. "I am writing in haste," she told Ellen. "It is almost inexplicable to me that I seem so often hurried now – but the fact is whenever Arthur is in, I must have occupations in which he can share, or which will not at least divert my attention from him – Thus a multitude of little matters get put off till he goes out and then I am quite busy." Inevitably, her creative work was affected. "I have not so much time for thinking," she confessed to Margaret Wooler; "now that I am married I do not expect to be an object of much general interest. Ladies, who have won some prominence (call it either *notoriety* or celebrity) in their single life – often fall quite into the background when they change their names."[11] In a frequently quoted letter to George Smith written after her death, Arthur himself innocently revealed how he impinged on Charlotte's time and space:

> One Evening at the close of 1854 as we sat by the fire listening to the howling of the wind around the house my poor wife suddenly said, "If you had not been with me I must have been writing now." She then ran upstairs, brought down & read aloud the beginning of her New Tale [the unfinished fragment, *Emma*] – When she had finished I remarked, "The Critics will accuse you of repetition as you have again introduced a school." She replied, "O I shall alter that – I always begin two or three times before I can please myself." But it was not to be.[12]

"If you had not been with me I must have been writing now." Even before Mrs Gaskell met Arthur, she warned Charlotte "You had better do all your writing before you are married, you will do none after." Mrs Gaskell was not making a general comment on the condition of all married women, for she had no problem with Mr Gaskell. It was rather her perception, shared by Thackeray, that for all her independence of mind Charlotte was easily dominated by men. Charlotte may have recognized this too, for she intimated to George Smith at the time of her engagement that her writing life was over. "In the course of the year that is gone – Cornhill and London have receded a long way from me – the links of communication have waxed very frail and few. It must be so in this world. All things considered – I don't wish it otherwise."

Mrs Humphry Ward saw a different meaning in this letter: it reflected, she felt, the "deep exhaustion" which Charlotte felt on the completion of *Villette*, perhaps even a "final renunciation" of creative work, and "above all a deep need for rest."[13] Was Charlotte burned out, turning to Arthur as one might enter a convalescent home? There is no simple answer to such questions. Part of the power of Charlotte Brontë's fiction derives from the collision of two opposing images of women: Shirley Keeldar, strong, independent, her mind filled with visions of titanic females bestriding the earth, and Helen Burns, passive and submissive, ever obedient to some superior will. In her fiction, Charlotte separated and dramatized the collision, but in her own life these two aspects of her remained inseparable, causing constant stress, of which her recurring bilious headaches were a probable symptom.

The passive side of Charlotte's nature contributed to the myth of Arthur Bell Nicholls as the man who had murdered a great literary talent, a myth to which, late in life and full of bitterness, Ellen Nussey contributed. In describing the single visit that she paid to Haworth after Charlotte's marriage, Ellen told Thomas Wemyss Reid how one day she had accompanied Charlotte and Arthur on a walk over the moors.

> In the course of their conversation she asked Ch if she was writing another book. "No," replied Ch, "Arthur says I have no time for writing now as I must attend to my duties as a clergyman's wife." She said it in such a tone as to convince her friend that she was not satisfied with her husband's decision, and Miss N, plucking up her courage, remonstrated with him upon his refusal to allow Ch to exercise her great gift. Mr N's response was short and to the point. "I did not marry Currer Bell, the novelist, but Charlotte Brontë, the clergyman's daughter. Currer Bell may fly to heaven tomorrow for anything I care."

Reid was skeptical about the "absolute truth" of this tale but he was "quite sure [Ellen] believed it to be true."[14] Many years later Arthur strenuously denied to Clement Shorter that he had ever discouraged

Charlotte from writing, and he was even more emphatic in an 1899 letter to Mrs Humphrey Ward.

> I must say that I fail to see any confirmation in them [Charlotte's post-marital letters] of the statement that "I encouraged her to give up novel writing."
>
> There was no such understanding between us – of course. We talked of her Literary Work – on one occasion she read for me the MS (afterwards published in "The Cornhill"); when she concluded I merely said "I fear the critics will accuse you of repetition" – but not a word of discouragement …
>
> I never interfered in the slightest degree with her liberty of action – I shall feel obliged if you will endeavour to remove the misconception which you say exists in this respect.
>
> There is also another misconception, which I am told by a Literary Friend [probably Shorter], prevails – "that her married life was unhappy" – I should have thought that her own words written from her deathbed had made such a statement incredible but I am told that it exists.
>
> I can only say that during the few months of our married life we were never separated for a day and that during that time a hasty or unkind word never passed between us.[15]

Of course Arthur was hardly likely to concede that he had stifled his wife's creativity, but his boast that they were never separated for a day shows how ignorant he was of the novelist's need for time to herself. Patrick's biographers, John Lock and W.T. Dixon, saw him as "the enigma of the Brontë story. He was the intruder from the outside world who penetrated the Brontë fastness, yet he loved a woman and not a legend … He saw Charlotte's courage, not her genius, her loyalty, not her fame, he brought her happiness not praise. It was a perfect match, because it was brief. Had the fates protracted the union, it could have ended in disaster."[16] The shortness of their marriage, which lasted only nine months until Charlotte's death, has licensed every subsequent commentator to speculate on the extent to which Arthur had suffocated, or would have suffocated, Charlotte's creative powers. Reading those letters in which she describes, sometimes in an almost bewildered way, how her private time has been purloined, it is difficult not to conclude that being married to Arthur did stifle his wife's strongest creative impulses. His obsessive husbanding of her every action suggests the neurotic fear, characteristic of anxious attachment, that the beloved will vanish at the slightest opportunity and must, therefore, be kept under constant surveillance and control. But we can never know what effect marriage would have had on Charlotte's career had she lived another ten, twenty, or thirty years. She might have fought for her own space as, in the end, she fought with Patrick for the right to be courted by Arthur, and Arthur might have eventually recognized that she must always be given time to sit alone, as he had allowed her to do on the cliffs of Kilkee. But the short duration of the marriage allowed neither of these possibilities to emerge.

What *is* clear, however, is the slow transformation of Charlotte's feelings for her husband. On 11 April 1854 she refers him as "Arthur" for the first time but then reverts to "Mr N." He remains stuck in that formal mode until 7 September, when she excuses herself to Ellen for referring to him as "Arthur – it has grown natural to use it now." On the 14th she is back to Mr N, but writing to Margaret Wooler five days later, she calls him "my dear Arthur." From then on, "Arthur" triumphs. Slowly but surely, familiarity was breeding love. Not, however, a blind, romantic love: Arthur continued to cleave to his Puseyite religious views, while Charlotte continued to treat him, as she had the fictional Mr Macarthey, with a gently sarcastic humor. "He is just gone out this morning," she informed Ellen, "in a rather refractory mood about some dissenters. On Sunday we had a pair of very sweet sermons indeed – really good – and touching the better springs of our nature. Just before going to Church – he menaced me with something worse than the preceding Sunday – I was agreeably disappointed."[17]

The tenor of social life at the parsonage was subtly altered. Arthur's clerical friends were frequent visitors, often staying overnight. But there was a limit to Charlotte's tolerance. When Arthur went off to the consecration of Heptonstall Church, she did not accompany him: "I hardly like coming in contact with all the Mrs Parsons." Contact with her own circle of friends was circumscribed. Ellen Nussey made only one visit to Haworth in the fall, and then only when it was convenient to Arthur. Charlotte herself planned to visit Ellen at Brookroyd, but never managed the trip before her final illness. Ellen felt shut out from a long intimacy and, understandably, blamed Arthur for excluding her. And although Charlotte often asked Mrs Gaskell to come over to see her, the latter never went, "partly because it required a little courage to face Mr Nicholls, as she had told me he did not like her intimacy with us as dissenters, but that she knew he *would* like us when he had seen us."[18]

Arthur may or may not have smothered Charlotte's life as a novelist; he certainly affected her personal correspondence, particularly with Ellen Nussey, which she had employed since their schooldays to work out emotional problems. In October, Mary Taylor's brother, Joe, his wife Amelia, and their daughter Tim paid a visit to Haworth. In a letter to Ellen before Christmas, Charlotte described Amelia's "strained – odd – unnatural" behavior. Arthur was so "out of patience" with her that he "threatened to bolt" whenever she came again, but "we got on with them better than I expected." Tim declared a "decided preference" for Patrick's white hair over Arthur's black "and coolly advised the latter to 'go to the barber, and get his whiskers cut off.'" Whether or not Arthur was amused by tiny Tim's behaviour, he was upset by Charlotte's detailed account of it to Ellen.

> Arthur has just been glancing over this note. He thinks I have written too freely about Amelia, &c. Men don't seem to understand making letters a vehicle of communication – they always seem to think us incautious. I'm sure I don't think I have said anything rash – however you must *burn* it when read. Arthur says such letters as mine never ought to be kept – they are dangerous as lucifer matches – so be sure to follow a recommendation he has just given "fire them" – or "there will be no more." Such is his resolve. I can't help laughing – this seems to me so funny. Arthur, however, says he is quite "serious and looks it, I assure you – he is bending over the desk with his eyes full of concern. I am now desired "to have done with it –[19]

This image of him bending over the desk scrutinizing her correspondence is chilling; it is Arthur at his worst. Despite Charlotte's effort to treat the matter lightly, Ellen could hardly do so. Over the years she had preserved almost everything her old school friend had written, and after Currer Bell became a major literary figure must have realized their future value, not only financially, but also as a means of assuring herself a place in posterity. Then along came this dark intruder, menacing everything. He had already interrupted her friendship; now he threatened to destroy her vicarious fame. It was the beginning of an enmity that would grow and continue to the end of her life.

Ellen's response failed to satisfy Arthur, who complained that

> you do not distinctly promise to burn my letters as you receive them. He says you must give him a plain pledge to that effect – or he will read every line I write and elect himself censor of our correspondence.
>
> He says women are most rash in letter-writing – they think only of the trustworthiness of their immediate friend – and do not look to contingencies – a letter may fall into any hand. You must give the promise – I believe – at least he says so, with his best regards – or else you will get such notes as he writes to Mr Sowden – plain, brief statements of facts without the adornment of a single flourish – with no comment on the character or peculiarities of any human being – and if a phrase of sensibility or affection steals in – it seems to come on tiptoe – looking ashamed of itself – blushing "pea-green" as he says – and holding both its shy hands before its face. Write him out his promise on a separate slip of paper – in a *legible* hand – and send it in your next.[20]

Ellen's reply, addressed "To the Revd. The Magister," was surcharged with scorn: "As you seem to hold in great horror the ardentia verba [burning words] of feminine epistles I pledge myself to the destruction of Charlotte's epistles henceforth, if You, pledge *your*self to *no* censorship in the matter communicated." "Arthur thanks you for the promise," Charlotte told Ellen. "He was out when I commenced this letter, but he is just come in – on my asking whether he would give the pledge received in return – he says 'yes we may now write any dangerous stuff we please to each other – it is not '*old friends*' he mistrusts, but the chances of war – the accidental passing of letters into hands and under eyes for which they were never written." Arthur could not have known how prescient his words were of future trouble for both him and Ellen. To Charlotte, this initial duel seemed "mighty amusing." She tried to explain Arthur's concern as "a man's mode of viewing correspondence – Men's letters are proverbially uninteresting and uncommunicative – I never quite knew before *why* they made them so. They may be right in a sense. Strange chances do fall out certainly. As to my own notes I never thought of attaching importance to them, or considering their fate – till Arthur seemed to reflect on both so seriously." But for Ellen the situation was far from amusing. As Margaret Smith observes, Ellen "intended to conceal her own promise and Nicholls's pledge in response to it. … [S]he did this by deleting as thoroughly as she could" that part of the letter "from 'Arthur thanks you' to 'each other,' and adding a footnote in pencil: 'he never did give the pledge.'"[21] While we may condemn her dishonesty and her subsequent editorial distortions, we remain forever in Ellen's debt for having failed to burn Charlotte's letters.

In this battle of wills Arthur's terror of any expression of feeling that might upset the established order of things is once again revealed. Whether his rigidity was the product of the culture of his time, or of his own particular childhood, can never be determined. Almost certainly both influences were at play. One aspect of the industrial revolution was to enhance people's fear of chaos and there is an obvious homology between social and personal control. The stock image of the terse, thin-lipped Englishman appears only at the beginning of the nineteenth century: Wellington was perhaps its first exemplar; formerly the English were considered among the most violent and emotional people in Europe. Arthur's need for stability was almost certainly what turned him into a Puseyite and, paradoxically, what made him such a stable friend and lover. The dark side of this emotional control, as the anxious-attachment diagnosis would suggest, was a stifling possessiveness arising out of fear of loss and separation.

Charlotte was caught in its grip, but although it left her at times with a sense of being smothered by Arthur's attention, she was simultaneously seduced by the depth of his passion and tranquillized by his reliability. "Papa has taken no duty since we returned [from Ireland]," she told Margaret Wooler, "and each time I see Mr Nicholls put on gown or surplice – I feel comforted to think that this marriage has secured Papa good aid in his old age."[22] There may also be, as Juliet Barker has suggested when describing Charlotte's relationship with M. Heger, a masochistic element at work in her submission to Arthur's will.[23]

When Sir James Kay-Shuttleworth came for a weekend in November, Charlotte had further proof of Arthur's dependability. Trained as a physician, Sir James became known as the father of English elementary education for his work as secretary to the committee of the Privy Council on Education. When he retired in 1849 on account of ill health, he was made a baronet. A literary groupie before his time, Sir James had invited Charlotte to visit him and his wife as soon as he discovered that the celebrated author of *Jane Eyre* and *Shirley* lived close to their country house, Gawthorpe Hall. Charlotte had been impressed by the hall, 250 years old, "grey, antique, castellated and stately … the arms and the strange crest of the Shuttleworths [his wife's family name, which he had been obliged to tack on to his own at marriage] … carved on the oak-panelling of each room," but she was less impressed by Sir James: "I wish he may be as sincere as he is polished. He shows his white teeth with too frequent a smile," she told Ellen. When she visited London in 1851, he was almost excessively attentive. Now, when he heard that she had married a lowly clergyman, he conceived that through his patronage, he might snare Charlotte as his own pet writer. He told a friend that Charlotte, "described her husband as a sensible man of high principles, and whose attachment to her had borne the trial of several years delay. I found him all and more than I had been led to expect."[24] Charlotte thought his main purpose was to see the Rev. A.B. Nicholls – "a gratifying proof of respect for my dear Arthur" – but Sir James's real motive was to use her dear Arthur as a means of securing her as his curate's wife. He offered Arthur the living of Padiham, which carried a stipend of £200, twice his current income. Arthur declined, true to his pre-nuptial agreement to continue at Haworth as long as Patrick lived.

Charlotte's appreciation of her "dear Arthur" in September continued, progressing to "my dear Arthur" in November. At the end of December she called him tenderly "my dear boy … dearer now than he was six months ago," adding that "every day makes my own attachment to him stronger." Love appeared to be good for her health. "It is long since I have known such comparative immunity from head-ache, sickness and indigestion, as during the last three months." After a visit to Charlotte and Arthur, George Sowden commented on how well she looked and the complete happiness of the newly married couple. Even Ellen Nussey admitted that "after her marriage – a halo of happiness seemed to surround her – a holy calm pervaded her even in moments of excitement."[25]

These brief months of health and domestic happiness were not to last. One morning at the end of November, Arthur called Charlotte out for a walk on the moors. The weather being fine they went a considerable distance to view her favourite waterfall, after a winter melt "a perfect torrent raving over the rocks white and bountiful." Suddenly the weather changed. It began to rain, and Charlotte arrived home soaked to the skin. Always susceptible, she caught cold and although she soon appeared to have made a complete recovery, she had to cancel a visit to Ellen at Brookroyd. She herself was ready to go but "these matters are not quite in my power now – another must be consulted – and where his wish and judgment have a decided bias … I make no stir."[26] Subsequent biographers, beginning with Mrs Gaskell, have suggested that this was the beginning of her terminal illness, thus leaving the impression that Arthur was the unwitting agent of his wife's death. But his wish that Charlotte not visit Ellen at Brookroyd, where there was the possibility of typhus, surely shows concern for her well being, maybe even that they thought her pregnant.

At the beginning of January, Arthur and Charlotte again visited Sir James Kay-Shuttleworth and again Sir James asked Arthur to accept the living of Padiham, "but *that* is out of the question," Charlotte noted. When Sutcliffe Sowden's name came up as a second possible choice, Arthur's inherent fear of publicity was revealed when he told Charlotte to keep absolutely silent. "If a whisper gets out – these things fly from parson to parson like wild fire."[27]

Sir James had written a novel and insisted on reading long passages from the manuscript. To escape the baronet's endless recitation, Charlotte went out in the rain in her slippers, perhaps aggravating a chill she had already contracted. On their return to Haworth, James Adamson Bell, whose guests they had been at Cuba House during their honeymoon, paid a short visit. Charlotte was once again impressed by the gentility of her husband's Irish relatives: "the visit was a real treat – He is a cultivated, thoroughly educated man with a mind stored with information gathered from books and travel – and what is far rarer – with the art of conversing appropriately and quietly and never pushing his superiority upon you."[28]

James Bell was to be Charlotte's last guest. Around the 9th of January "the stomach seemed quite suddenly to lose its tone – indigestion and continual faint sickness have been my portion every since."[29] Charlotte clearly regarded this as an early sign of pregnancy for she warned Ellen: "Don't conjecture – dear Nell – for it is too soon yet – though I certainly never before felt as I have done lately. But keep the matter wholly to yourself – for I can come to no decided opinion at present." The morning sickness continued. Charlotte took to her bed and Arthur, wishing "to have better advice than Haworth affords," sent for the well-reputed Dr Macturk of Bradford. Another planned visit to Brookroyd had to be canceled, for Charlotte was now so ill that she asked Arthur to keep Ellen informed. Dr Macturk's opinion when he saw Charlotte at the end of January was that "her illness would be of some duration – but there was no immediate danger." His prognosis may well have been offered to calm Patrick and Arthur for, except for a brief improvement at the beginning of March, her condition grew steadily worse. "Let me speak the plain truth," she wrote Amelia Taylor, "my sufferings are very great – my nights indescribable – sickness with scarce a reprieve – I strain until what I vomit is mixed with blood. Medicine I have quite discontinued – If you *can* send me anything that will do good – *do.*" When Martha Brown, who shared with Arthur the tasks of nursing, tried to cheer her patient up by reminding her of the child to come, Charlotte could only reply: "I dare say I shall be glad sometime, but I am so ill – so weary." Since Arthur had taken over most of her correspondence, her own notes were few and short, but they all contained at least one sentence describing his care and her deepening affection. "No kinder, better husband than mine it seems to me can there be in the world. I do not want now for kind companionship in health and the tenderest nursing in sickness ... I find my husband the tenderest nurse, the kindest support – the best earthly comfort that ever woman had. His patience never fails, and it is tried by sad days and broken nights ... My heart is knit to him – he is so tender, so good, helpful, patient."[29]

On 17 February 1855, as it became clear that she was close to death, Charlotte made her last will and testament. Her earlier, cautious marriage settlement was revoked, and everything of which she was possessed was left to Arthur, "to be his absolutely and entirely." This new will was a measure both of her love and her "absolute faith in her husband's integrity."[30]

Charlotte lingered on to the end of March. Despite acting throughout as her intensive-care nurse, Arthur still managed to perform his regular clerical duties until the last week of her life, when he took up a round-the-clock vigil at her bedside. On the 30th, Patrick summoned up the strength to send a note to Ellen, telling her that Arthur was not "sufficiently strong, and composed as to be able to write" and that Charlotte was "on the verge of the grave." His reference to Arthur's lack of strength and composure suggests that he still retained an element of contempt for what he considered Arthur's unmanliness at the time of his proposal. It was probably at this point, when all hope was lost, that Patrick walked into the kitchen and said softly, "I told you, Martha, that there was no sense in Charlotte's marrying at all, for she was not strong enough for marriage." Not strong enough, he meant, for childbearing. Nearly sixty years later Tabitha Brown, Martha's younger sister, recalled that Charlotte was so worn and thin "that light showed through her hand when it was held up, and her face was so drawn that she looked like a little old woman. When her father came into the room, she put forth all her strength and said, 'See papa! I am a little better; don't you think I look better?'"[31]

Mrs Gaskell has left a description of her final days.

> Long days and longer nights went by; still the same relentless nausea and faintness, and still borne on in patient trust. About the third week in March there was a change; a low wandering delirium came on; and in it she begged constantly for food and even for stimulants. She swallowed eagerly now ["opening her mouth," said Tabitha Brown, "just like a little throstle for them to put the food in"]; but it was too late. Wakening for an instant from this stupor of intelligence, she saw her husband's woe-worn face, and caught the sound of some murmured words of prayer that God would spare her. "Oh!" she whispered forth, "I am not going to die, am I? He will not separate us, we have been so happy."[32]

When death finally came, early on the 31st, Arthur "sprawled across the bed in a convulsion of grief," sobbing loudly. Patrick stood upright with dry eyes. Then, completely under control, he quietly turned and left the room, leaving Martha and Tabitha wondering at his hardness of feeling. After Martha closed Charlotte's eyes, the women left the room, leaving the shattered husband alone with his beloved. Thinking that Patrick had gone down to his study, Tabitha opened his bedroom door and then stopped abruptly. "Patrick was kneeling by his bed in an attitude of prayer and crying in agonized tones, 'My poor Charlotte! My dear Charlotte!' As Tabitha would later admit: 'I understood Mr Brontë better then: I never understood him before.'"[33]

There has been considerable speculation concerning the cause of Charlotte's death. Mr Ingham, the local surgeon, wrote "phthisis" on the death certificate (31 March 1855) signifying either a wasting away, or tuberculosis of the lungs. The subsequent diagnostic debate has been due largely, in Juliet Barker's view, to Arthur's "reluctance to cite pregnancy as the cause." In a letter to Ellen, he had simply said, "its cause is yet uncertain." Yet, a comment by Thackeray in 1860 in his introduction to *Emma* that "the heart newly awakened to love and happiness, and throbbing with maternal hope," indicates that it was probably generally accepted then, as now, that Charlotte was pregnant. The most likely diagnosis of her symptoms is *hyperemesis gravidarum* (excessive vomiting in pregnancy) probably caused by a hydatidiform mole, "a rare complication in which the fertilized ovum develops into a bag of cysts instead of a foetus."[34]

At Charlotte's funeral, which took place on 4 April 1855, the church overflowed, and the churchyard was filled with parishioners who had come to pay their respects.

CHAPTER FIVE

Her Will Be Done

After Charlotte Bronte's death, the two widowers lived alone on the edge of the moors "in that forlorn house, planted on the very clay of the churchyard, [that] living sepulchre," as Harriet Martineau described it in her *Daily News* obituary of Charlotte.[1] Each must have harbored secret resentments against the other. Patrick's remark to Martha, that his daughter should never have married, suggests he felt that Arthur had been an indirect agent of her early death. But he contained himself. Arthur, too, at least outwardly, treated the old man with care and respect. For the moment they were united in grief.

Arthur's clerical friends gave him a brief respite from his duties, but he was soon back in the pulpit, taking the weight off Patrick's shoulders just as Charlotte would have wished. Yale professor James H. Hoppin, who visited Haworth during this period, described Arthur preaching from the first verse of John as "a dark-complexioned man, rather thin, with black hair and beard. It was a short, practical sermon, and the tones of his voice, especially in the service, were grave and pleasant, and, as I conceived, with a touch of sadness."[2]

Arthur would have wished to mourn his wife in the utmost privacy, far from the intrusive glare of public curiosity. But he could not turn back the flood of letters of sympathy that poured into the parsonage. Nor could he prevent the tide of newspaper and journal articles dealing with Charlotte not only as a great literary figure, but also probing into the intimate details of family life: details Juliet Barker describes as "increasingly prurient and speculative," fueled by Harriet Martineau's "well-meant but highly coloured obituary."[3] Even Matthew Arnold, who had met Charlotte when she was staying with Harriet Martineau at Ambleside, was moved to compose a threnody, "Haworth Churchyard," in which Arthur makes a brief appearance.

> Another grief I see,
> Younger: but this the Muse,
> In pity and silent awe
> Revering what she cannot soothe,
> With veil'd face and bow'd head,
> Salutes and passes by.[4]

Arnold caught precisely how Arthur would have preferred to live the rest of his life. But there were others who saw Charlotte's posthumous fame as an opportunity to acquire vicarious immortality by association, or simply to make money. In the case of John Greenwood, the Haworth stationer, both motives seem to have been at work. He represented himself to Mrs Gaskell and Harriet Martineau as an intimate of the Brontë family, which was far from the case, although Charlotte had taken Mrs Gaskell to meet him and it was he who wrote Mrs Gaskell informing her of Charlotte's death. Although his letters have not survived, it is clear from Mrs Gaskell's side of the correspondence that he was anxious to set up a marble tablet in the church commemorating Charlotte and to make a daguerreotype of Richmond's portrait, presumably for public sale. It was the beginning of a campaign by one part of the community to turn Haworth into a Brontë shrine.

Of course, Greenwood knew that Arthur would be against these projects, and it is clear from Mrs Gaskell's replies to his letters that he had set out to paint Arthur in the worst possible light. He repeated an inaccurate report from the *Literary Gazette*, that the quarrel between Patrick and Arthur over Arthur's marriage proposal had been patched up through the intervention of the vicar of Bradford, who offered "to secure Mr Nicholls the incumbency [of Haworth] after Mr Brontë's death." The implication was that Arthur was more interested in clerical advancement than in the high Puseyite doctrines he professed. Mrs Gaskell had not yet met Arthur, although she knew something of him from what Charlotte had told her. As a Unitarian she was apprehensive about his religious views, and without having known anything about Arthur's censorship of Charlotte's letters, she confessed to "a panic about the husband seeing my letters."[5]

Although now dependent on Greenwood's gossip she nevertheless, in this instance, came strongly to Arthur's defense.

> I have looked for Mr Macarthey's character in Shirley, and I find it exactly corresponds with what you have told me of Mr Nicholls, & also with what she herself has said to me before now. Yet it shows something fine in him to have been able to appreciate her. And I know of better curacies being offered to him, & one living indeed, the refusal of which also seems to prove that he is not a worldly man, so that I can not understand how he should slight any one for another, inferior in character & attainments, but superior in fortune. A man who could do that would have snatched at opportunities for improving his own worldly condition. I don't like to believe him guilty of meanness because I could not then respect him as I like to respect *her* husband.

She was to use Greenwood as a major source of information when writing her biography of Charlotte, but Mrs Gaskell was already aware of his unreliability as a witness. "One can see," she told George Smith, "that poor John Greenwood takes things according to the impulse of the moment, from the contradictory accounts of Mr Nicholls that he sends." She also knew that there was no love lost between the curate and the stationer. Following a visit to Haworth in July 1855, she apologized to Greenwood for not having looked in on him after going to the church, but was "baulked" by Arthur having taken her there.[6] Aware of Greenwood's hostility, she was already behaving in a furtive manner as she gathered material for her life of Charlotte. It is a pity that she could not overcome her fear of Arthur, for it led her to rely on dubious sources for her information.

Ellen Nussey was also anxious to advance her particular version of the Brontë myth, partly out of genuine affection, partly because as Charlotte's closest friend and chief correspondent, she would inevitably share in the publicity attending any published material. Charlotte's letters, most of which Ellen had preserved, would make her the chief source for any future biography. But she knew that Arthur would not agree to her publishing them. His natural reserve was increased when he began to go through Charlotte's papers and saw that his late wife's

> lack of discretion in writing to her friends had placed potentially explosive material in the hands of others who did not share his wish to keep her private life private … He realized that there were confidences made before her marriage which she had not shared with him. The one that most upset him was the discovery that James Taylor had proposed to her, and that Charlotte had seriously considered accepting him. What emotions would her letters to M. Heger have aroused, had she kept copies? His first reaction was to go over to Brookroyd to ask Ellen for further information; she was not at home, but at least he believed he had her promise not to let anyone read Charlotte's letters and to destroy them in due course.

The other correspondent with whom Charlotte had shared her most intimate thoughts and feelings was Margaret Wooler, her old headmistress at Roe Head School. From her Arthur had nothing to fear. She had destroyed Charlotte's letter concerning James Taylor as soon as she heard of her engagement to Arthur. "There is something peculiarly revolting," she told him, "in the bare idea of those communications being laid open to the public gaze, which were intended only for the eye of a confidential & sympathizing friend."[7]

How was Ellen to break down Arthur's opposition? She struck on the idea of an authorized biography, which would set right the misrepresentations and distortions that had been gathering about the Brontë household. Some of the elements of the Brontë legend began with gossip passed on from Lady Kay-Shuttleworth to Mrs Gaskell, based originally on the tales of a dismissed Brontë servant, according to which Patrick was a

> strange, half mad husband … [who] vented his anger against *things* not persons; for instance once in one of his wife's confinements something went wrong, so he got a saw, and went and sawed up all the chairs in her bedroom, never answering her remonstrances or minding her tears. Another time he was vexed and took the hearth-

> rug & tied it in a tight bundle & set it on fire in the grate; & sat before it with a leg on each hob, heaping on more colds [sic] till it was burnt, no one else being able to endure in the room because of the stifling smoke ... [He] never taught the girls anything – only the servant taught them to read & write.[8]

These lurid materials coloured Harriet Martineau's much-reprinted obituary, but an article in *Sharpe's London Magazine* (June 1855) provided the opportunity Ellen had been looking for to overcome Arthur's resistance. She argued that

> both you and Mr Brontë will feel acutely the misrepresentations and the malignant spirit which characterises it. Will you suffer the article to pass current without any refutations? The writer merits the contempt of silence, but there will be readers and believers. Shall such be left to imbibe a tissue of malignant falsehoods, or shall an attempt be made to do justice to one who so highly deserved justice, whose very name those who best knew her but speak with reverence and affection? Should not her aged father be defended from the reproach the writer coarsely attempts to bring upon him?

She suggested that Mrs Gaskell would be best qualified to set the record straight, and assured Arthur that where "she lacked information, I would gladly supply her with facts sufficient to set aside much that is asserted." Arthur's reply indicates how he would have liked to handle all such incidents. He agreed that the article was full of errors, but the writer's motive was not malicious.

> His design seems rather to be to gratify the curiosity of the multitude in reference to one who had made such a sensation in the literary world. But even if the article had been of a less harmless character, we should not have felt inclined to take any notice of it, as by doing so we should have given it an importance which it would not otherwise have obtained. Charlotte herself would have acted thus; and her character stands too high to be injured by the statements in a magazine of small circulation and little influence – statements which the writer prefaces with the

> remark that he does not vouch for their accuracy. The many laudatory notices of Charlotte and her works which appeared since her death may well make us indifferent to the detractions of a few envious or malignant persons, as there ever will be such.

As for Patrick, the article "excited in him only amusement – indeed, I have not seen him laugh as much for some months as he did while I was reading the article to him. We are both well in health, but lonely and desolate."[9]

Patrick's laughter contained more bitterness than amusement. Less than a week after Arthur had counseled Ellen to a policy of silence, the "we" in his letter implying Patrick's agreement, Patrick took his own separate initiative. He accepted Ellen's advice and addressed himself to Mrs Gaskell. Finding "that a great many scribblers, as well as some clever and truthful writers, have published articles in newspapers and tracts respecting my dear daughter Charlotte since her death, and seeing that many things that have been stated are untrue, but more false," he and Arthur would give her whatever information they could if she would do what in effect would be an authorized biography. Arthur told Ellen that he would still prefer "to take no steps in the matter, but I do not think it right to offer any opposition to Mr Brontë's wishes."[10] Juliet Barker has suggested that the author of the *Sharpe's* article, whose distortions Mrs Gaskell was being asked to rectify, was none other than Mrs Gaskell herself. This would make a pretty irony indeed. But in fact, evidence cited in the *Gaskell Society Journal* suggests that the author was Frank Smedley, a former *Sharpe's* editor.

Mrs Gaskell had already determined on a memoir of some kind and was writing down everything she could remember about Charlotte "before its vividness faded from my mind," but even before Patrick authorized her involvement, she foresaw difficulties. She wanted to publish everything about Charlotte's life in the belief that "the more she was known the more people would honour her as a woman, separate from her character of authoress."[11] Arthur wanted to keep Charlotte's private life private, and allow her public reputation to rest entirely on her written work. In our own time, when enthusiastic self-disclosure of trivia by ephemeral figures such as Madonna or Princess Diana has become the norm, his passion for privacy is attractive. Still, one cannot help wishing he had been able to distinguish between those matters that help us appreciate Charlotte's literary work, and those that merely serve to stimulate scandalmongers.

A long drawn-out battle had now begun between Arthur on one side and Mrs Gaskell, Ellen Nussey, John Greenwood and George Smith on the other, with Patrick playing an ambiguous role somewhere in the middle. On 23 July 1855 Mrs Gaskell visited Haworth with her friend Catherine Winkworth, intent on literary loot. She found the two widowers still in a state of grief. "It was a most painful visit. Both Mr Brontë and Mr Nicholls cried sadly. I like Mr Nicholls." She explained that if she were to do a proper job of Charlotte's biography and reveal her "most unusual character (as taken separately from her genius)," she would have to inform her readers of "the circumstances which made her what she was." Having decided to authorize the work, Patrick seemed mainly concerned that she should get on with it. "No quailing Mrs Gaskell! no drawing back," were his parting words to her. But Arthur "was far more aware of the kind of particulars which people would look for; and saw how they had snatched at every gossiping account of her, and how desirable it was to have a full and authorized history of her life if it were done at all. His feeling was against it's being written; but he yielded to Mr Brontë's impetuous wish." Nevertheless, when the time came for producing the documents "he brought me down … about a dozen letters addressed principally to her sister Emily; one or two to her father & her brother; and one to her aunt. The dates extend from 1839 to 1843." Charlotte – or perhaps Arthur after her death – had destroyed most of the letters she received, including those Arthur had written during his 1853–54 exile from Haworth. He had certainly destroyed her letters to him and when he went through her papers after her death, he probably destroyed others. We will never know how extensive the damage was. He also withheld from Mrs Gaskell all the Brontë children's juvenilia, the manuscript of *The Professor*, and a fragment of Charlotte's unfinished novel, "Emma".[12]

Literary historians will always regard Arthur's destruction of this material as a heinous offence. But despite his protectiveness, he did tell Mrs Gaskell that Ellen Nussey was "the person of all others to apply to." In this he may have been a trifle disingenuous. After all, years ago he had asked Ellen to destroy everything Charlotte wrote to her, and even after Charlotte's death, he had instructed her that "Any letters you may have of Charlotte's you will not show to others."[13] And he informed

Ellen of Patrick's decision to allow Mrs Gaskell to write a biography, and alerted her that she might visit in search of data. "The greatest difficulty seems to be in obtaining materials to show the development of Charlotte's character. For this reason Mrs G. is anxious to see any of her letters, – Especially those of an early date – I think I understood you to say that you had some – if so we should be obliged by your letting us have any that you may think proper – not for publication, but merely to give the writer an insight into her mode of thought."[14]

Having failed to prevent the biography from being written, he was still hoping to limit the publication of intimate material, particularly that touching on Charlotte's later life. Having given in to Patrick's wish, his role was limited to damage control. It may have been his ignorance rather than his knowledge of what lay hidden in Charlotte's past that made him so fearful of publicity He knew nothing of her curious relationship with George Smith, or of her passionate attachment to Constantin Heger. Nor, despite what some of Charlotte's biographers have suggested, and his discovery of letters from James Taylor, is there any evidence that he knew of her ambivalent feelings about Taylor's courtship. Since all the evidence of her feelings concerning those three men lay in her letters to Ellen, how could he know unless she herself had told him, or unless she had preserved some of Taylor's letters to her? But he must have known it would be difficult to suppress the story of his own proposal, Charlotte's rejection, Patrick's fury, and the public loss of control of his feelings. In the end, Arthur's reticence and lack of cooperation was counter-productive, while his injunction that the letters were not for publication was simply ignored.

The following year Mrs Gaskell was busy gathering material. She visited Ellen twice, once when Margaret Wooler was staying with her. She was able to see some 350 of the 500 odd letters in Ellen's possession. Like Arthur, Miss Wooler was inclined to be retentive about material concerning Charlotte, but Ellen had cunningly engineered her visit to coincide with Mrs Gaskell's, the result being that Mrs Gaskell came away with a packet of Charlotte's letters to Miss Wooler which she liked "better than any other series of letters of hers that I have seen." George Smith was less forthcoming. He sent her a few letters mainly concerned with the publishing business, withholding the correspondence that she was most anxious to have, that which he described as of "too purely personal a nature to be generally interesting." Mrs Gaskell was not amused, and wrote Ellen: "He is very civil, more civil than satisfactory … I am sure I have not got half of what Mr Williams and he together *might* give: and what they *shall* give, or I'll know the reason why." Smith more than matched her determination, however, and she got nothing further from him. But she had more luck in Brussels where she visited the Hegers. Knowing Mrs Gaskell to have been a friend of Charlotte's, and offended by Charlotte's fictionalized portrait of her in *Villette,* Madame refused to see her, although she had recovered some of Charlotte's passionate letters to her husband from a wastebasket and carefully sewn the torn bits together, presumably for future us. By contrast, M. Heger not only received Mrs Gaskell cordially, but provided her with "certain confidences that placed her under a moral obligation to suppress them. Judging of her absolute integrity, he showed Charlotte's poignant letters to him." As a result of this visit and her own careful reading of *Villette*, she had a pretty accurate picture of Charlotte's passionate regard for her Brussels schoolmaster.[15]

By the middle of 1856 Mrs Gaskell was well into Charlotte's biography, but she had not been back to Haworth since the previous summer, nor had she even bothered to communicate with Arthur and Patrick to let them know how she was getting on: it was an uncharacteristic reticence on the part of such a prolific letter-writer, and one that argues a bad conscience. Arthur found it curious that neither he nor Patrick had heard anything from her, but at Christmas he told Ellen that he had "every confidence that she will do ample justice to Charlotte." Patrick was puzzled too. He wrote Mrs Gaskell in January 1856, that he wondered how she would write Charlotte's life given "the few facts you have of a biographical nature. We so frequently talk over and meditate on these things, that we are forced at last to solve the difficulty by saying that you must draw largely on the resources of your own mind … I often think that if you would write a running critique of her *works* as well as her *life* it would be highly popular and render your task easier, by an accession of subject matter." The truth was that Mrs Gaskell was "literally *afraid* of" the parsonage, partly because her portrait of Patrick was hardly an attractive one and partly because she knew Arthur's wish to keep Charlotte's private life private. Yet there were some documents she desperately wanted to see that only Arthur could provide: the manuscript of *The Professor*, which she knew he possessed, the novel fragment, and perhaps some of M. Heger's letters had been preserved (although she feared he had destroyed them). She thought that everything depended on Arthur and that Patrick's "consent or opinion … had very little weight with Mr Nicholls. I am vexed with Mr Nicholls," she told George Smith. In her frustration she turned to Ellen for help, and although Ellen could only suggest that she convince Arthur that "it is wisest, best, & kindest to tell the whole truth to you in everything that regards her literary life or her domestic virtues," she corrected her correspondent's misunderstanding of the relationship between Arthur and Patrick, advising Mrs Gaskell to convince *Patrick*, and "for a quiet life Mr N. will have to yield where Mr B. is urgent and impatient."[16]

In the end, Mrs Gaskell came up with a different, if more heavy-handed, strategy. She recruited Sir James Kay-Shuttleworth to her cause and at the end of July 1856, he and Mrs Gaskell made a surprise raid on the parsonage. Her account shows how easily, in that class-dominated culture, a baronet could overawe a couple of lowly curates.

> I have had a very successful visit to Haworth … accompanied by Sir J P.K. Shuttleworth, to whom it is evident that both Mr Brontë and Mr Nicholls look up. – & who is not prevented by the fear of giving pain from asking in a peremptory manner for whatever he thinks desirable. He … coolly took actual possession of many things while Mr Nicholls was saying he could not possibly part with them. I came away with the 'Professor' the beginning of her new tale 'Emma' … & by far the most extraordinary of all, a packet … full of paper books of different sizes … in this indescribably fine writing … They give one the idea of creative power carried to the verge of insanity.

Mrs Gaskell emerged triumphant, but also a trifle shame-faced on account of Sir James's lack of "delicacy or scruple." He also "coolly introduced the subject of the portrait [Richmond's of Charlotte], as if he had known nothing of Mr Nicholls' reluctance, asked Mr Brontë's leave to have it photographed, which was readily granted with a reference to Mr Nicholls for an ultimate decision, so then Sir James said 'Oh! I know Mr Nicholls will grant it'… and he so completely took it for granted that Mr Nicholls had no time to object. But I cannot feel quite comfortable in absolutely wresting things from him by mere force of words." Had Charlotte looked down on this scene she would have seen it as confirming the estimate she made of Sir James in 1850: "In observing his behaviour to others – I find that when once offended his forgiveness is not to be again purchased except perhaps by servile submission. The substratum of his character is hard as flint."[17]

Sir James told Mrs Gaskell that the manuscript of *The Professor* ought to be published and that *he* would revise it. Mrs Gaskell felt it "inferior to all her published works," but still of interest as providing "a very curious link in her literary history, as showing the *promise* of much that was afterwards realized." Both she and Sir James thought parts of the story "disfigured by more coarseness – & profanity in quoting texts of Scripture disagreeably than any of her other works." Examples of what they considered coarse were the frequent use of "Hell" by one of the characters, and some "irreverent" quotations from the Bible by another. In this estimation they were only reflecting the fastidiousness of the mid-Victorian sensibility. Mr Gladstone devoured *Jane Eyre* in a single evening, but found it "jarring," while his fellow high-churchman, Sir Abraham Elton, noted in his diary that *Shirley* possessed "a quaint rough flavour and vigour with touches of vivid painting – but a coarse, offensive taint."[18]

Mrs Gaskell was not in favour of publication herself; moreover, she had enough delicacy to realize that Arthur would have to be consulted, and that he would have the last word. "This Sir James seems entirely to lose sight of." On 30 July 1856, she wrote to both George Smith and Arthur, pointing out that Charlotte would not have liked Sir James to be in charge of revision. She probably thought that Arthur would refuse publication, but in this she had misread the nature of his wish for privacy: it was Charlotte's *personal* life, particularly that part which touched his own, that he wished to keep from scrutiny. In fact, when he received an offer from George Smith to publish *The Professor*, he read the manuscript to Patrick and they decided jointly that "with the exception of two or three strong expressions which might be open to misinterpretation, no revision … is necessary. Indeed if any extensive alteration had been necessary we could not have consented to the publication of the tale. We have erased the few seemingly objectionable phrases."

To modern eyes, the original phrases are hardly objectionable. In Chapter V, "God damn your insolence!" was replaced by "Confound;" and in Chapters XIV, XXII, and XXIV, the word "God" was cut out. Three short passages "probably implying physical intimacy" were also deleted. But the passages from scripture, which Mrs Gaskell felt Charlotte had quoted disagreeably, were left intact. Arthur sent the manuscript to Smith with a short note of his own appended to Charlotte's preface, but modestly declined to have his name appear as editor, although he carefully checked each proof against the manuscript. When it came to setting a price on the work, he based his fee on the amount Smith had paid for *Villette* (£500) and asked for £220, which reflected the proportionate length of *The Professor*. Smith promptly paid this, plus an additional £50 for "Foreign Copyright and Sheets to America." Ironically Mrs Gaskell, who had so feared Arthur's wish not to publish anything, now bewailed his failure to "extirpate" and "expunge." "But oh! I wish Mr Nicholls would have altered more!" she told George Smith. "I fear from what you say he has left many little things *you* would & I would have taken out, as neither essential to the characters or the story, & as likely to make her misunderstood. For I would not, if I could help it, have another syllable that could be called coarse to be associated with her name."[19]

Meanwhile, Mrs Gaskell herself was hard at work finishing the *Life*, still relying on John Greenwood and Ellen Nussey as her principal sources. The second half of the book was to be based largely on Charlotte's letters to Ellen (carefully controlled and edited by Ellen), and would involve "merely copying." Nonetheless, she foresaw a major impediment. "I do not wish the letters to assume a prominent form in the title or printing; as Mr Nicholls has a strong objection to letters being printed at all; and wished to have all her letters (to Miss Nussey & every one else) burned. Now I am very careful what extracts I make; but still her language, where it can be used, is so powerful & living, that it would be a shame not to express everything tha[t] can be, in her own words. And yet I don't want to alarm Mr Nicholls' prejudices." That was undoubtedly the chief reason why neither Arthur nor Patrick saw the manuscript before publication. But Ellen was not to be so deprived. On 11 December, Mrs Gaskell told George Smith that Ellen was "about the only person who would care to see it in MS, because she wants to know what extracts I have taken from all her letters." Since Patrick had admonished her not to show the manuscript to anyone other than her husband, family, publisher, and compositor, she disingenuously circumvented his request by inviting Ellen to Manchester where she read the manuscript aloud to her. At least that is what she told George Smith in December, although a month later she told his editor, W.S. Williams, that "Miss

Nussey was here last week reading the MS. I was gratified to hear her repeatedly say how completely the life at the Parsonage appeared to her reproduced. Much of this was owing to the remarkable extracts from letters; but she said several times how exactly and accurately I had written about the life and characters."[20]

Ellen's own account of this visit, given to George Smith, differs materially from Mrs Gaskell's.

> I had a very cordial reception from Mrs Gaskell but in a few moments I received a heavy blow to my sense of right, Mrs Gaskell telling me Mr Brontë had requested her not to let anyone see her M.S. except Mr Gaskell – I said you gave me your *promise* I should see any extracts you made from my letters – Oh yes! she replied I shall keep my word. The first part of the work describing this neighbourhood was already in your [George Smith's] possession. I did not mind [that] (but I have since been blamed by many for letting Mrs G. give such a picture) I saw sheet after sheet of the rest as it was being sent off to you. Mrs Gaskell was ill and kept her room during part of my stay – I discussed and perusal [sic] was all I could effect. Mrs Gaskell was not disposed to alterations but I entreated her in person and afterwards by letter to omit some passages – one more especially where I thought Mr Nicholls appeared too prominently – if she would not listen I begged her to consult Mr Gaskell feeling sure he would see the subject in the same light as I saw it – I conclude this was not done.[21]

Although Arthur and Patrick remained ignorant of how heavily Mrs Gaskell was relying on Charlotte's letters and how extensively she was intending to quote from them, she must have revealed this to someone other than Ellen Nussey and George Smith, unless Smith himself had let the information out. In any case, Henry Chorley, literary critic of the *Athenaeum*, knew what she was doing and warned her: "Remember correspondent's permission to publish goes for nothing; the legal power over any deceased person's papers lies with the executors; this having been settled in the case of Dallas and Lord Byron, by Lord Byron's executors; and thus Mr Nicholls *may*, if he likes turn sharp round on you, and not merely protest, but *prohibit*." Mrs Gaskell was distraught. "Now I did *not* know all this; and Mr Nicholls is a terribly tickle person to have to do with; if I asked him for leave to make large extracts from her letters … he would ten to one refuse it, – if I did not ask him, but went on, as I am doing, I *think* he would sigh & submit." She assured Smith she had been "*most* careful to put nothing in from Miss Brontë's letters that can in any way implicate others." But this was less than the truth. She had reproduced parts of the letter in which Charlotte described Arthur's trembling, painful proposal and another in which Charlotte looked forward to her marriage as something that "will not be generally regarded as brilliant." More problematic was the fact that, while Ellen had been given the opportunity to select, edit, and even alter the letters she sent to Mrs Gaskell, and had subsequently read large parts of the manuscript, Arthur and Patrick had been excluded from the whole process. She was in a quandary: "what shall I do if Mr N were to prohibit all I have written from appearing … I shall have to re-write a considerable portion of the memoir." Nonetheless, Mrs Gaskell would not admit she had been unfair to Arthur, transforming her avoidance of him into anger, as though she were the injured party. She cited Arthur's request for the return of a photo of the Richmond portrait, even though it had been broken and "he knows it to be engraved, & consequently numerous copies circulated," as an example of "how 'inconséquent' a man he is, with all his warm affections and humble qualities. Sir J.P. Kay-Shuttleworth manages him the best, though in not a pleasant way."[22]

Sir James had overwhelmed Arthur with his aristocratic arrogance. George Smith now proposed to subdue him with sheer bourgeois will power, presenting Mrs Gaskell with two possible solutions to their situation. The one she chose (what the alternative was is not known, but it probably required re-writing large sections of the book) required Arthur to sign "a business form of application" under which he would surrender copyright in certain of his wife's manuscripts to her. To be of any use, the agreement would have had to include all the letters used in the biography. Arthur had not seen the manuscript and had no idea how extensive her direct quotations were. Being asked to sign away his rights sight unseen he not surprisingly declined Smith's first request:

> not because I have or ever had the slightest intention of making any pecuniary claim on Mrs Gaskell on account of the work on which she is engaged; but simply because, if I did so, [i.e., sign the

business form of application] I should be thereby precluded from making any further use of the MS. referred to.

As you seem to ascribe to me a greater share in getting up the memoir than I can lay claim to, allow me briefly to explain the circumstances out of which it arose. Soon after my wife's death several notices of her appeared in the public print all more or less inaccurate. Of these I took no note as I was well aware how the subject of them would have acted. Mr. Brontè [Arthur habitually spelled Brontë with an e grave] however was annoyed by the falsehoods published about both himself and his daughter, and expressed his determination to ask Mrs Gaskell to compile a memoir of my wife. I objected to his doing so, but as he seemed very anxious about it, I at length acquiesced. He accordingly made the proposition to Mrs Gaskell, and after some correspondence, she came over her[e], and the subject was discussed. I told her plainly that I did not approve of the project, but that out of deference to Mr. Brontè's wishes, I should give every facility in my power, adding that if such a work was undertaken at all I would rather she did it than anyone else, as I knew her kindly feelings toward my wife. I have accordingly from time to time forwarded to her some MS., but never with any idea of giving her exclusive right to them. This is all that I have had to do with the matter.

Arthur's refusal struck not only at Mrs Gaskell's memoir, large parts of which she would have to re-write, but also at George Smith's pocket-book. In Juliet Barker's words, Smith now revealed "the steel that underlay his genial manner." He sent off a letter which must have employed every argument he could muster to alter Arthur's decision: the damage it would cause to the quality of Mrs Gaskell's work and thus to his wife's reputation, the pain it would cause Patrick not to see his daughter's memory properly preserved, and even, perhaps, a threat of legal action, although he knew it was groundless. Its effect was, as Mrs Gaskell put it, "a great deal more than I hoped for." Three days after his initial refusal Arthur came to heel.

I have signed the enclosed document, as it seems to be taken for granted that I am to do so, tho' why it should, I know not as

> I never entered into any agreement with Mrs Gaskell to convey to her the copyright of any of my wife's MS. for the purpose of the Memoir or any other. I trust I shall not be required to do anything more in a matter which from beginning to end has been a source of pain and annoyance to me, as I have been dragged into sanctioning a proceeding utterly repugnant to my feelings, indeed nothing but an unwillingness to thwart Mr. Brontë's wishes could have induced me to acquiesce in a project, which in my eyes is little short of desecration.

In a second letter he added: "I allowed Mrs Gaskell to peruse certain documents, but before attaching my signature to the note you sent, I never authorized her to publish a single line of my wife's MS and correspondence; such a thing was never mentioned, in fact until the receipt of your not[e] I was not even aware that it was contemplated."[23]

Even George Smith, used to the toughness of the publishing business, described this correspondence as "fierce." Mrs Gaskell was simply relieved that the task had fallen on his shoulders, not hers;" I should have been daunted at once." But she must have felt some guilt about the way she had treated Arthur, for when Smith paid her £800 for the English copyright of the *Life*, she asked him to send £100 to Mr Nicholls "for the parish of Haworth – I shd like a village pump; they are terribly off for water."[24] However bitter Arthur may have felt about Mrs Gaskell's cavalier use of Charlotte's letters, he would have welcomed this gift, for he and Patrick had been active for some years in a community movement to improve the town's water supply.

The Life of Charlotte Brontë, published in March 1857, was the immediate centre not only of critical attention, but also of threats of legal action. Juliet Barker observes that Mrs Gaskell had vindicated Charlotte "by blaming her family and her upbringing in Haworth" for the "coarseness" which had offended many of her readers. It was Patrick who suffered most from Mrs Gaskell's carelessness in portraying him as a demented patriarch who had ruined Charlotte's life. Whatever his real feelings, Patrick was initially restrained in his reaction, praising the book to George Smith and Mrs Gaskell and limiting himself to the observation that there were "a few trifling mistakes which … may be corrected in the second edition." Later, perhaps as the full impact of Mrs Gaskell's misrepresentations began to sink in, he was more explicit in detailing the changes he wished to have made. He had never imposed a vegetarian diet on his daughters; he had never burned rugs or cut up chairs. He even signed a testimonial stating that Nancy and Sarah Garrs – two servants while the Brontë children were young – had been honest, kind to the children, and not wasteful. To Mrs Gaskell he continued restrained and courteous, but he must have been cut to the quick when a reviewer in the *Christian Remembrancer* stated that "Charlotte Brontë's … home held a monster whom the strong ties of an inordinate family affection constrained her to love and care for and find excuses for." Arthur's reaction, in a note to George Smith, was more candid:

> I have read the work with inexpressible pain. – Mrs Gaskell has done justice to her subject – she has however fallen into many errors but fewer perhaps than might have been expected. She has moreover inserted some things, which ought never to have been published. It was not without reason that I instinctively shrank from the proposal of a Biography. But I suppose it matters not, provided the curiosity of the Publick be gratified.
>
> Haworth Church and Parsonage are commonplace enough, but not quite such queer things as they are represented in the view.[25]

Although understandably bitter about Mrs Gaskell's account of his marriage proposal and Charlotte's less-than-passionate response, he made no demand that she retract her description of these events. However, two weeks later, when Mrs Gaskell was in Europe avoiding the controversy, he did send Mr Gaskell a list of alterations he wished to be made to the third edition. These all referred to Patrick except "a passage in a letter about an intimate friend of my wife, which I consider an act of treachery to have published." He also told George Smith that, before publication, either Patrick or himself should be shown the section describing "'the characteristics of Haworth' as Mrs Gaskell's information has not been reliable." He had a double reason for this request (which was disregarded): the citizens of Haworth and of the West Riding were offended by Mrs Gaskell's account of them as "a wild, rough population … Their accost is curt; their accent and tone of speech blunt and harsh." They felt that she had presented them as a barbarous foreign hinterland unlike with the gentler South, and their resentment was intensified by the knowledge that Mrs Gaskell herself was a resident of neighboring

Lancashire. "Some of the West Ridingers are very angry," Ellen Nussey told her, "and declare they are half a century in civilisation before some of the Lancashire folk, and that this neighbourhood is a paradise compared with some districts not far from Manchester." Ellen also complained that *she* had been blamed for allowing Mrs Gaskell to paint the region in such unflattering colours. Others saw Arthur as the culprit. Having tried to stop the project in its infancy, he was understandably bitter that he was now taken to be the source of such slander.[26]

Mrs Gaskell also faced two legal actions arising out of the book. The woman with whom Branwell Brontë allegedly had an affair while tutor to her children was unmistakably identifiable as the former Mrs Robinson, now Lady Scott. In his wife's absence and on the advice of lawyers, Mr Gaskell issued a retraction, printed in the *Times* and the *Athenaeum*, of everything in the *Life* having to do with her. Thinking no doubt of his own treatment as much as Lady Scott's, Arthur observed that

> Mrs Gaskell has been rash; she seems to have forgotten that she was dealing with *living* persons. I shall ever regret that I did not ask to see the *MS.* as I think I could have convinced her of the injudiciousness of some things in it. [There is a veiled criticism of George Smith here as well.] Besides Lady Scott's affair, she has mentioned a very disgraceful occurrence that took place in a family in this neighbourhood, some members of which are still here, indeed one is a magistrate in Keighley – [he refers to a young girl who was seduced by her sister's husband] – the charitable folks say of course that I supplied her [Mrs. Gaskell] with the information tho' I am not aware that I ever heard of the transaction until I saw it in print. Again those ridiculous anecdotes about Mr Brontè are utterly with[out] foundation. The character given him is quite unreal.[27]

A second possible legal action involved Arthur in controversy from April to August of 1857. For a short period in the 1820s, the Brontë sisters had attended the Cowan Bridge Clergy Daughters' School. In *Jane Eyre*, Charlotte had fictionalized the school as Lowood, a kind of female version of Dotheboys' Hall; Mrs Gaskell had reversed the fiction and named real names. The picture that emerged of William Carus Wilson, director of the Cowan Bridge School and model for Mr Brocklehurst in *Jane*

Eyre, was of an authoritarian, meddling, and ultimately incompetent administrator. Carus Wilson's son rose to his father's defense. Letters from him and his supporters appeared in the *Daily News*, the *Times*, and in northern provincial papers such as the *Leeds Intelligencer*, the *Leeds Mercury*, and the *Halifax Guardian*.

For the only time in his life, Arthur broke his policy of public silence and entered the profitless, hair-splitting world of letters-to-the editor. None of the participants emerges a clear victor from this series of angry exchanges, but when sufficiently aroused Arthur reveals himself to be an effective defender of his wife's reputation. "If Mr Wilson's friends had confined themselves to a legitimate review of Mrs Gaskell's work," he wrote, "I should never have written a line on this subject, but when they attacked the dead, and adopted the questionable course of disseminating their vile slander anonymously through the post-office (actually sending a copy to Mr Brontë), I should indeed have been inexcusable had I allowed their assertions to pass unchallenged." He tried to bring the exchange to an early end, declaring that the *Guardian*'s readers "would soon be as tired of us … as the poor girls were of their burnt porridge," but Sarah Baldwin, another ex-pupil of Cowan Bridge, entered the lists in the school's defense, and the war of letters not only continued but became increasingly brutal. When Arthur referred to Mrs Baldwin as "evidently a stranger to that delicacy of feeling which causes a lady to shrink from having her name paraded before the public," she responded in kind, describing his letter as written in a style "coarse and unusual among educated people." Finally, on 8 August, Arthur brought his own part to an end. "I have discharged a painful but necessary duty. Henceforth Charlotte Brontë's assailants may growl and snarl over her grave undisturbed by me." The *Guardian* tried to draw Patrick back into the controversy but he refused to be drawn, although he was active behind the scenes, trying unsuccessfully at one point to get George Smith to publish one of Arthur's letters in the *Times*.[28]

However much Patrick and Arthur may have wished for peace and quiet, the controversy was far from over. "I don't think there was ever such an apple of discord as that unlucky book," Mrs Gaskell complained. Angered by her treatment of Patrick, William Dearden, an old family friend, published letters in the *Examiner* and the *Bradford Observer* defending "this venerable clergyman, now on the verge of the grave" whom Mrs Gaskell had "tarred and feathered" on the basis of false and malicious "country gossip." He quoted Patrick as having said "I did not know I had an enemy in the world; much less one who would traduce me before my death. Everything in that book … which relates to my conduct to my family is either false or distorted." In a bitter moment of private conversation Patrick probably did say something along these lines, but he hastened to send Mrs Gaskell a denial.

> I never said anything to Miss Martineau, him [Dearden], or any other intimating in the remotest degree that I considered you an enemy; that I fully believed you were a friend to my Daughter as she was to you, and that you were no enemy to me, and that when I did speak of an enemy, I alluded only to false and malignant informants, and a few prejudiced, ruthless, and unjust critics who, like soldiers of fortune, make their bread by the sword of destruction. My real, or pretended friends seem, in their gossiping skill, to have combined to present me not as a single, but a double Janus, looking, and smiling or frowning, with my four faces in opposite directions.[29]

Patrick's reference to Harriet Martineau revived a painful part of Charlotte's past. The two women met in London in 1849 and the following year Charlotte was Martineau's guest at Ambleside. A close friendship developed in which Martineau played a dominant and Charlotte a submissive, though not uncritical, role. When, in 1851, Martineau and Henry Atkinson published *Letters on the Laws of Man's Social Nature and Development*, a positivist account of mankind as "a portion of the Universe, resting on the security of its everlasting laws, certain that its Cause was wholly out of the sphere of human attributes," Charlotte reacted with "instinctive horror." To her credit, she did not allow what she mistakenly took to be Martineau's atheism to end their relationship, even when urged to do so by Margaret Wooler. The break, when it did occur, followed the publication of *Villette*. Charlotte asked for Martineau's opinion "as frankly as if you spoke to some near relative whose good you preferred to her gratification." Martineau responded with a double discharge. In a review of *Villette* in the *Daily News* she criticized Charlotte for presenting all her female characters as obsessed with "one thought – love … It is not thus in real life. There are substantial, heartfelt interests for women of all ages …

quite apart from love." She was equally frank in telling Charlotte directly: "I do not like the love, either the kind or the degree of it; and its prevalence in the book." This blunt response, coupled with Charlotte's discovery through George Smith that Martineau was the author of the *Daily News* review, brought the friendship to an abrupt end. She marked the offending passage with red ink and returned it to the author with the comment that it "struck me dumb – I know what love is as I understand it – & if man or woman shd. feel ashamed of feeling such love – then is there nothing right, noble, faithful, truthful, unselfish in this earth?"[30]

This exchange, and the rupture it caused, remained private until the first edition of the *Life* appeared. Mrs Gaskell had used several letters in which Charlotte had described her friendship with Martineau and its collapse. What outraged Martineau was not that Mrs Gaskell portrayed Charlotte as shocked by what she took to be Martineau's atheism – she knew that Charlotte was incapable of sharing those views – but Charlotte's tone of almost sanctimonious pity for what she conceived to be Martineau's isolation after the publication of Atkinson's *Letters on the Laws of Man's Social Nature and Development.* It was galling to see, in print, Charlotte's pious refusal to give up her friendship even though "hundreds have forsaken her [Martineau]," and Charlotte's belief that she "secretly" suffered from this abandonment, and that she was "one of those whom opposition and desertion make obstinate in error; while patience and tolerance touch her deeply and keenly, and incline her to ask of her own heart whether the course she has been pursuing may not possibly be a faulty course." "Hallucination," she wrote in the margin of the second edition of the *Life*; and where Charlotte had written that God, not Man, must judge her "for her sin", she scratched "Fie!"[31]

To set her side of the record straight, Martineau published a letter in the *Daily News* attacking Charlotte as an unreliable witness: "When I find that, in my own case, scarcely one of Miss Brontë's statements about me is altogether true, I cannot be surprised at her biographer having been misled in other cases of more importance." These were strong, indeed challenging words, but still Patrick (and Arthur) refused to be provoked, at least in public, although Patrick vented his spleen privately to Mrs Gaskell: "Notwithstanding Miss Martineau's strange and unhappy illusions, which mystify and bewilder her Atheistical brain, I had thought she was a Woman, naturally kind, and just and generous, who would not knowingly or unwillingly injure the memory of anyone, especially that of the dead."[32]

In September the third, revised, edition of the *Life* appeared, the first two editions having been withdrawn. Those sections dealing with Patrick's "eccentric" behavior had been excised. There were also additions, including more than a page inserted at Martineau's insistence containing parts of her *Daily News* review of *Villette* and her letter to Charlotte on the same subject.[33] Martineau interpreted these changes to mean that *her* version of the relationship between herself and Charlotte had been accepted as the correct one, and that what she had said about Charlotte in the *Daily News* letter was now vindicated. It was at this point that Patrick at last decided to speak. On 5 November 1857 he wrote Martineau, initiating what Mrs Gaskell called "a warlike correspondence."[34] His letter contains the characteristic mixture of old-fashioned gallantry and thinly disguised vitriol that Mrs Gaskell so disliked, and which was to earn him the undying hatred of Martineau. "I should not have troubled you," he begins,

> had it not been that you have publicly stated my Daughter Charlotte to have said or written some things of you that were not true. This is a somewhat heavy charge made against one, who has been generally considered, and who, I firmly believe was a woman of candour and veracity and who if she had been disposed for malevolent misrepresentation, would have placed you amongst the last she would have misrepresented. I have ever heard her speak of you, in terms of kindness, and veneration, and when any one spoke of you otherwise, she took your part.

Then, referring to Charlotte's statement that Martineau had lost all her friends as a result of her co-authorship of the Atkinson *Letters*, which he and Charlotte had taken to be pure atheism, he began to rub salt into her wounds:

> whatever you may think or say to the contrary, your unfortunate book on Atheism made you many opponents and enemies, and gave a shock to those who gave you credit for reasoning powers, that would have kept you from descending to say, "there is no God." What you have written respecting my Daughter, has,

> perhaps, been written hastily, and without much regard to consequences. But even if it were so, it was wrong; since you must be aware that whatever you may write, the world will read; but it may be well to remember also, that whilst it reads, it will also criticise, and bring both the writer, and the persons and things, written about, to the bar of its judgment.

Martineau, who described Patrick's letter as "vicious" and filled with "vehement insult," reacted instantly. Her reply, also dated, almost certainly in error, as 5 November, underlines the speed and passion of the exchange: twelve letters fired off in ten days between two remote settlements not yet connected by rail is also a tribute to the efficiency of the Victorian postal system. She stuck to her assertions in the *Daily News.*

> I have no doubt whatever of the kindly disposition and even of the personal affection of your daughter Charlotte towards myself: but it is not the less true that, as I have publicly and privately said, there is scarcely a statement concerning myself in her letters which is altogether true: and I may add that some of them are more like hallucinations than sober statement. It is not necessary to enter into… the causes of her inaccuracies. Mrs Gaskell is supplied with the particulars of the mis-statements – some of trifling and some of considerable extent; and many of them are specified in the new edition of the "Life," which is equivalent to the correction of them. Mrs Gaskell has done everything in her power to remedy a mischief which is indeed of very slight importance and which I have no desire to magnify.

In a postscript she set Patrick straight on her religious and philosophical views: "I ought to add, as I perceive you have not read the Atkinson *Letters,* that it is not an atheistical book, and that I have never said 'there is no God'." Margaret Smith notes that Martineau "might more fairly have been called an agnostic – a term not in use until 1869,"[35] and a distinction beyond Patrick.

"Hallucinations," "inaccuracies," "mis-statements": Patrick had thrust his snout into a mass of porcupine quills, and he decided to leave the prickly beast to his son-in-law who, as Charlotte perceived in the case of Mr de Renzy, was more pugnacious. Arthur told Martineau he had looked over the third edition of the *Life*, especially "over that part of the work where you are referred to, and amongst other new matter I find a paragraph, supplied by you, purporting to be an extract from a letter addressed by you to Miss Brontè on the publication of 'Villette', and to which Miss Brontè took exception." The extract in the third edition and the extract published in the Wise and Symington Shakespeare Head edition of the Brontë correspondence are identical, but Arthur told Martineau that he possessed the complete original and that "this passage does not occur in it." He let her know that he intended to "adopt the same means that you have to inform the public that the individual who accuses my wife of *inaccuracies* has herself been guilty of a much graver offence." He also sent Mrs Gaskell a copy of the letter in question, and Charlotte's reply to it.

Martineau was briefly rattled: "I suspect there is a mistake about the letter you refer to. The one I reported to Mrs Gaskell had red ink marks made by C.B. to indicate the part she objected to, when she sent it to me for a second reading, at my desire … I gave the passage to Mrs Gaskell … as what I wrote, as nearly as I could remember, soon after the original was written and am sure there could be very little difference between the original and my recollection of it." Then she took the offensive.

> You have now given me *a right to require* a sight of the note or of a certified copy of it. I do require it, and without delay.
>
> I shall be sorry if public notice is drawn to the numerous inaccuracies I find in C.B's statements regarding myself, from her entering my house, to the last mention of me in her letters. It was never her intention to do or say anything but what was friendly, and none of the statements are injurious to myself, as far as I know, though some of them are to my friends … Mrs G's corrections and explanations in the 3d edition shd suffice: but my memoranda are complete; and there is plenty of corroboration at my command from my neighbours and friends.

She went on to justify her *Daily News* letter as a defense of Patrick against Dearden's claim that he felt "traduced" by Mrs Gaskell. "I was most unwilling to refer to myself: but silence on the statements in the *Life* must have been received as assent to them. I entered my dissent as briefly

& gently as possible. And now my plea for justice on Mr B's behalf is answered by insults from himself & threats from you." This expression of concern for Patrick's reputation was disingenuous at best. What she really thought of him was expressed in a letter to Catherine Winkworth: "She [Mrs Gaskell] sent me Mr Brontë's letter on the publication of the [first edition] of the *Life*. The old monster! ... I do mourn that Mrs Gaskell ever came in the way of that awful family."[36] She concluded her note to Arthur with a mixture of veiled threat – "This is the first step. We shall then see what next." – and self-pity: "I write by another hand [her niece] as I am (as you no doubt know) deep in my last illness." Martineau had been "deep in her last illness" since 1855, when a London specialist had told her she had an enlarged heart. She was to remain in a highly productive terminal condition until 1876.

Arthur's reply enclosed a copy of the disputed passage, noting that it was "essentially different from that inserted in [the third edition of] the Memoir." His complaint was that "relying on your imagination to supply the deficiencies of your Memory, [you] shd. publicly charge my wife with making statements, scarcely one of which is *altogether* true ... Your intention in writing to the *Daily News* may have been very kind: but will you pardon me for saying that your interference was wholly gratuitous? Mr Brontè being quite competent to take care of himself: He would moreover have willingly dispensed with a vindication which was made the occasion of bringing a charge of general untruthfulness against his daughter."

The original letter with Charlotte's red underlining has not survived. All we now possess is the extract Arthur sent to Martineau, and a fragment she reconstructed, which is reproduced in the third edition of the *Life*, and in the Shakespeare Head edition of the Brontë correspondence. The wording differs but the meaning of each version is virtually identical.[37] To Arthur's implying deliberate falsehood, she replied on 10 November as follows.

> You are aware that Mrs Gaskell was anxious to see the letters received by C.B. and that she and I had a particular desire that she should have a sight of the one in question – on account of its bearing on the discontents it excited in C.B's mind, & because Mrs Gaskell saw here her reply to that letter, & all her other letters to me. You informed Mrs Gaskell, when she began the Memoir,

that you had destroyed all C.B's papers: & Mr Greenwood wrote, in reply to an enquiry from myself, that my letters to C.B. had been burnt, his information having been doubtless obtained from yourself. Our endeavours to obtain a sight of the letter being thus baffled, the only course that remained was for me to supply Mrs Gaskell with the passage wanted, as nearly as I could recal[l] it. This I did.

Now, when I received your first note, the question was whether you had mistaken one letter for another or whether your assertion that the passage I had given Mrs Gaskell "does not occur in it," was an advantage craftily taken of some difference in the wording, when the substance was the same, – (which was all that I professed.) As I feared, the case turns out to be not one of mistake, but of craft: & very sorry I am to see it.

I omitted to say before that C.B's mistakes in her statements about me were not of my own discovery, – though of course I could best judge of them. It so happened that I did not see the book until the second edition was appearing: &, weeks before I saw it, my relations, friends and neighbours were talking about the extraordinary representations of me, my ways, position, & experiences, that appeared in C.B's letters. The matter was notorious before it came to my knowledge at all. I have put the facts on record, in case of any call being made for the facts after I am gone. Otherwise, the thing is too personal, & of too little consequence to require any further effort than to obtain corrections in the 3d edition.

And now, – see how you stand. Mr Brontë has gone out of his way – leaving the subject he was writing on, – to charge me with an atheistic profession which I never made: & you, Sir, palter with a passage in a letter which is as clear as daylight, – *not* in reply to my assertion about C.B's correctness, but to charge *me* with some offence not specified, which had no connection with the subject of Miss Brontë's letter. It is no pleasure to me to see clergymen showing such a state of temper & of conscience; but it is of importance to yourselves that you should see your conduct as others see it. If such conduct had been exhibited in two priests in the diocese of Tuam[38] you would have known how to estimate and characterize it. I hope you may learn it in your own case.

Arthur was not intimidated by these fierce words. "I never told Mrs Gaskell that I had destroyed all Charlotte's papers," he replied the next day, "but only her letters to myself." Then he pretended that he didn't know which "Greenwood" she referred to,

> there being many persons of that name in this village – two small stationers and several operatives – but with no one of them have I ever had any communication whatever on the subject of your letters, but you do not hesitate to say that the information with which you were furnished was obtained from me – thus falling into the error, imputed by you to Miss Brontè, of making statements not altogether true.
>
> I regret to see that you consider it a very venial weakness to substitute one passage [in a letter] for another – I know how your two priests in the Diocese of Tuam would deal with you in such a case if they had you in their power.

He knew exactly which Greenwood. Indeed, he immediately extracted a confession from the poor stationer that "I never had any communications with Mr Nicholls concerning the correspondence in question" and that he only "*believed* Mrs Nicholls made it a rule not to keep letters, except those of "importance," and sent on.

Patrick made his second and final intervention also on 21 November.

> You say that I stepped out of my way in charging you with Atheism, & that I could not have read your book … or must have misunderstood it. I have read it, thought of it, & understood its contents, and so have many others; and they, & I have felt convinced, that you maintained there was no God. Hardly anything would give me greater pleasure, except your entire orthodoxy, than … your own public asserting to all the world, that we were mistaken. I conceive I did not go out of my way in mentioning the circumstance. In your article in the Daily times [sic], you forced me to do it; where you said, that you had not lost a friend on account of the book in question, thus bringing my daughter under the disagreeable charge of officious meddling. You rather amuse me when you make a kind of comparison of Mr Nicholls and me, with the liberal minded priests of Tuam.

> Now, trust me, Madam, when I assure you, that here at least, you have made an egregious mistake – Why? – Mr Nicholls & I, had we full power over you, would not injure a hair of your head, or put you into the least pain, either of body or mind, whilst, were [you] in the power of the priests of Tuam ... and Mr Nicholls & I in their power, they would apply the thumbscrews and tighten it [sic], till we cried out in our agony, not only that we believed there is a God, but that the Virgin Mary is a Goddess & that both she and all the Saints in the Calendar are objects of worship & prayer. But to return to my Daughter Charlotte ... In her case what most astonishes me, is the real, or apparent prejudice you have against her ... I well knew her character for veracity and candour, and had many proofs of her affection for you, I entreat you ... to do justice to her in all you may think, say or write ... Beware of the designs of prejudiced, or reckless Informants.

The question of who had said what to whom and when, now involving five people, had become ludicrously complicated. Arthur shot off a note to Mrs Gaskell accusing her of telling Martineau "quite falsely" that he had destroyed all of Charlotte's papers. She replied that it was just a misunderstanding, and obviously hoped that this would bring matters to an end.[39] By contrast, Martineau apologized for nothing. She contended that it had been her "natural supposition" that John Greenwood, whom she described as Charlotte's "*one* friend at Haworth," must have derived his information from Arthur. She referred to Greenwood twice as Charlotte's one Haworth friend, underlining the "one" each time as a thrust at Arthur's previous pretense that he did not know which of several Greenwoods she had dealt with. Then she switched once more to the offensive.

> I was remiss in not at that time, April 1855, exerting my right of requiring the return of all letters from myself to Charlotte Brontë. I once had occasion ... to obtain a legal statement of the rights of writers and receivers of private letters ... private letters are the property (– to keep or destroy, but not to publish –) of the receiver during life ... they become the property of the writer, or his or her heirs, on the death of the receiver. Within the last week I have made inquiry again, in order to be sure of my ground; & this

> morning I receive the dictum of an able lawyer that "letters continue the property of the writer, who has a right to reclaim them, if preserved, on the death of the person they were addressed to."
>
> I now thus reclaim my letters to Charlotte Brontë. Any of hers to me which may be in existence at the time of my death will be returned to you according to ordinary custom.
>
> I need hardly add that your omission of this customary observance in the spring of 1855 would have dispersed all doubts of the accuracy of the information I had received, if I had had any reason to doubt it. – To this omission is also due all the trouble we have respectively had in regard to the passage in my letter about "Villette." As soon as I receive the original letter, I shall send the passage, (certified as from the original), to Messrs Smith & Elder, to be substituted in any future edition for the one furnished from memory – avowedly from memory, to Mrs Gaskell.

Talk of lawyers was bound to disturb Arthur, and on 14 November he sent the letters by return post, assuring Martineau that she "should have had them in 1855, had I known of the custom referred to by you," and that, with the exception of the letters relating to *Villette*, he had read none of them. (This is doubtful. How could he have unearthed the *Villette* letters had he not gone through at least some of the others?) As for Martineau's contention that Greenwood was Charlotte's one friend in Haworth, he observed with supercilious hauteur that Greenwood's position was "not such as would have enabled him to know anything of Miss Brontë's private affairs, further than what he [may] have learned by gossiping with servants & his relation to Miss Brontë consisted in being the recipient of her bounty & advice when in distress from the claims of a large family." This was Arthur at his worst – pompous and remote. Indeed, Martineau seized on this comment to remark "he now utterly forfeits our interest & esteem by his insolent and mean tone."[40]

Their correspondence came to an end somewhat less belligerently. Arthur sent Martineau a final note which he requested her to burn, and which she described as "*wholly* self-excusing. I mean that it did not relate to myself, any further than he desired to obtain my good opinion before we parted." She took him to be "a weak man of narrow experience, who vents his irritation, when he has got into difficulty, in bluster, which contrasts curiously enough with the anxiety to justify himself into which he subsides at last. I am really sorry for him, however, & so I told him as kindly as I could." Forty years later, still innocent of her real opinion, Arthur told Clement Shorter: "Miss Martineau and I parted good friends."[41] Age had not diminished his capacity to transform the unpleasant aspects of his past.

In her final note to Patrick, Martineau wrote: "In regard to the Atkinson Letters you have missed their aim and doctrine. The existence of a First Cause is distinctly stated … as a matter of necessary human belief & the same conception underlies the whole work." In her autobiography she claimed that Charlotte had "accepted my explanation that I was an atheist in the vulgar sense – that of rejecting the popular theology – but not in the philosophical sense of denying a First Cause," although Charlotte's religious outlook might not seem to have permitted her to make the distinction. Martineau's antipathy to Patrick was far stronger than she ever allowed him to see. To a friend she wrote: "I now not only believe him heartless … but entirely distrust his sincerity … & I have a painful impression that Mr Dearden's story is no less true than Mr Brontë's opposite expressions to Mrs Gaskell."[42]

And so this intense ten-day exchange came to an end. Neither Patrick nor Arthur came out of it well, Patrick willfully blind to the religious distinctions Martineau made, Arthur discharging poorly aimed ammunition that ricocheted against him. Both men had allowed their anger over the *Daily News* attack on Charlotte's veracity to cloud their judgment. On the other hand, despite her recourse to legal threats and the self-pitying reference to her "final illness," Martineau compels one's admiration for her sturdy self-defense.

The two clergymen, bruised by their encounter with this female porcupine, returned to the quiet rhythm of their clerical lives only to find that Haworth, after the appearance of the *Life,* was becoming a literary shrine. A steady stream of tourists poured into the town to gawk at the church, the graveyard, and the parsonage. Although Arthur felt it "would be a great nuisance if they were to intrude on us," some did manage to obtain an interview, including the Duke of Devonshire and E.W. Benson, who in 1882 would become Archbishop of Canterbury. Arthur was generally more protective of his privacy than Patrick. When Thomas Akroyd, a Liverpool clergyman, asked Joseph Redman, the parish clerk, "if he thought Mr Brontë would see me if I called. He 'couldn't tell – Mr Brontë wur gettin' old and rather infirm now – didn't see monny folks; but he wur far readier than Mr Nicholls.'" Akroyd did succeed in talking to Patrick, and then, as Martha was escorting him to the door,

> another wish clamoured to be gratified. So in the most seductive tone I could summon I said: "Martha, could I not see the portrait of Miss Brontë?" "I don't know, Sir," she replied, "it is in Mr Nicholls' room and he doesn't like folks going in. But … I'll go and ask him." The clerk had previously told me of Mr N's reluctance to admit visitors into the parsonage, how he had recently declined the request of the daughters of Lord John Russell to see the picture, churlishly remarking that "the house was not a picture gallery."

However Akroyd was admitted, as were others, including several Americans, whom Patrick seemed to favour. When one of them, Henry Jarvis Raymond, the editor of the *New York Times*, observed that he found the town and surrounding country "less sombre and repulsive than Mrs Gaskell's descriptions led me to expect, Mr Nicholls and Mr Brontë smiled at each other, and the latter remarked: 'Well, I think Mrs Gaskell tried to make us all appear as bad as she could.'" Similarly, when Akroyd suggested that readers "should not perhaps take everything for gospel that Mrs G. has said about your family," Patrick replied: "Mrs Gaskell is a novelist, you know, and we must allow her a little romance, eh? But the book is substantially true, Sir, for all that. There are some things in it, to be sure – there are some about myself, for instance – but the book is substantially true, Sir, substantially true." Mary Taylor concurred with this judgment, noting however that Mrs Gaskell "seems a hasty, impulsive person, and the needful drawing back, after her warmth gives her an inconsistent look … Libellous or not, the first edition was all true… Of course I don't know how far necessity may make Mrs Gaskell give them [the contested materials in the first and second editions] up. You know one does not always say the world moves."[43]

Despite the bruises she had suffered from the critics and the legal threats that the *Life* had stirred up, Mrs Gaskell had not lost her interest in the Brontës. The reviews were mostly positive, and sales brisk. In March 1858, she suggested to George Smith that it might help sales of the planned cheap edition if Charlotte's unfinished novel were added as an appendix. But she feared that Arthur would refuse permission, since he had so much disapproved of the *Life*. Once again she reiterated the myth of Arthur opposing Charlotte's career as an author: "it [the fragment] was begun a year or so before her marriage and Mr Nicholls always *groaned literally* – when she talked of continuing it." More than one critic has wondered how Mrs Gaskell knew that he always groaned. Charlotte could not have told her, since their last meeting had been in September 1853, well before the marriage, and there is nothing of this in her subsequent letters. The most likely source, if indeed there was one, was Ellen Nussey, always ready to paint Arthur in the worst possible light.

Still, her carelessness was matched by her generosity; genuinely interested in seeing the fragment published, she suggested to George Smith that he might include it in the *Cornhill Magazine*, which he was about to inaugurate. And recognizing that she would be unlikely to secure Arthur's permission, she suggested, as she had before with Charlotte's letters, that Smith should make the request himself.[44]

Arthur agreed, eagerly transcribed the original manuscript, and proof read and edited the galleys. Lyndall Gordon has observed that "he proved remarkably free of prudery in restoring a final scene which Charlotte herself had cancelled. The suggestiveness of this scene, where a male character carries a little girl to bed, was typical of what the Victorians found 'coarse' in Charlotte Brontë."[45] *Emma*, as this last fragment was now called, appeared in the spring of 1860 with a short preface by Thackeray. In a touching note, Arthur begged Smith to return the original manuscript. "I prize it much as being the last thing of the kind written by the Author." He also offered some Brontë poems to Smith, and in the next eighteen months two by Charlotte and one by Emily were published in the magazine. How many other poems Arthur copied, and the quality of the transcriptions, is contentious. Christine Alexander suggests that on his return to Banagher after Patrick's death in 1861, Arthur did not simply pack away his Brontë manuscripts but continued to transcribe them steadily. In comparing his transcriptions with the originals, Victor Newfeldt has demonstrated that however enthusiastic a copier he may have been, Arthur was far from accurate. However, he was certainly a conscientious preserver of the sisters' literary reputation. "I would not however publish anything," he told Smith, "that could possibly detract from the fame [Charlotte] has already achieved."[46]

In his dealings with George Smith Arthur revealed sensitivity, good taste and discretion. He was quite another person in his relations with petty officials like William Brown, Joseph Redman, and John Greenwood. To his chagrin, the tourists who crowded the narrow streets of Haworth wanted Brontë mementoes, and the local population was only too happy to provide them. The chemist displayed photographs for sale in his windows and Sexton William Brown, who had succeed his brother in 1855, invited tourists to see Charlotte's signature in the marriage register and showed them his own photos "with an intimation that they were for sale."[47]

These enterprises disgusted Arthur and strengthened his old intolerance, sometimes to the point of the absurd. In 1858, Patrick ordered a new family memorial tablet to replace the original, which was so filled with the names of the Brontë dead that Charlotte had to be remembered on a separate plaque at its foot. According to William Brown, "Mr. N. made him take the old tablet-stone, and with a hammer break it into small pieces, which he then bade, and saw, him bury 4 ft. deep in the garden: for fear any one should get hold of a piece for a relic."[48]

The following year John Greenwood proposed to have his newborn son baptized "Brontë," presumably to perpetuate the myth of himself as one of Charlotte's local intimates. Knowing Greenwood had provided Mrs Gaskell with malicious rumours about his family, Arthur refused to perform the ceremony. Apparently the poor infant remained unimmersed for some six months, until – according to Mrs Gaskell – "its great delicacy coming to Mr Brontë's knowledge, he sent for it privately and christened it in his own room. When Mr Nicholls came upon its name upon the register book, Mr Greenwood says that he stormed and stamped, and went straight home to the parsonage to Mr Brontë to ask him for his reasons in going so directly against his wishes." ["So I see you have christened your namesake!" Mrs Greenwood, in telling the story to Mrs Gaskell's daughter, Meta, has him exclaiming.] Fortunately Mr Brontë had the excellent defence of saying that if the child had died unchristened Mr Nicholls' case would have been extremely awkward and that he had thus saved him from a great scrape." Meta Gaskell saw this as just one more "specimen of Mr N's sullen, obstinate rooted objection to any reverence being paid to Miss B. one might almost say at any rate to people caring to remember her as an authoress.[49]

When he had first read *Shirley*, Arthur had stamped his feet in delight as he recognized himself in Charlotte's description of how "the thought of an unbaptised fellow-creature being interred with Christian rites … could make strange havoc in [Mr Macarthey's] physical and mental economy." Although one can sympathize with Arthur's anger when he saw John Greenwood about to appropriate his wife's name, and understand his desire to prevent Haworth from becoming a Brontë Lourdes, it is hard to excuse this lapse in clerical duty. And then Mrs Gaskell, perhaps feeling guilty about her treatment of Patrick who, unlike Arthur, had received the *Life* with public restraint and surface good humour, decided to pay the parsonage a visit.[50]

When she and Meta arrived in November of 1860, the old man was bedridden. Although "touchingly softened by illness," Mrs Gaskell found that he "still talks in his pompous way, and mingles moral remarks and somewhat stale sentiments with his conversation on other subjects. Mr Nicholls seems to keep him rather *in terrorem. He* [Arthur] is more unpopular in the village than ever; and seems to have even a greater aversion than formerly to any strangers visiting his wife's grave; or, indeed, to any reverence paid to her memory." During this visit, Patrick showed that he was perfectly aware of Mrs Gaskell's dislike of Arthur. Meta relates that at a certain point Patrick had said: "'There are certain circumstances, you see,' looking very knowing, 'which make it desirable that when you leave in 5 minutes or so, we should shake hands – and I give your daughter free leave to make a sketch, or do anything *outside* the house. Do you understand Latin? Mrs Gaskell does at any rate, well, *verbum sap*, a word to the wise,' and then he chuckled very much; the gist of it was … that he feared Mr Nicholls' return from the school – and we were to be safely out of the house before that." William Brown confirmed their impression that Patrick and Arthur were not exactly intimate: "Aye, Mester Brontë and Mr Nicholls live together still *ever near* but *ever separate*."[51]

Other evidence paints a different picture of relations between father and son-in-law. On 20 June 1855, Patrick made his last will. Aside from two specific bequests – £40 to his brother Hugh "to be equally divided amongst all my Brothers and Sisters to whom I gave considerable sums in times past," and £30 to Martha Brown – he left everything to "My beloved and esteemed son-in-law, the Rev. Arthur Bell Nicholls, B.A.," and he made Arthur his sole executor. This is hardly the act of someone who lived "in terror" of his son-in-law, or felt "ever separate" from him. On Arthur's side, too, there are signs that however resentful he may have been of Patrick's treatment of him during his courtship of Charlotte, trust and a solid friendship had subsequently developed. After Charlotte died, Patrick's health slowly declined, and Arthur was party to Martha Brown's care of him. Patrick still managed to preach one sermon – his homilies had always been short and ex tempore – every Sunday until October 1859. After that he was pretty well bed-ridden, although he lingered on for many months beyond the Gaskells' visit, the *Bradford Observer* publishing periodic bulletins on the state of his health until it announced his death on 7 June 1861. During those last months, Arthur told George Smith that his father-in-law "had a good deal of physical suffering but for some days before his death he was remarkably free from pain. Early on the morning of the 7th he was seized with convulsions: when I got to him he was unconscious & continued so until his death."

Despite being deeply affected by Patrick's death Arthur, with his customary efficiency, arranged for a funeral of Spartan simplicity, as Patrick had wished: no tolling bells, no sung Psalms. The church was full and hundreds more stood outside in silent respect as Patrick's coffin was followed in by Arthur, Martha and Eliza Brown, their mother and Nancy Garrs. Juliet Barker notes that anyone "who might have doubted the personal affection which had arisen between Patrick and his son-in-law had only to observe Arthur's conduct: he was so 'deeply affected' that he had to be physically supported by William Cartman," who assisted Dr. Burnett, the vicar of Bradford, who conducted the service.[52]

Patrick's death was the first of three blows Arthur suffered in 1861. In August his closest friend in the district, the Rev. Sutcliffe Sowden, suffered a heart attack or some sort of fit, fell into the canal at Hebden Bridge, and drowned. Arthur took over at that service, though he wrote to Sutcliffe's brother, Thomas, that "it will be hard work for me to read the Service over one whose intimate friendship I have enjoyed for many years, and whom I have looked upon more as a relation than a friend." Indeed, he was so overcome with emotion burying Sowden that, at times, he was "wholly inaudible."[53]

The third blow changed his entire future. The previous summer, Haworth church had witnessed its first confirmations since 1824. Patrick had been looking forward to the occasion but was so weak that he could not attend it. At the time, the *Bradford Observer* reported that when he died, Arthur would succeed him. Arthur had immediately issued a denial that he had "any expectation of obtaining the appointment," but after sixteen years of service in the parish it is difficult to believe that he did not feel that the incumbency would be offered him. And now the time had come.

The process of selecting the perpetual curate of Haworth was a curious one. Although the power to nominate a candidate lay in the hands of the vicar of Bradford, he did not control the income to pay his stipend; when Edward VI dissolved the chantries in 1547, the curate of Haworth was left without income until, on Elizabeth's accession in 1558, the people of Haworth had raised £36 by subscription, purchased land at nearby Stanbury, and used the income, administered by twelve trustees, to pay their curate. The current vicar, Dr Burnett, was thus the patron in name only, since "in the event of the Patron appointing a person not approved by the trustees or their majority, they [could] withhold the endowment and leave the incumbent to live on air, or meditations among the tombs."[54] This was not a mere paper prerogative. The twelve trustees, independent and fractious, had exercised their power several times in the past: in 1741, when they had rejected Bradford's choice and insisted on William Grimshaw; in 1791, when they overrode the vicar in securing Patrick's predecessor, James Chadwick; and in 1820 when they appointed Patrick himself after a year-long struggle.[55]

A meeting to discuss Patrick's successor had in fact been scheduled for the very day of his funeral but was, on that account, adjourned for several months, during which Arthur performed all the normal clerical duties. This long delay could only have strengthened his expectation that he would be appointed Patrick's successor. What happened after that depends on the testimony of an anonymous correspondent of the *Bradford Review*, signing himself "N," and on a report in the *Bradford Observer*. Either "N" was himself a trustee or he had the confidence of at least one member of the board. His corrections of "certain inaccuracies" in the report of the *Bradford Observer* are probably reliable, so in what follows, I have altered the *Observer's* story to conform to them. Arthur had been the first choice of Dr Burnett who was falsely rumored to have promised him the incumbency on his marriage to Charlotte. When the trustees reassembled in early October, Arthur's name was put forward, but he received only four votes, with five opposed, and one trustee, a dissenter, abstaining. Two other trustees were absent at the time. Dr Burnett, familiar with the trustees' history of unmanageability, decided that Arthur would have to be sacrificed in the interest of parochial peace. He therefore brought forward a new candidate, John Wade. And at a third meeting, with all trustees present, Wade received seven votes to Arthur's five.[56]

This rejection, after sixteen years of faithful service, assuming most of Patrick's duties, building up the local National School, and attending to all the other obscure but important works that fall to a curate's lot, cut Arthur to the bone. That he really had been expecting the appointment despite his earlier denial is clear from the fact that, after Patrick's death, he had begun to sign himself "O.M." (Officiating Minister), instead of "Curate." He must have wondered who the seven trustees were who opposed him, and why. The reason given by Lock and Dixon, Patrick's biographers, is simple but unsubstantiated: "the people of Haworth in general, and the trustees in particular, were heartily sick of him. Indeed, they had only waited for their old parson's death before taking immediate steps to rid themselves of their moody curate." Their "ready-made" excuse concerned the way Arthur had handled, or failed to handle, the funeral of Michael Heaton, their late chairman. In 1856, an Order-in-Council had closed all graveyards and burial grounds in the parish of Bradford. The Heaton family, one of the more distinguished in the locality, had come to Patrick for permission to bury Michael in the family plot. The ailing Patrick referred them to Arthur who, with the rigid scrupulosity that often characterized him when dealing with matters of protocol, told them that nothing could be done. The Heatons then applied directly to the Secretary of State, who gave them permission to inter the old fellow beside his wife. The burial service was conducted by Joseph Grant of Oxenhope, Arthur, having refused. But when Patrick died, Arthur himself applied to the Secretary of State in order to place him in the family vault. This apparently inequitable treatment might well have given the Heaton family grounds for opposing him. But as Juliet Barker notes, "if there was any truth in the incident at all, the matter had been forgiven and forgotten by those most concerned" since the chairman of the trustees, himself a Heaton, had been one of the five voting in Arthur's favour.[57]

According to Lock and Dixon, "Arthur Nicholls, who had waited so patiently for the living of Haworth and who had kept his promise to Charlotte that he would remain with her father until the end, went slowly down Kirkgate with all his belongings (including those many precious Brontë manuscripts); and there was not one who was sorry to see him go!" There is no doubt that, over the years, he had irritated several members of his congregation by his uncompromising behaviour. But aside from Mrs Gaskell, the Greenwoods, and the Browns, only one other negative view of Arthur has been recorded by his contemporaries. Charles Hale, an American who visited Haworth shortly after Arthur's departure, implied that Arthur's refusal to christen Brontë Greenwood was due to "a strange feeling about his wife's separate reputation – He hated that she should be remembered in any other relation than as his wife; as an author or as the chief personage of Haworth he could not bear to have her thought of." Nothing could have been farther from the truth. Arthur did not object to public scrutiny of Charlotte as an author; his aversion was to prurient, intrusive curiosity about her private life, especially her marriage. Hale was probably repeating what he was told by the Greenwoods, but he was undoubtedly correct when he noted how strongly Brontë Greenwood's christening "affected the popular estimate of the two clergymen. Mr Brontë was sincerely and truly beloved. The sexton said he was the most truly kind and considerate man for the feeling of others, while Mr Nicholls was just the opposite." And Hale's story that Arthur "threatened the law against the farmers for alleged neglect in maintaining the flagstones across several fields on the path leading from the back of the parsonage to the moors" certainly sounds authentic. Even Mabel Edgerley, a sympathetic memorialist writing long after his death, states that he "was not altogether liked by the parishioners," that "he was not genial, and at times was deficient in tact," and that compared to Patrick, "who minded his own business, was apt to rebuke backsliders, and was intolerant of Dissenters. Now there were at least three Chapels in the village, in which their members took a keen interest. The Haworthians were independent in thought and conduct, and did not relish Mr N's interference." Baptismal statistics provide an indirect confirmation of this view. In 1862, the first year after Arthur's departure, the number of children baptized jumped to 250, suggesting that the new minister, John Wade, had picked up "children who had not been brought during Brontë's last years, a fact which seems to confirm the relative unpopularity of Nicholls."[58]

Among other things, Arthur was an ardent devotee of exercise and the benefits of the outdoor life, and his insistence on imposing his personal regimen as well as his religious beliefs on others might have caused resentment. Patrick Brontë could always be identified by the high white stock he wore to ward off colds and like all good Haworthians, he kept the parsonage windows tightly closed. Arthur, on the other hand, deplored closed windows, especially in bedrooms. The village carpenter's son provides a good description of him going for a "sharp walk" on the moors in the early morning,

> running to get up the circulation, swinging his arms, and in the winter beating them across his chest until he got himself into a glow. Then he would hurry into the schoolroom at 9 o'clock to take the Scripture, and would insist on all the windows being open, forgetting that the teachers and scholars had not had his experience and were not in such an excellent condition to stand the draughts and cold morning air. He was a hard worker and made others work and … was generally considered a hard man, conscientious to a fault.[59]

He might have been a hard man, but there is a persuasive volume of counter-evidence suggesting that Arthur had the support, respect, and even affection of most of the members of the community. Mabel Edgerley observes that "he was greatly loved by the old folks, and the little children. They did not argue and did not have to be scolded; for the old were past sinning time, and the very young had not seriously started." To illustrate his rapport with the young, she relates the recollections of an aged member of the congregation long after Arthur's death.

> It was usual for Mr N to go every morning to the Church School and instruct the children in religious matters. He often had a large dog with him called Plato…. Then, too, Mr N always had a pocketful of sweets for the children, and those fortunate enough to meet him on the moors would get a ride on Plato's back. One day – it was during his married life – he saw a little girl crying; she had been punished for a fault. He bent down and whispered: "Come to my house after school." The little girl was hardly able to wait, and after school was over she rushed to the Parsonage. There was a beautiful new "pinny" for her. What a joy for the child! And 87 years after it was still remembered.

She adds that "by more discerning adults he was also very favourably judged, for they saw how hard and how conscientiously he worked." An old villager, recalling Arthur's rejection, told Edgerley that "all the church folk wanted to have him, but a trustee who had a casting vote and who was a Dissenter, gave it against him." The hostess of the Black Bull was probably doing no more than reflecting local opinion when she told a visitor soon after Charlotte's death that "the people all liked Mr Nicholls."[60] One remembers, too, the strong demonstration of esteem when he left Haworth in May 1853 before his marriage. And when he took Plato and Flossy for long walks on the moors he was often accompanied by members of the congregation. One old parishioner, a plasterer who had worked on the church schools, remembered rambling over the moors with his curate:

> Ay, I've been with Mr Nicholls mony a time on t'moor and catching trout. He was fearful fond of going to Smith Bank and we gate mony a lot. We'd no rods or lines but just put our hands under them as they lay under the stones in the pools and laiked [played] with them, and when we gait hod on them we threw them as far as we could into t'field. Poaching do you say? Nay, there were no preserving, not there there worn't, at that time: we could wade up and down the stream as we liked. And after he wor married Charlotty – Mrs Nicholls – used to come and all. She'd take a board and put it across two stones and car down on t'green, while Mr Nicholls and me were wading up and down t'stream. He wor a verra good hand at it, a better hand nor me … Ay, we'd often go on t'moor together. He'd a retriever, a girt brown un, he'd go in t'water anywhere. It just suited him to see t'dog run after t'birds, t'moor game, and it would creep within a yard of them and it had had no training, nobbut what he'd given it. It worn't like dogs that have been trained and beaten. Did he beat it? Nay, it wor a reight petted dog, a house dog, but it wor a reight clever dog – it would go sideways through stile-hoils when it wor carrying a stick … A very quiet man wor Mr Nicholls, never much talk; a dark-complexioned man, hair black as a coil.

Fifty years after Arthur's departure the old fellow was indignant about his rejection: "I never thought but he would ha' had it and he did himself. All t'church folk wanted him to have it, and he would ha' had it but for one o' t' trustees, a girt manufacturer and a Metody, and he'd t' casting vote." The congregation wanted him to "come back and preach for t' rush-bearing Sunday [the festival of the church's dedication] but he wouldn't. He thought he'd been done out o' t' church and he'd never face it again." Even William Brown, who had filled Elizabeth and Meta Gaskell with stories of how Arthur was disliked, completely reversed himself seven years later when he told a visitor that "Mr Nicholls was very well liked by the people. A true gentleman he was, though very shy and reserved."[61]

With so much conflicting testimony it is hard to reach a simple, clear conclusion about the reasons for Arthur's rejection. The closeness of the vote shows that the trustees were not strongly united against him. Juliet Barker speculates that there "may have been a wish to end the Brontë associations with the church and appoint a minister who would not be a celebrity because of his personal connections." Another reason may have been that Arthur was totally dependent on his stipend. John Wade, who was "unsympathetic, if not actually hostile, towards the Brontës," enjoyed an independent source of income and would not be a drain on the parish.[62]

Arthur himself said nothing publicly or, so far as one can tell, privately about what had happened, but the editor of the *Bradford Observer*, a Dissenter with no sectarian axe to grind, denounced the decision as shabby and heartless.

> It is not many months ago since Patrick Brontë went down to the grave in ripe old age; he was the last of his race, but he wanted not in his latter helpless years the watchful kindness of a son.
> Mr Nicholls his curate, and the widowed husband of Charlotte, smoothed the old man's dying bed and saw his head laid in the grave. He had for many years laboured in every sense as the Pastor of Haworth. His character is above reproach and his faithful discharge of the duties of his office well known. What was more natural than that the people of Haworth would wish the incumbency to be conferred on the man that had gone out and in before them for such a long time, and who stood in the relation of husband to her that first made their district known to fame.
> Outsiders never doubted for a moment but that the congregation

> would do all in their power to perpetuate by the only remaining link the connection that fortune had formed between them and a child of genius. It is therefore with a feeling different from surprise that we now learn the unexpected issue.
>
> We have naught to say against the gentleman preferred … but the trustees will be asked by the country not whether their choice is a better man, but whether Mr Nicholls is unfit for the incumbency of Haworth? They are responsible first to the parishioners, and next to all England for an answer. Have they interpreted the feelings of the parishioners correctly? Is it possible that the people of Haworth wished to turn adrift in a thankless manner a gentleman, no longer young, who had been for so many years their teacher in divine things? On the face of the appointment there is a shabbiness and heartlessness which only the highest purity of motive can justify … They are bound to prove that the choice of Charlotte Brontë was not the choice of the Churchmen of Haworth.

A correspondent from Haworth wrote to support these views, denying "that the congregation would not tolerate Mr Nicholls, or that the people *generally* wished for his removal." He pointed out that church attendance after Patrick's death had been as large as before. An impressive indication of Arthur's popularity was that on the day before the trustees' last meeting, a petition in his favour had received "upwards of five hundred signatures in a few hours." Five hundred, noted the *Observer*, was more than two-thirds of the seating capacity of Haworth Church. "When the trustees met to disgrace themselves in the eyes of all England, it was known to them that the majority of the congregation were in favour of Mr. Nicholls's settlement." These strong words were dismissed by the anonymous "N," who insisted that the "spiritual good of the people" should be the only criterion for selecting a curate and that the importance of the Brontë tie to the community was irrelevant. "N" also questioned the importance of the petition, since there was no way of knowing how many signatories were actual members of the congregation. He concluded that the trustees' choice was "in harmony with the views of the vast majority of the Parishioners." Finally, in an appeal to local patriotism, he revealed that of the five who voted for Arthur one came from Lincolnshire, and another from a distant part of Yorkshire.

Although he refrained from entering the controversy, Arthur did reveal a small part of his feelings when, back in Banagher he remarked that the editor of the *Observer* had given "great offence to some people in Haworth. His strictures however were well merited."[63]

In exploring all the possible motives for Arthur's rejection, Juliet Barker finally suggests that "the trustees' choice … seems attributable chiefly to that bloody-mindedness which is characteristic of Yorkshiremen and more especially of the people of Haworth. They seem to have wished to assert their own authority in the face of a general expectation that they would prefer the curate." While "bloody-mindedness" does not seem an extreme description, a more violent collision between the Trustees and the Vicar of Bradford had occurred over Patrick's appointment, when the trustees rejected a popular preacher simply because they had not been consulted before his nomination. With a retarded and probably intoxicated chimney-sweep at its head, the congregation had ejected the unfortunate man from the pulpit, covered him in soot, and driven him out of town. Yet a few years later they welcomed him back as a visiting preacher because, after all, their quarrel had not been with him, but with the vicar. Boswell mentions difficulties with northern juries as widespread, and a century later Trollope comments that an advocate 'in the north of England has a finer scope, because the people like to move counter to authority. A … jury will generally be unwilling to do what a judge tells them."[64] It may well have been this hard introduction to the West Riding that taught Patrick, who got the living in default, to deal gently with his obstinate parishioners.

The new appointment was announced on 18 September, and John Wade intimated that he wanted to take over on Sunday 22, four days later. Arthur prepared to leave immediately, packing all the surviving Brontë manuscripts and letters, Charlotte's portrait by Richmond, some of her clothes, including her wedding dress, and a few pieces of furniture. With the exception of items he gave to Martha and Tabitha, the rest of the household effects were auctioned off in the first two days of October for £115. 13s. 11d. Arthur had Charlotte's bed broken up and discarded before the auction, another example of his protectiveness of anything touching her personal life. Then he took his leave of Haworth where he had labored so conscientiously, fallen in love so passionately, suffered so deeply. But he did not go alone. Martha Brown, whose earlier hostility had changed to respect and affection, went with him down the steep

Kirkgate. Behind them came Plato and Cato, Patrick's dogs, who had replaced Emily's Keeper and Anne's Flossy, and with whom Arthur had enjoyed so many walks on the moors. And except for one brief visit in July 1863 when he acted as witness at the marriage of Martha's sister Mary, he never saw Haworth again.[65]

CHAPTER SIX

Return to Banagher

When he left Haworth Arthur was forty-three years old. At an age when most men are moving into their most productive period, he found himself unemployed, a curate without a curacy and, since the vicar of Bradford made no effort to find him a new place, with little prospect of getting one. Being thus doubly rejected must have been a severe blow to his self-respect and it undoubtedly influenced him to return to the warmth and affection of his adoptive family.

Although he had been living in England for over sixteen years, his frequent Irish vacations had allowed him to keep in touch with life back home. He had been a witness to the devastating potato blight and famine of 1846–47. In 1848, he had seen his young cousin James assume the mastership of the Royal Free School and thereby return the family to Cuba House. By 1850 Susan and Frances, two of Harriette's four daughters, were dead. In 1854, following his honeymoon visit, young Harriette, the cousin who had previously declined Arthur's proposal, married another cousin, John Evans Adamson (1822–1869), and began to bring up her own family outside Clifden in Connemara. Of the remaining sons, Alan (1821–1868) was senior chaplain to the British forces stationed at King Williamstown, South Africa; Arthur (1828–1891) was a medical officer with the RAMC in India where he died "having sacrificed his life in a terrible visitation of cholera;" Joseph, (1831–1891), after a brilliant career at Trinity, went on to a distinguished career in the Church of

Ireland; and William (1839–1870) became a surgeon in the Royal Navy, dying like his brother Alan, at the Cape.[1]

When James Bell married shortly after Arthur's honeymoon with Charlotte, Aunt Harriette and her daughter, Mary, had moved out of Cuba House, first to a house in Banagher, and later to the Hill House. Still habitable, it is situated quite close to Cuba House on twenty acres of land above the town, which Harriette had inherited on the death of her husband. It was here, with this tiny remnant of his adoptive family, that Arthur settled down to spend the rest of his life.

He made no effort to find another living in Ireland, giving up the cure of others' souls and devoting himself to the cure of his own. The speed with which he adapted to his new surroundings suggests that the healing process was rapid.

> I am busy farming in a small way; we have two cows, a heifer and a calf. It affords me some little employment. On the whole I have been better since I came here, but the Rheumatism is still troublesome … the prospect for the winter is very gloomy – the potato crop, on which the poor principally depend, has been a failure; more than half of the tubers being diseased. Moreover owing to the wet autumn in these parts very little peat has been got off the bogs – coal is quite beyond the means of the great bulk of the people.[2]

To Harriette and Mary, Arthur's arrival was welcome on several counts: he was a family member returned, he was someone who could look after their affairs, and he might, if things were managed properly, some day serve Mary as a husband. But Arthur was in no condition to think of taking on a new wife. Over the previous decade his feelings had been bruised by the passionate Brontës and the bloody-minded folk of Haworth. All he wanted now was support – maternal or sisterly, it was all one to him. A portrait made in 1861, just after he left Haworth, shows a dark and gloomy man, staring down blankly, as though stunned by everything that has happened to him. It makes a painful contrast to his honeymoon photo in which he looks up and out with vigor and hope. With Charlotte dead and the incumbency of Haworth denied him, that hope had been extinguished.

Yet he could not rid himself of Haworth. Hardly had he returned to Ireland when news arrived from an unexpected quarter. John Greenwood, with whom he had quarreled for so long, sent him a long letter "on the sayings and doings at Haworth." Perhaps, as Lock and Dixon suggest, Arthur represented the last link with the Brontës, but there must have been another motive. Greenwood's letter has not survived, but Arthur's reply makes it clear that the community, which had divided over the question of Patrick's replacement, was still in a state of turmoil.

> I sincerely trust that you may not be subjected to any further annoyance from the proceedings of the persons you mention. It would be more creditable to them to let bygones be bygones and set themselves to restore peace and harmony to the parish – as far as I am concerned I have benefitted very much by the change – My health is much better than it has been for some time – Martha also is stronger than she was, so that on the whole I am quite satisfied with the turn matters took, tho' [and here he could not conceal the raw wound] I should rather not have got such an insight into the dispositions of some of my former neighbours.

A letter to Mr Sutcliffe dated 5 November 1861 indicates what some of the "annoyances" were, and makes it clear that Arthur was still *au courant* with affairs in Haworth. "Matters have been going on strangely at Haworth – some miscreant has injured the monuments in the chuchyard belonging to Mr G. Merrall and Eliza Brown's mother. I do hope he may be found out. There are extensive repairs going on at the parsonage, I understand. I dare say I shall scarcely know it when I see it, but it will not be the same to me."[3]

Although technically Arthur held the curacy of St Paul's in Banagher between 1870 and 1885 during the rectorships of his two cousins, he would never again perform the rigorous duties he had undertaken when at Haworth. But he was an active fundraiser in 1870, when the Church of Ireland was disestablished and the Protestant Orphans Society lost the bulk of the income it had previously received from the state. To make up the shortfall, money had to be raised through voluntary contributions. Church members were invited to subscribe to a "sustentation fund" at two per cent of their annual income. Arthur was very busy with this campaign, raising most of the endowments for the parish of Rynagh.[4]

James Bell's daughter, Harriet, claimed that he retired from the church because of throat trouble, yet he often assisted his cousins by reading the lesson in his "unusually deep and resonant voice," so perhaps the throat trouble was an excuse to withdraw from public life. Arthur was fundamentally healthy, but he had a tendency towards psychosomatic disorders, as Charlotte had observed in the weeks prior to their marriage; a doctor had told him he had a weak heart when he was young, "and for the rest of his long life his [second] wife used to detect him every now and then surreptitiously feeling his pulse, much to her quiet amusement." He would have been distressed to learn that he shared this neurotic anxiety with the redoubtable Harriet Martineau, as he would have been amused to know he shared another habit with many distinguished Victorians. He returned to Ireland a committed Puseyite, and James' daughter remembered as a child hearing "a deep groan of disapproval issuing from the Hill House Pew when something that was said by the preacher … excited [her uncle's] displeasure."[5] According to Leonard Woolf Tennyson the painter, Watts, and Virginia Woolf's father, Sir Leslie Stephen, also "groaned freely."[6]

Arthur did not allow his Anglicanism to isolate him from the surrounding Catholic population. In the 1880s he was a generous contributor to the Banagher Gaelic Athletic Association, whose membership was overwhelmingly Catholic, although his support for the GAA ceased in the late 1880s, when it fell under the control of the Irish Republican Brotherhood.[7] And the brusque reserve of which some in Haworth had accused him, seemed to disappear when he left the West Riding. A photograph, taken toward the end of his life, shows him standing in the middle of Banagher's main street talking to an acquaintance: a man at ease among his own people. This easy-going geniality was nowhere more marked than in his friendship with Martha Brown. Although Martha never settled permanently in Banagher, she became an intermittent member of the Hill House family and even when she was absent, a room known as "Martha's room" was reserved for her. Her position in the household was an ambiguous one. "I do not know whether she had any duties," one of Mary's nieces recalled; "she seemed to spend a great deal of time in making the most delicious sponge cakes and ginger-bread biscuits I have ever met with. Immediately the hall door opened one seemed to be met with an odour of fresh cakes, and a large slice accompanied by a glass of creamy milk was always brought to the youthful guest … Tall and spare, with dark eyes and hair looped back over her ears, her Yorkshire accent seemed to me almost as remarkable as her talent for making sponge cakes."[8]

Martha shuttled back and forth at least six times between Haworth and her Irish family. In early 1863, she had to return to Yorkshire to look after her ailing and widowed mother, who was trying to supplement her income by taking in lodgers. In July of the same year Arthur made his only post-1861 visit to Haworth to be a witness at the wedding of Martha's sister Mary to John Jopling. For most of the next three years, Martha was housekeeper to Dr Ingham, the Haworth physician who had attended Charlotte during her final illness, but after her mother's death in August 1866 she went back to the Hill House.

Whenever Martha was away from Banagher Arthur kept her regularly informed, and through these letters we see how he had reduced the circumference of his life to the ordinary events of his own little world. He writes Martha that Ann, a servant at Cuba House, has "married an old pensioner. He is only 76. They had a great wedding." As a convenience for the servants Arthur has had a new pump installed near the house. "The old women at the Hill are all well; but Mrs Coghlan is nearly blind, she can hardly find her way into the kitchen." Dick, a hired hand, "got up as usual … got a great pain in his shoulder and back, and expired in a few minutes." Little Ann, a new servant, "has been coming on badly … Her temper is fearfully bad." Another servant, Mary Anne, "goes on pretty well, but she is a great smasher. She has broken a multitude of things." Poor Plato died in April 1866. He "had become very helpless, wasted away like Keeper."[9]

Arthur also helped Martha look after her finances. When she received £50 after her mother's death, he was conservative. "I really don't know how to advise you as to [its] investment … Under ordinary circumstances [he is writing in 1868 after the financial crisis of 1867] I should say that Railway Stock was as good as any: but so much distrust has been created by the revelation of the mismanagement of some of the principal lines that I hesitate to recommend you to trust your money on such security. The Savings Bank is the best; but the interest is small." Martha must have ignored his counsel, for whenever she was in Haworth he forwarded her railway dividends. She was less judicious when she invested in a spinning venture set up the husbands of her sisters, Ann and Hannah. After its bankruptcy in 1870, Arthur hoped she would "not be induced to lend any more of your money. Even small interest, if sure, is better than the promise of much more." In addition to acting as her trust officer, keeping her stock certificates and other financial papers in Banagher, he sent her gifts of money as a "Christmas box" or, in the early years, to buy wine for her ailing mother. When Martha herself fell seriously ill in 1870, he sent her £3: "You will want plenty of nourishment when you get up, so don't neglect to get whatever the doctor thinks good for you. If you require money don't hesitate to let me know and I shall send you whatever you require."

Arthur's friendship with Martha Brown reveals once again his capacity for forming solid, lasting attachments. There was never anything sexual in this relationship although Martha was not unattractive; when she was about thirty she was described by an Irish visitor to Haworth as "an interesting looking girl with very dark eyes and hair, [who] would be pretty but for the loss of nearly all her front teeth."[10] Arthur's connection with Martha was consistently avuncular; at one point, in 1864, he even found himself acting as her marriage counsellor: "I don't think Jemmy Witham would be a good match for you. You must be careful how you commit yourself in that way." This was sound advice since her suitor was a forty-seven-year-old carrier whose wife's death earlier that year had left him with two young daughters. He was clearly looking for a nursemaid rather than a wife.

Sometimes Martha was still a servant. When Mary planned to spend five or six weeks in Dublin during the summer of 1866, Arthur was anxious that she come over during Mary's absence to "make the women do the cleaning properly." But normally he dealt with her as a valued friend. "I fear Haworth does not agree with you as it is cold and damp," he wrote when Martha found herself unwell for an extended period in 1868. "I wish you could make up your mind to live with us. I don't mean as a servant, but to make this your home … I don't think there is any necessity for you to be working when your health is not good, and you know that your Mistress and Master [he means Charlotte and Patrick] would not have wished you to do so; neither would I." Thirteen years after Charlotte's death and seven after Patrick's, Arthur was still the faithful executor of the Brontë will. Martha, however, continued to shuttle between the Hill House and Yorkshire, dividing her time in England between her three sisters in Ludgate, Bradford and Saltaire until 1877, when she moved back to Haworth. She died there of stomach cancer in January 1880, aged fifty-one. Like a good trust officer, Arthur had seen to it that Martha made a will on one of her Banagher visits in 1875. After her death he sent it, along with her railway shares, to her sister Tabitha's husband. With Martha's death he lost his last intimate connection with the Brontës.

Arthur's cautious advice to Martha over the years reflects his protective and private nature. In this sense, his decision to give up the clerical vocation was a matter of psychological recoil. At the Hill House he found himself a safe haven. Still, he was in the prime of life and needed to find some occupation to supplement the income he derived from Charlotte and Patrick's estates. So he started looking after his aunt's affairs, and farming her small property assisted by Pat, the hired man, and the occasional casual labourer at harvest time. It was small farming indeed. He began with two cows, a heifer, and a calf. He added another cow at a cost of £14, and then some pigs. "I had your old friend the sow killed last week," he wrote Martha. "Pat sold her in Birr." Soon he reported that he had two lambs and expected more.[11] At first he felt that he needed a property larger than his aunt's twenty-acre holding to fully occupy his time, but when she transferred the house and land to his name in 1864 he settled down at the Hill House for the rest of his life, spending most of his time in the fields. A niece pictures him in his later years as "a handsome, white-bearded old man, with black slouch hat and heavy policeman's cape, sauntering down the field paths, accompanied by his sheep-dog Stray." But he must have done more than gentlemanly supervision, for he told Martha in the wet summer of 1877, as he approached sixty, that he left some of his hay uncut because he "was so tired out with it." The following year he asked her to have the Haworth shoemaker make him "a pair of light clogs as my feet often get wet when I go down the fields, and I am afraid of Rheumatism."[12]

Besides farming, a steady flow of visitors kept Arthur busy. A favourite among these was James Bell's son Alan who, as a young man in the 1870s, had joined the Royal Irish Constabulary and served in several towns in central counties of Ireland. He had the dubious distinction of arresting the American single-tax advocate, Henry George, who, on a lecture tour of Ireland, was suspected of activity in support of Michael Davitt's Land League. Arthur was often amused by his nephew's endless fund of stories based on his experiences as a resident magistrate, stories which, according to family sources, formed the basis of Somerville and Ross's classic *Reminiscences of an Irish R.M.*

Arthur would have been horrified had he known how the life of this amusing young man would end. Bell had acquired a reputation as an expert in unraveling the finances of secret societies, so he was brought out of retirement in 1920, in the midst of the Irish War of Independence, for this purpose. As resident magistrate of Dublin, he was put in charge of an enquiry with extraordinary powers requiring bank managers to appear before him and reveal all documents relating to their dealings with a long list of suppressed organizations, such as Sinn Fein and the Irish Volunteers. The enquiry was aimed at the funds of the provisional Irish republican government, funds that had been squirreled away in the accounts of sympathetic private individuals by Michael Collins, the provisional government's brilliant and elusive minister of finance. When, on 7 March 1920, the *Freeman's Journal* revealed his name as the enquiry's central figure, he became a marked man. Collins, who regarded him not just as a civil servant but also as "high in British Intelligence in Ireland," ordered his flying squad, the dreaded Twelve Apostles, to eliminate him. On the morning of 27 March as he sat reading the morning paper in a tram on his way to the Castle, two men took hold of him. "Come along, Mr Bell," said one, "your time has come." He was dragged into the roadway, surrounded by eight or ten armed men, and shot dead while the terrified passengers looked on paralyzed with horror.[13]

Another frequent visitor to the Hill House was Aunt Harriette's brother, Colonel Joseph Adamson, a heavily be-medalled veteran of the Crimean War who, with his daughter Minnie and son Robert, usually arrived about five weeks before Christmas and stayed through the holiday season. After the colonel died in 1890, Minnie became a permanent (and permanently languishing) Hill House resident. The colonel loved to play whist, and Arthur sometimes joined Mary and his aunt to make up a foursome. One evening Martha came into the drawing room and "stood transfixed upon the threshold. 'The Meenister playing cards!' she exclaimed. '*What* would the people o' Haworth say!'"[14]

In this warm and sociable atmosphere that Arthur discovered his true home, with his aunt to mother him and Mary to take care of his modest domestic needs. Mary was twelve years his junior, "a handsome, dark-eyed woman, a real Celtic mixture of humour and melancholy and full of solicitude for the welfare of others … extremely energetic in her house, and over-anxious for the perfection of everything." According to a great-niece, Arthur "always had a strong brotherly affection" for her but Mary's feeling for Arthur went a good deal deeper, and "she lived in hopes that he would ask her to marry him. However, Arthur was being well looked after and seemed quite content to leave things as they were." Arthur's inertia was the subject of correspondence between Mary's sister Harriette (the Harriette Arthur had once proposed to) and her sister-in-law, Emma Bell, in South Africa. The letter has not survived, but a descendant said that it contained remarks about Arthur's "strange attitude" towards Mary, remarks so intimate that "even at this late date [the 1950s no less] I refrain from repeating them." Arthur would probably have spent the rest of his life indifferent to or unaware of Mary's feelings, had not the colonel's son Robert fallen in love with her and proposed. Mary was fond of him, but "wanted to be quite sure that there was no hope of Arthur before accepting. It was a delicate situation and something had to be done quickly, so she and her mother decided that the best way was to ask Arthur's advice … Arthur's reaction was typically masculine. It had not occurred to him that Mary could possibly want to marry anyone else. 'But Mary belongs to me!' he exclaimed, much dismayed." The women's stratagem was successful, and Arthur and Mary married on 25 August 1864. Harriette Bell, having witnessed the union of her nephew and last unmarried daughter, transferred the Hill House property to Arthur's name the following year.[15] This hardly turned Arthur into a wealthy man, but when added to his Brontë inheritance it at least gave him enough elbow room to help Martha when she was in difficulties.

By every account this second marriage was happy, a happiness based on solid companionship and mutual understanding rather than passion. Arthur was perfectly open with Mary about his feelings, telling her "he had buried his heart with his first wife," and taking her to North Wales on their honeymoon just as he had once taken Charlotte." Even after they returned from their honeymoon, when Martha wrote asking for one of the tiny "Angria" booklets for John Greenwood's wife, Arthur confessed, "when I looked at the handwriting I could not bring myself to part with it." Luckily, Mary had the generosity of spirit to understand how profoundly her new husband had been shaken by that relationship, for she was to live with the Brontë ghosts for the rest of her marriage. In fact, one of Mary's nieces, Frances Bell, described her aunt as herself "devoted to [Charlotte's] memory," for whenever one of her Clifden nephews visited the Hill House, she "would solemnly take him by the hand and lead him to the drawing room to stand before the [Richmond portrait of Charlotte] and tell him, 'That was your Uncle Arthur's first wife; she was a very clever woman.'"[16]

As the years passed, the Hill House seems to have been transformed into a little Brontë shrine. In addition to the Richmond portrait, and those of Thackeray and Wellington which George Smith had sent Charlotte, the drawing room walls were covered with the Brontës' childhood sketches. Patrick's rifle leaned against a corner of the dining room. His old grandfather clock stood half way up the stairs; near it hung the Leyland plaque of Branwell's profile. In an upstairs drawer, Mary preserved Charlotte's snowdrop wedding dress, one-buttoned gloves, and sandaled shoes. (Before he died, Arthur instructed a niece to burn Charlotte's wedding clothes, but many years later two members of the Irish section of the Brontë Society got their hands on the dress and reverently reconstructed it.) And the Richmond portrait hung behind a sofa where Mary took her afternoon nap? One day it broke free from its hanger and fell on her. Mary emerged unscathed, but one can easily imagine what significance Emily would have read into the incident.[17]

Thus, with the ghost of Charlotte hovering around them, the little household continued for over forty years. Old Aunt Harriette Bell retained a splendid appetite to the end of her life. When the Galway fish cart was in the neighborhood, a niece recalled her tucking into hot lobster, "Uncle Arthur carefully concocting a small glass of punch for each lady, but refraining himself: Aunt Mary intent on the refilling of plates, and deeply pained when appetites fell short of her Victorian ideal. Sometimes my uncle would look across the table with 'Well, how come'ee on now?' To which Aunt Mary would give the expected reply, 'Moderate, thank thee, and how art thou?'"[18]

As it had been in Haworth, Arthur's legendary reclusiveness was selective. He hated anyone who intruded uninvited on his privacy, especially American tourists, by whom he felt "tormented." "They used to ignore dear Mary Bell," one local visitor recalled, "although as always there was a gorgeous tea. She used to laugh about it, but Mr N hated their rudeness." Increasingly, he absented himself from Mary's tea parties, although young people usually lured him out of his study. A certain Miss Haire, who used to practice the organ at the church, remembered that when she dropped in "he would be in his study and ask the maid who had come to tea. She would say 'only Miss Haire' – that was me – and he would come in and be delighted. They were the kindest and dearest pair and so happy." The daughter of the rector of St Paul's remembered him in old age, "his love of children and animals … his playful gentleness with the young people who knew him not as the 'stern and bigoted' Mr N but as 'dear Baboo Nick,' the old man who went for walks with them and was fond of lump sugar."[19]

CHAPTER SEVEN

The Struggle over Copyright

Back at Haworth in 1857, Arthur had concluded his long public correspondence over the Cowan Bridge School with a vow that henceforth he would leave others to "growl and snarl" over Charlotte's grave. Then he had figuratively buried himself in distant Banagher where he was able to maintain this resolution pretty successfully. But he could not stop the continuing public interest in the Brontës, an interest that inevitably involved him. Whenever he lapsed into a silence lasting for days, Mary knew that he had "seen some reference to himself in print and realized what his reserved nature was enduring … It was a trial to her that her husband had become more and more of a recluse as he grew older." His sensitivity to anything that might recall his Brontë past was so acute that even his young nieces, frequent visitors to the Hill House, were conditioned to respect it. One of them had been given permission by her Aunt Mary to read the Brontë novels that were kept in the glass-fronted bookcase in the drawing room, "but I always had a fear of hurting my uncle if he should see me reading one of them, so I would hastily conceal it in his presence."[1]

While Arthur was isolating himself in Banagher, Ellen Nussey, his old contender for Charlotte's affections, spent much of her time promoting her own version of the Brontë story. Her motives were mixed: a genuine love for Charlotte, a desire for reflected glory, and a determination to present a self-sacrificing image of Charlotte, an image cleansed of bitterness, anger or even joy. There was also, of course, some hope of financial gain. In her hands, Ellen had the means to realize all these ambitions: the great treasure trove of letters stretching from their school days to Charlotte's death. All that stood in her way was that dreadful man in Ireland who had alienated her from her oldest and dearest friend and who now, as his wife's literary executor, held her copyright. Ellen's correspondence with George Smith, Thomas Wemyss Reid, and others interested in the Brontë project, bristle with venomous outbursts against Arthur, but it is only fair to remember that this dislike was mutual and had begun before Charlotte's death, when Arthur tried to censor his wife's letters. A letter Ellen wrote to George Smith gives her version of how the struggle over Charlotte's letters continued:

> Mr Brontë wrote to me very shortly before dear Charlotte's decease saying, the Doctors said "there was no hope … I started to Haworth by the first available Train after Mr B's letter (I had begged *to go before*, but Mr B and Mr N objected, fearing the excitement of a meeting on poor Charlotte). She had breathed her last sometime before I arrived. Mr B did not appear at first but he sent me a message requesting me to stay [for] dear Ch's interment, which was to take place on the 4th day – I did stay for the interment, and left about an hour after. The very day of my arrival Mr N said to me (I believe in these precise words) "Any letters you may have of Charlotte's you will not show to others and in course of time you will destroy them." I was surprised at the request timed as it was, but I simply and honestly replied, *Of course.* Nothing was ever further from my intention than deviation from this promise … I did not think Mr N had any *right* to make the request for I considered he had no property in his wife's letters written before their engagement, but the request so harmonised with my own views in regarding correspondence as perfectly sacred to the one addressed that I do not think any power less than a husband's would have wrenched any of the correspondence from me. It was Mr Nicholls who wrote to *ask* for Mrs Gaskell to see the correspondence – he expressed his repugnance to a memoir but said he yielded to Mr B's determination to have one. About the same date I had a similar request from Mrs Gaskell telling me she had been to Haworth & that she was intrusted to apply to me for

> materials for the Life. It appeared to me that I ought not upon this double request to consider my own predilection, that I had no right to decline compliance with these requests since the *Father* determined & the Husband acquiesced.[2]

Someone reading this letter in isolation would be astonished to be informed that, far from maintaining a "predilection" not to publish Charlotte's letters, Ellen spent thirty years trying to do exactly the opposite. She describes how her relations with Arthur continued to deteriorate in another letter to Smith, nine years later.

> Charlotte said before her marriage that she would destroy all former correspondence but I was led very seriously to doubt her having carried out this intention from some little episodes in Mr N.'s subsequent behaviour. He discovered something about your Mr Taylor which sent him over hither in an excited state about a month after his wife's death: he did not find me at home, happily – but he wrote to Miss Wooler on the subject, fortunately she knew little. His next move was to get me into his neighbourhood to stay with some intimate friend of his, which I declined. It was a shock to me discovering that he had been ransacking his wife's things, so speedily after losing her, unfavourable impressions deepened still more, afterwards, by what seemed a most selfish appropriation of everything to himself, and when there were near relatives living both on Mr and Mrs Brontë's side. His notes to me became less and less civil in time till the time of Mr B.'s death when I ceased to write at all. I feel an insuperable aversion to write to him even for the obtaining (if I could) of my own letters.[3]

When the first edition of Mrs Gaskell's *Life* appeared, Arthur had blamed Ellen for allowing Mrs Gaskell to use certain passages from Charlotte's letters which were embarrassing to him, but Ellen maintained that she had lent the letters only at his "urgent request." This is at best lacking in candor. On 24 July 1855, following Mrs Gaskell's first visit to the parsonage, Arthur had told Ellen that Mrs Gaskell was "anxious to see any of her letters, – Especially those of any early date – I think I understood you to say that you had some – if so we should feel obliged by your letting us have any that you may think proper – *not for publication* [my emphasis], but merely to give the writer an insight into her mode of thought." He had added that "the course most consonant with my own feelings would be to take no steps in the matter, but I do not think it right to offer any opposition to Mr Brontë's wishes."[4] This is hardly an urgent request; on the contrary, there is a distinct injunction *not* to publish. In any event, Ellen used Arthur's recognition that the letters still existed as sufficient excuse not to destroy them and so, whatever her motives or subsequent behavior, especially her self-serving suppression of critical material, we have Ellen to thank for one of the finest correspondences in the English language.

In 1863, determined to publish Charlotte's letters despite her knowledge that Arthur's consent would be necessary, Ellen turned to Constantin Heger with the suggestion of a collaborative edition. Heger turned her down with ponderous tact. Since the letters hid nothing of "the innermost movements of her thoughts, and in a way, the beatings of this poor sick heart," he questioned whether it was proper to "deliver them up as food for the malignant curiosity of readers."[5] His rebuff checked, but did not extinguish, Ellen's ambition. In 1868 she got in touch with George Smith, ostensibly to enquire about his mother and sisters but really to suggest publishing her letters. Smith asked her whether she knew anything about Arthur, and Ellen replied: "I have not had a line from him since Mr Brontë died and then it was an ungracious reply to enquiries which I made … about Mr Brontë – he seems to have been in a savage humour with me ever since the 'Life' came out – but he had no just reason for such conduct." Smith then repeated what others had told her already: that the right to print Charlotte's letters belonged to Arthur. "The letters themselves are your property and Mr Nicholls cannot claim them from you, but you cannot print them without his permission." This was not what Ellen wanted to hear. She was "a little vexed" that Arthur had "*any power* whatever" over the letters.[6]

Always the astute publisher, Smith suggested a solution: if Ellen could let him have some pieces about her early friendship with Charlotte incorporating a few passages from the letters, "I think that Mr Nicholls could not make any objection to such a publication, especially if it took place in the 'Cornhill Magazine.' Indeed I would venture to print your articles in the Magazine without communicating with him."[7] Although this plan would have allowed Ellen to avoid the unpleasantness of corresponding with Arthur, it failed to match the scope of her ambition. She wanted the freedom to publish the letters with herself as their editor. So she tried to involve Smith in what amounted almost to blackmail.

> I have some letters which most people in his [Mr. Nicholls's] place would give almost a fortune to possess – besides one from Mr Brontë written under the soubriquet of the old favourite dog. [See above: LBC, IV, 35, PB to CB, January 19, 1835; Charlotte had passed part of this letter to Ellen with instructions to burn when read.] If you think it right you can give him a hint that he has not all the power on his side – and that there is an obligation in kindness which is never ignored by true-hearted people.

This was too much for the patient Smith, who replied: "the doubt I felt as to Mr Nicholls's approving the publication of some portions of these letters is confirmed by the tone of your allusions to him. I … should not have thought of writing to him on the subject of your letters, as any application to him would more properly come from you; especially as you desire to get back any letters of yours."[8]

Ellen ended her second attempt at publication by remarking she felt "an insuperable aversion to write to him even for the obtaining (if I could) of my own letters." Wise and Symington observe that Arthur was opposed on principle to publication, but probably as well "strongly resented the commercial element behind Miss Nussey's endeavours … and maybe, too, he considered that Miss Nussey was intellectually incapable of doing justice to them. Charlotte herself had said of Ellen 'She is no more than a conscientious, observant, calm, well-bred Yorkshire girl'."[9] Accurate enough perhaps, but Wise, the forger and industrious merchant of Charlotte's correspondence, was hardly the person to comment on Ellen's mercenary motives.

In 1870, Ellen finally found an outlet beyond Arthur's control. In the United States, where foreign authors did not enjoy copyright protection until 1891, Scribner's *Hours at Home* published material from some 114 of Charlotte's letters, soon to be followed in *Scribner's Monthly* by Ellen's "Reminiscences." Both were designed to emphasize Charlotte's self-sacrifice and religiosity. If Arthur saw these pieces, he would have been wounded to find that Ellen had published Patrick's gently satirical lines describing his expulsion of the washerwomen from the Haworth graveyard.

The same year Ellen met a new collaborator for her Brontë project. Thomas Wemyss Reid had visited Haworth in 1866. On a visit to Leeds four years later, he was amazed to find a "positive antipathy" to the Brontës, and a widespread feeling that Charlotte's novels were "a disgraceful libel upon the district," a feeling more probably attributable to Mrs Gaskell's description of the West Riding than to anything Charlotte herself wrote. In the Brontës' defense, Reid delivered a public lecture which attracted Ellen's attention, and she invited him to her home in Birstall where she complained that Mrs Gaskell "had mixed up the sordid and shameful story of Branwell with that of his sisters; and she protested against the way in which the local traditions that had nothing to do with the character of the gifted sisters, in whom there was not a single drop of Yorkshire blood, had been imported into Mrs G's narrative." She urged Reid to write a book which would correct "the over-colouring" of the *Life* and, as an incentive, she offered to let him use her correspondence with Charlotte, "including the letters relating to her courtship and marriage, which Mrs Gaskell had never seen." He published two *Macmillan's* articles in 1876, and then *Charlotte Brontë: A Monograph* the following year. Despite rough treatment by the critics, it went into three editions in Britain, was a bestseller in the U.S., and according to Reid's own less-than-modest claim, started "the Brontë cult which has since spread so widely."

Despite his access to the letters in Ellen's possession describing Arthur's marriage proposal and its emotionally revealing sequel, Reid "shrank from [using them] because I was not in sympathy with the public curiosity which aspired to know everything that there was to tell about the Brontës without regard to its intrinsic interest, or that decent reticence which even the dead have a right to expect from us. And of course Mr. Nicholls was still living, and I felt that these letters could not decently be published." In his 1905 *Memoirs*, he notes with a touch of acerbity that C.K. Shorter published the letters twenty years later "not only during the lifetime of Mr. Nicholls, but with that gentleman's full consent."

Reid was less reticent about Charlotte's relations with Constantin Heger, describing his "singular influence … over the untrained young woman" and quoting the letter to Ellen in which Charlotte says "I returned to Brussels after aunt's death against my conscience, prompted by what then seemed an irresistible impulse. I was punished for my selfish folly by the total withdrawal for more than two years of happiness and peace of mind." Charlotte's friends, Reid continues, believed that "her future husband dwelt somewhere within sound of the chimes of St. Gudule ... We know now how different was the reality. The husband who awaited her even then was about to begin his long apprenticeship of love at Haworth." This was prudent enough, but then Reid added:

> Yet none the less her spirit, if not her heart, had been captured and held captive in the Belgian city ... The secrets of her inner life could not be trusted to paper. This stay in Belgium was ... the turning point in Charlotte Brontë's career, and its true history and meaning is to be found, not in her 'Life' and letters, but in 'Villette', the master work of her mind, and the revelation of the most vivid passages in her own heart's history.

Reid also used the frank letters to Ellen in which Charlotte discussed her ambivalent feelings about James Taylor.

When he read all this Arthur was understandably agitated. Reid's reading of *Villette* was more perceptive than he himself perhaps realized, and although Charlotte had never told Arthur how deeply her emotions had been involved in Brussels, after the publication of *Villette* he could hardly have been unaware that something important had happened there. (How important he would never know, since it was not until 1913 that the Heger family allowed the *Times* to publish Charlotte's letters to Constantin.) But even the letters to Ellen, which Reid thought he had used with discretion, upset Arthur, who felt that Reid's assessment of the relationship with Heger was "from its obscurity ... liable to misconstruction. Had I known these letters were in existence I should have asked her [Ellen] to destroy them." He partly blamed himself for not having told her that Charlotte's letters were not "hers for publication – I could not however imagine that she would have been so unmindful of what was due to the memory of the dead and the feelings of the living." He also objected to Reid's description of Patrick as "very much overdrawn," insisting that Patrick "had never uttered an unkind or angry word" to him. This was at best technically correct. Patrick may have never *spoken* unkindly, but the passage of time and his own preference for peace and quiet had allowed Arthur to forget the harshness, contempt and cruelty with which, according to Charlotte, Patrick had treated him after his proposal.[10]

Reid did describe the brief happiness of Charlotte's married life, but the evidence of the letters drew from him a portrayal of Arthur as a narrow philistine who had crushed his wife's creative life. "Her husband was now her first thought; and he took the time which formerly had been devoted to reading, study, thought, and writing. But occasionally the pressure she was forced to put upon herself was very severe. Mr. Nicholls had never been attracted towards her by her literary fame; with literary effort, indeed, he had no sympathy, and upon the whole he would rather that his wife should lay aside her pen entirely than that she should gain any fresh triumphs in the world of letters." He felt that Charlotte, too, was constrained by similarly conventional views.

> Brought up as she had been among those who regarded any literary pursuit, and above all the writing of a book as something beyond the limits of the rights and duties of her sex, she had never quite escaped from the notion that in putting pen to paper she was in some way offending against the proprieties of society ... She seemed to feel that in writing novels she had sinned against the conventional canons, and that she was in consequence looked upon not as a great woman who had taken a lofty place in the republic of letters, but as a social curiosity who had done something which had made her notorious.[11]

Reid discussed with Ellen depositing her letters with the British Museum, but he told her that he was "forced to act very cautiously because of the possibility of Mr Nicholls appearing on the scene." Wherever Ellen turned in her never-ending crusade to make use of what she continued to think of as *her* letters the hated figure of Mr Nicholls frustrated her efforts. In 1878 she turned again to George Smith, who responded with cool formality: "As to the particular enquiry you make ... respecting the marketable value of the private letters from the late Miss Brontë in your possession ... if the Revd Mr Nicholls be alive, or if ... he has left an executor, it is doubtful if you can legally sell his late wife's letters to the Trustees of the British Museum without his sanction"[12]

Her next source of irritation with Arthur had nothing to do with the letters. In 1879, a controversy erupted in Haworth over the Rev. John Wade's plan to replace the old Haworth church with a larger structure. In the eyes of those who felt that everything connected to the Brontës deserved to be treated as a holy relic, Wade was a "vandal" who had begun by altering the parsonage so "as to destroy every vestige of the gifted family who made it famous," and was "wantonly" bent on destroying the old church "because he was jealous of the achievements of the three Brontë sisters." Wade had five children to bring up; being no Brontë cultist, he had enlarged the parsonage to accommodate them. Nor could he see why he should hold open house to the crowds of tourists flooding into Haworth; by the end of the nineteenth century they numbered around 7,000 per annum. He would have been "heartily pleased" said one observer, "if an end can be put to these pilgrimages of enthusiastic strangers by which the dismal calm of the old church is daily broken."

Michael Merrall, the head of the largest textile firm in Haworth (the same Merrall who, as chairman of the board of trustees had supported Arthur in 1861), agreed to donate £5,000 to underwrite the cost of the new structure. This led opponents of the venture to suggest that Wade was backed by a small number of the village "aristocracy," while a majority of the local population was opposed to his plans. A public meeting attended by 500 people, including T.W. Reid and Lord Houghton, favouring the preservation of the old church "by judicious restoration or enlargement," appeared to lend credence to this view. But a recent study argues that the meeting, which was not held in Haworth, was not "representative of the parish." Moreover Wade's chief opponents, W.B. Ferrand, Lord of the Manor of Haworth, and General Rawdon, owner of the Bull Hotel and most of the surrounding property, both had an interest in the tourist industry. In spite of them, Wade succeeded in building his new church, although the square tower of the old church was preserved. He told his parishioner that his duty "was not to maintain a showplace for strangers, but a house of prayer for the praise of God." He reassured those concerned about desecration of the Brontës' remains, which lay in the old church crypt, that great care had been taken "to locate the family vault exactly, so that the building work did not affect it." Furthermore, he had corresponded with Arthur about the matter, and had gained "his entire approval of what was proposed to be done, so that there was now no further question that the Brontë family would object."

Ellen saw Arthur's co-operation in this project as proof of his lack of reverence for Charlotte's memory. One of her friends, Sydney Biddell, a country gentleman whose "greatest achievement was being one of the oars in the first Boat Race," carried his animosity against Arthur to such lengths that he penciled out every mention of him in his copy of Mrs Gaskell's *Life*. "A most deplorable event," he wrote in the margin where Arthur's marriage to Charlotte is described. In 1882, Biddell helped Ellen raise funds for a Brontë memorial in the new church. When he wrote to Wade seeking his support, "he seemed to have had his head bitten off." Wade must have told him to mind his own business since Arthur himself "was contemplating erecting a memorial ... but to Charlotte's memory only." Biddell wrote furiously to Ellen: "If anything could show up Mr Nicholls as being a monster, it surely would be his luke-warmness in the matter. He cares to do nothing, and in one respect I am glad of it, for if he did I certainly would have nothing to do with it." Wade must have told Arthur that Ellen was involved, hence his "luke-warmness." His dislike of her was as deep and long-lived as hers of him. (Even after her death in November 1897, when an unidentified correspondent sent him some obituary notices, he observed that "Miss Nussey seems to have been much respected by her neighbours – though I find it hard to 'forget & forgive' her for her proceedings in reference to my dear Wife.")[13]

The next chapter in Ellen's long struggle against Arthur's control of copyright involved the Yorkshire antiquarian, J. Horsfall Turner, whom Ellen entrusted with the bulk of the letters, heavily censored by her. Between 1887 and 1889 he set 1,000 copies in print. It would appear that she intended to allow him to publish these as the second part of a work on the Brontës, but in 1889 she suddenly and unaccountably changed her mind, and paid Turner £100 to return not only the original letters, but also everything he had printed. All but a few copies of the Turner printing were eventually burned. On the advice of Augustine Birrell she contemplated an American edition instead. Birrell was sensible enough to advise her that, although she could do this "without asking anybody's leave," no copies could be imported into the UK without Arthur's permission. After lengthy negotiations with Scribners the American project lapsed in 1892.[14]

Meanwhile, in 1889, Ellen had met Clement K. Shorter, a self-taught journalist and Brontë enthusiast, who was soon to become editor of the *Illustrated London News* and founder of the *Sketch, Sphere*, and *Tatler*. Shorter has been variously characterized as "a man who was always making other men do what they did not want to do," "importunate and acquisitive," and "the type of literary man who would print a famous writer's blotting-pad in a limited edition if he could get hold of it." He described himself as "self-made [he left school at fourteen] and therefore badly made." Shorter presented Ellen with a fresh solution: his friend, Thomas J. Wise, well known as an eminent bibliophile although later exposed as a forger of first editions, would pay her £100 (later raised to £125) to house the letters with his Ashley Library. At his death he would bequeath them with his own splendid collection to the South Kensington Museum (later the Victoria and Albert) where they would be "safe for the use of future generations."[15] Ellen was now seventy-eight and living in straitened circumstances. Her determination and resources exhausted, she gave up the letters, this time for good.

Sometime, perhaps earlier, she had given Shorter a copy of the Horsfall Turner printing of her letters and asked him if he "would write something around what might remain of the unpublished letters." Before taking on the project, he first took the trouble to look at Charlotte's will and realized at once that "the possibility of a veto" lay in Arthur's hands. He quickly discovered Arthur's address (probably through William Robertson Nicoll, editor of the *Bookman*, who had met Martha Brown in Haworth in 1879), and accomplished with consummate ease what Ellen had been trying to do for thirty-five years.[16]

> I had heard of his [Arthur's] disinclination to be in any way associated with the controversy which had gathered round his wife for all these years; but I wrote to him nevertheless, and received a cordial invitation to visit him in his Irish home.
>
> It was exactly forty years to a day after Charlotte died – March 31st, 1895 – when I alighted at the station in a quiet little town in the centre of Ireland to receive the cordial handclasp of the man into whose keeping Charlotte Brontë had given her life. It was one of many visits, and the beginning of an interesting correspondence. Mr. Nicholls placed all the papers in his possession in my hands. They were more varied and more abundant than I could possibly have anticipated. They included MSS. of childhood, of which so much has been said, and stories of adult life, one fragment indeed being later than *Emma* ... Here were the letters Charlotte Brontë had written to her brother and to her sisters during her second sojourn in Brussels... letters that even to

> handle will give a thrill to the Brontë enthusiast. Here also were the love-letters of Maria Branwell to her lover Patrick Brontë, which … have never hitherto been printed.[17]

J.M. Bulloch, the editor of Shorter's autobiography, describes this as "the most gratifying pilgrimage he ever took. I shall never forget the intense delight with which he returned, bringing back tidings of the material which he turned into his books on the Brontë sisters."[18] That he could so easily win Arthur's trust speaks eloquently of his amiable qualities. A niece described how at their first meeting "his vivacity, and his skill in drawing out my uncle, made the luncheon hour very pleasant, and the latter showed no trace of his usual self restraint." Shorter may have been charming but he was also a scoundrel, and his motives in coming to Banagher were strictly practical. Still, his account of his first meeting with Arthur shows that he was genuinely drawn to the old man. "I found him in a home of supreme simplicity and charm, esteemed by all who knew him and idolised in his own household. It was not difficult to understand that C.B. had loved him and had fought down parental opposition in his behalf."[19]

But Shorter needed more than his charm to get Arthur to reverse his deep-set retentive habits and he had another powerful weapon of persuasion. He knew that there were at least ten unburned copies of the Horsfall Turner edition of Charlotte's letters. By suggesting that "without some authoritative editing" a "misunderstanding of many things might arise" from the wider circulation of these copies, he was able to convince Arthur to do what no one else had been able to. Besides, Shorter recognized that at seventy-seven Arthur was too old for farming, and that money was "not too plentiful in the Banagher household, and when I offered Mr N some hundreds of pounds for certain little books of the Brontës, with the rights of publication, he not unnaturally accepted my suggestion. They had been tied up in a brown-paper parcel for forty years and had I not gone to Banagher he assured me he intended to burn them all." Everything converged fortuitously for Shorter who found Arthur "at the 'precise psychological moment' when he was ready to talk, not only about Charlotte, but about business."[20]

This "precise psychological moment" had been prepared by another event that also worked in Shorter's favour. A Brontë Society had been formed in Haworth whose first honorary secretary was J. Horsfall Turner.

In the summer of 1894 he had visited Arthur in Banagher, partly out of simple curiosity, partly to seek Arthur's help in establishing the authenticity of certain Brontë memorabilia for the planned parsonage museum. "I should not have known him from the photograph," he wrote, referring probably to the gloomy portrait taken sometime after 1861.

> This is nothing less indeed than a caricature. You would fancy him as you look at it a curt, snarling, heavy-jawed, morose Hibernian. But I had learnt something of him from Martha Brown … and the moment I felt the hearty grip of his hand I was at home with him … a genial, well-built, healthy, ruddy-faced, strong-haired gentleman, in manner, mind and matter as different from the usual portrayal of him as cheese from chalk. *Suaviter in modo, fortiter in re* is the best description I can give of his bearing. I could get on with him well; nay, I already revere him. He is the country gentleman, not only cultured, charitable, manly, but Christ-like.

In the *Yorkshire Post* account of their meeting Turner also wrote about the silence Arthur had preserved over the decades since Mrs Gaskell's *Life* had appeared, but said nothing of Arthur's reasons except to remark that "I now believe Mr. Brontë and Mr. Nicholls had the best of motives for this silence, and exercised the rare gift of Christian charity in preserving it. Mr. Nicholls has borne obloquy with patience and courage: in the long run he will be fully appreciated." As the *Post* observed dryly, Turner "leaves Mr. Nicholls veiled … in a certain mystery which one hopes Mr. Nicholls himself will dissipate …"[21] Arthur would certainly have been inclined in that direction when Turner told him about his unhappy dealings with Ellen Nussey and the existence of a few copies of his printing of the letters. Shorter's arrival at Banagher soon after this interview could not, from Shorter's point of view, have been more timely.

Even so, the transfer of all these literary riches did not take place at once, as Shorter's account suggests. Since his side of the correspondence with Arthur has not survived, we do not know exactly what his first letter revealed about his intentions, but Arthur's response indicates that it would not be worth Shorter's while to come all the way to Banagher for the little information he could provide. Once there, however, Shorter was able to win Arthur's trust, and to carry away a great deal of manuscript material. He accomplished this so quickly that Arthur was left in a state of bewilderment which reminds one somewhat of a similar raid by Mrs Gaskell and Sir James Kay-Shuttleworth forty years earlier. "I should have liked to look over them before finally parting with them," he complained wistfully, "but it does not matter much."[22] That first haul, however, was far from complete. On 26 April 1895, Arthur wrote Shorter that he had found the manuscript of *The Professor* and "a considerable number of other little Books," evidently the Brontës' childhood writing. It is also clear from this letter that Arthur understood that, although Shorter would have the right to use any unpublished manuscripts in his own writings on the Brontës, the ultimate buyer would be T.J. Wise.

As well, Ellen Nussey must have told Shorter that Arthur had some of her letters to Charlotte and Shorter must have inquired about them, for Arthur responded on 26 April 1895, "You may tell Miss Nussey that her letters never came into my possession; in fact I cannot remember having ever seen a scrap of her handwriting." He had forgotten, or pretended to forget, her letter to him over the censorship of letters, and her letter of June 1855, which initiated the writing of Mrs Gaskell's *Life*.

Arthur's mode of storing documents resembled that of a forgetful squirrel. Under Shorter's patient prodding (sweetened by regular consignments of periodicals, much appreciated in remote Banagher) additional material kept turning up. On 7 May Arthur sent off a new batch of letters, asking that they be returned as soon as they had been read. On 22 May he dispatched twenty-five childhood booklets and announced that he had discovered six letters from Mary Taylor in New Zealand. When he came to mail them, he cautioned Shorter that they were "mostly very personal – I must rely on your discretion as to the use you make of them." One letter was of such "a very private nature" that he had not sent it off with the others. "I cannot bear the idea of making publick anything that could possibly hurt any person's feelings – I suffered too much from Mrs Gaskell's indiscretion." Shorter must have been on tenterhooks wondering what the old man would turn up next. "I believe there are some more MSS," Arthur announced in the same letter. "I shall have another look up – I have not met with a scrap of Emily Brontë's handwriting. It is just possible there may be some in a workbox which I have not yet examined."

Originally, Arthur had stipulated that none of Charlotte's eleven letters to her father should be published. Shorter must have asked him to reconsider, for on 4 June Arthur agreed that they "do not contain anything that would hurt people's feelings except perhaps the reference to the Cardinal." This occurs in a letter to Patrick from London, 17 June 1851, in which Charlotte describes Cardinal Wiseman at a meeting of the St. Vincent de Paul Society. It is Charlotte Brontë at her vivid best, her language unencumbered by pious doubts or ambiguities.

> He is a big portly man something of the shape of Mr Morgan [Charlotte regarded the Rev. William Morgan, an old friend of Patrick's, as "a stuffy and bombastic pedant"]; he has not merely a double but a treble and quadruple chin; he has a very large mouth with oily lips, and looks as if he would relish a good dinner with a bottle of wine after it. He came swimming into the room smiling, simpering, and bowing like a fat old lady, and sat down very demure in his chair and looked the picture of a sleek hypocrite.[23]

Despite Arthur's timid doubts, Shorter printed the letter in full in *Charlotte Brontë and Her Circle.*

The piecemeal discoveries continued. First manuscripts of Branwell's turned up, which Arthur mistook for work by Emily and Anne, and in which he supposed Shorter would have no interest. Shorter quickly disabused him. Then on 18 June 1895, Arthur forwarded what he thought to be "the remainder of my wife's MSS." These may have included a fragment written in 1852, and published by Robertson Nicoll in his edition of *Jane Eyre* under the title *The Moores.* Again, as with the Wiseman letter, Arthur cautioned Shorter that "there [are] some strong expressions which I would not wish to be printed." This material he had discovered "in the bottom of a cupboard tied up in a newspaper, where they had lain for nearly 30 years, and where, had it not been for your visit, they must have remained during my lifetime and most likely afterwards have been destroyed. I do not think there can possibly be any more, as I have rummaged every place that I thought likely."

At the end of June, Shorter forwarded a check from Wise. There is a pathetic irony in Arthur's comment on 24 June that he feared Wise, that rapacious conman who was drooling in London as each new parcel arrived from Banagher, would be "overwhelmed with MSS. – but as I understood from you that their ultimate destination was 'The South Kensington Museum' I was anxious to secure such a safe resting place for them." Whether or not Shorter too believed Wise's promise that the work would eventually go to the museum, he certainly repeated it, for Arthur mentions in a letter on 28 December that he is "quite satisfied with Mr. Wise's assurance that the letters and MSS. will be given to the Nation." But when Wise bought Shorter's papers after the latter's death in 1926, he pencilled a denial on both of these letters: "I never made such a suggestion. Shorter wanted me to add my books to those of Forster, and frequently pressed me to do so, but such a destination did not appeal to me at all" (on ABN to CKS, 24 June 1895), and "I gave *no* such assurance. Shorter was constantly pressing me to do so, and endeavoured to commit me to such a promise, but I made it quite clear to him that I had no intention whatever of meeting his wishes in this way" (on ABN to CKS, 28 December 1895).

Meanwhile, George Smith had got wind of the Shorter-Wise-Nicholls transactions and advised Shorter on 10 July 1895 that Smith Elder had "a proprietary interest in the subject." This probably meant that Smith considered the "business form of application," which he had extracted from Arthur in 1857, would still be in force in 1895. Arthur was lost in the legalities of publishing: "What does Mr. Smith mean … does he mean a legal interest or merely that as they were Mrs Gaskell's publishers they expected a preference in bringing out your book?" And after forty years he was still unclear about his own position, asking, "What is a 'Literary Executor'? What are his rights and duties?" But he was clear about his support for Shorter's enterprise, wishing him "every success" and indicating that he was "willing to sign a form giving you the exclusive rights to publish any manuscripts I send you on the terms stated in one of your letters." The terms were that Shorter's publishers would pay Arthur for use of the manuscripts in any publication. On 23 November Shorter, accompanied by his fiancée, the Irish poet Dora Sigerson, visited Banagher again, and came away with an agreement signing over copyright in "the Brontë letters, diaries and books, [and] all copyright in future Brontë letters and manuscripts which came to [Arthur] as the executor of his wife." It must have been a bitter pill for Ellen to swallow when she learned that the man who had introduced her to the swindler Wise, and had thus been instrumental in depriving her of her treasure-trove had now got control of everything from the man who, without lifting a finger, had for thirty odd years frustrated all her efforts at publication.

Shorter paid Arthur £150 for the copyright, acting for Wise, but the total amount Arthur received is unclear. In 1917 Shorter recorded that he had "purchased for Mr. Wise the whole of the little manuscripts for, I think, £400 … Mr. Wise obtained the whole collection, which he distributed from year to year, doubtless to his own great commercial advantage." Reference to "the little manuscripts" suggests that this payment covered the "Angria" manuscripts only. On 10 March 1907, Wise said that he had bought the Brontë manuscripts for £1,500, but later the same year he remarked that "the biggest purchase I ever made was the Brontë collection for which I paid in all £1,100.0.0 to Mr. Arthur Bell Nicholls."[24] These sums may seem picayune to us, but to an Irish farmer living in the 1890s they would have been considerable. In any case, Arthur's poverty was exaggerated; at his death, his estate was valued at £4,225.14s.2d, the equivalent in current terms of just over a quarter of a million pounds.

Shorter may have been a trifle duplicitous in his monetary dealings with the financially inexperienced ex-clergyman, but otherwise he appears to have acted honourably. When *Charlotte Brontë and Her Circle* appeared in 1896, Arthur thanked him "for the kind and loving spirit in which you have treated a difficult and delicate subject, but especially I feel grateful for the manly way in which you have disposed of the vile slander in reference to M. Héger [sic]. Of course the publication of many of the letters causes me intense pain – I shrink from the thought of their becoming the subject of common gossip and comment in the newspapers." When he wrote Shorter on 28 December 1896, his only criticism concerned a description of Charlotte as having "'a high and narrow forehead' – the fact being that her forehead was exceptionally broad – indeed so much so, that she endeavoured to cover it up by the arrangement of her hair." Shorter's description was apparently based on the Richmond portrait, while Arthur's comment supports (but does not confirm) the authenticity of two recently discovered photos in which a much broader face is revealed.

For his part, Shorter found his new friend "a peculiarly lovable man, [whose] qualities of gentleness, sincerity, unaffected piety and delicacy of mind" compelled him to alter the view he had expressed in his introduction to the 1889 Camelot edition of *Jane Eyre* that Charlotte's marriage had been a disaster. As to the charge that the unimaginative Arthur was not the ideal husband for a literary genius, Shorter countered with the quaint but interesting observation that if "women of intellect always waited for the ideal husband, most of them would die unmarried … We may leave that matter with the remembrance that Charlotte Brontë lived up to the adage, that in marriage it is better to begin with a little aversion, and clearly she had come to love her husband with very genuine devotion. Those who knew him in later years found that perfectly natural."[25]

Although he never met Thomas J. Wise in person, Arthur's experience of that shady gentleman was, by contrast, far from happy. Arthur was beginning to get suspicious of him as early as 21 January 1896, when he sent Shorter eight letters (six addressed to Emily) adding in an uncharacteristically peremptory tone: "you will please *return* these when you have done with them – Don't let Mr. Wise appropriate them." He repeated this request on 17 April and added in a later letter, "I shall ensure that they shall never be distributed." But the damage was done; the bulk of Charlotte's letters, whether acquired from Ellen or Arthur, was already in Wise's hands. And Arthur's suspicions were justified, for although Wise kept some of the manuscripts for his own Ashley Library, he had already begun to sell off his loot in bits and pieces. "Manuscripts by Branwell Brontë were split up and sold as Charlotte's, fragments were detached from other MSS and sold separately, collections of letters from other sources than Mr Nicholls' were sold together for no better reason than the variety of their signatures." Much of this business was conducted after Arthur's death, but Sotheby's catalogue of their 28 February 1896 sale alerted him that Wise was already at work. Several of Charlotte's letters were listed for sale there, and an extract was included from a letter to Ellen of 16 May 1853 in which Charlotte described how Arthur had lost control of himself at the Whitsun communion service and had stood before her "white, shaking, voiceless." Arthur asked Shorter to purchase the letter on his account "as the extract published contains personal matter of a very painful nature." Here we have a strange situation indeed: Arthur buying back at auction what he had already sold to Wise. "It is so cruel that your uncle Arthur, the best of men as we know, should be thus treated," his brother remarked about another such situation.[26]

Arthur's aversion to public scrutiny was so intense that on 28 December 1896, he asked Shorter "to put off the enquirers for my address." He had earlier turned down Shorter's request for a photograph to accompany an article in *The Woman at Home* because he would not part with the only one in his possession, which had belonged to Charlotte. When Shorter had an artist work from an outdated picture, Arthur wrote on 23 April 1896 to ask, "How did you develop my photograph into the portly figure in your illustration? It gave me a great surprise." Despite his reservations, when the article appeared he seemed pleased that a host of his Banagher friends bought the issue, "anxious to have a likeness of me."

Arthur never allowed his distrust of Wise to interfere with his friendship with Shorter. It never seems to have entered his innocent mind that there might be some kind of collusion between the two. So, for some time after the publication of Shorter's *Charlotte Brontë and Her Circle* in 1896, he continued to supply him with material, including further letters, although he made a point of asking that everything be returned. Shorter in turn kept the Hill House supplied with magazines and journals. In 1898 Shorter got hold of a lock of Charlotte's hair that Arthur had misplaced, and sent it to Banagher. Although Arthur was grateful to have the "little relic" restored, he found it "sadly reduced in size since I had it – a few hairs in stead of a long thick tress." Was Shorter himself responsible for the theft? Arthur never seemed to suspect him, although their correspondence continued less regularly after that incident. Arthur's last letter, dated 22 September 1902, acknowledges the receipt of "papers which reach me each week regularly – and afford much interesting reading."

Thoughtfully, Shorter continued to send the *Sphere* to Mary after Arthur's death. On 23 May 1904, she told him that Arthur had been burning a lot of old papers. One shudders to think what priceless manuscripts might have been consumed in those fires but he had not burned everything, for after his death in 1907 Mary released some of his "Brontë relics" for sale at Sotheby's. This material, including books from the parsonage and some of the tiny juvenile manuscripts, realized £718.2s. A second sale on 19 June 1914 brought in £613.14s. Among the forty-four items in this batch, *Emma,* Charlotte's final manuscript, claimed £105, the highest price. A third sale on 15 December 1916, after Mary's death, returned £173 to her estate.

A number of other Brontë items were given, or sold, to Alan Joseph Adamson, grandson of Arthur's adoptive parents and a nephew of Mary, who had been born in Kill House, near Clifden, in Connemara. For a few years as a child he had lived with Mary and Arthur, and even after emigrating as a young man to western Canada, he returned to Banagher several times to visit. In "Arthur Bell Nicholls and the Adamson Saga: New Discoveries of Brontë Memorabilia," Christine Alexander describes many items Alan Joseph brought with him to Canada from those visits.

They include a water-colour by Charlotte ("Annual Lavatera"), an ivory visiting-card case with a card, a gold brooch, manuscript leaves of juvenilia, and volume one of the first edition of *The Professor,* signed by Arthur to Julia Turriff Adamson.

An amethyst ring, known in the family as Charlotte's engagement ring, was given to yet another relative.[27] The Richmond portrait of Charlotte was donated to the National Portrait Gallery, as was Branwell's portrait of the three sisters. The belated discovery of the latter explains why Shorter had been receiving documents from Arthur so haphazardly. The circumstances are described by one of Mary's nieces.

> About 6 months ago a wardrobe was moved from one room to another, and some things on top of it were being taken down and dusted while Mrs Nicholls sat in a chair looking on (I may mention that these things had been frequently and regularly taken down and dusted by the servants, and they consisted chiefly of boxes and parcels). The dusting on this occasion was being done by Mrs Nicholls' companion, and coming on something which looked like two pieces of oilcloth, she asked Mrs Nicholls what it was (the backs of the pictures being turned outwards). On examination Mrs Nicholls recognised the portrait of Emily as one which had been cut out of a group by Mr. Nicholls, but the second picture, the group of the three sisters, she had never seen till then, notwithstanding the many years it must have been in the house.

For advice Mary called in Frances Bell, another niece. "Your uncle disliked them very much. He thought they were very ugly representations of the girls, and I think meant to destroy them, but perhaps shrank from doing so – you see, there is only one other existing portrait of Charlotte, and none at all of Emily and Anne." In the end, although Mary too thought the group portrait a poor thing, both paintings were presented "only reluctantly" to the National Portrait Gallery. This story is relevant to contemporary discussion about the authenticity of two photographs of Charlotte Brontë. Arthur surely would have known if a photograph of his wife had been taken, and he told Mary only one other portrait existed. That could only have been the Richmond painting, so one would have to conclude that a genuine photograph of Charlotte Brontë does not exist.[28]

Epilogue

In allowing Shorter to use so many of his valued Brontë relics, Arthur must have been preparing – albeit subconsciously – for his own death. As he grew older, he acquired the habit of settling into his chair after dinner muttering fragments of whatever was going on in his head. "I wonder how it will be?" was a question Mary frequently heard him asking himself. As the century came to an end, everyone at the Hill House was in a state of genteel disintegration. Minnie Adamson, the daughter of Colonel Joe, had become a permanent resident. Although the youngest member of the household, she was "dreadfully delicate and sick every day, takes little food and in the cold weather has great pain." In 1900, Arthur caught a bad case of the grippe from which he never fully recovered. Mary was feeling her years too. "Alas!" she told an American niece, "how dreadfully old I feel. We lead a very quiet life. I never go out but my neighbours are very good in coming to see me." Old Aunt Harriette was the toughest of this valetudinarian household. She continued gardening well into her nineties until, one day, she tripped over a mat and broke her thigh. Although she made a splendid recovery, she had to be carried up and down stairs by two maids, grunting because "she was very heavy." Once on level ground she was able to get about on crutches. "One day, to the horror of everyone, she was found to have made her way half way up the shallow staircase without any help. A friend who had come to tea had mentioned that her mother, a contemporary, could walk up and down stairs by herself. "What Mrs G. could do [Mrs Bell] was determined to do too." But even she could not put off the inevitable. "Gran has been very weak & poorly," Mary reported to a niece. "She is only able to sit up for a few hours now and takes little food. If she lives till the 6th of next month she will be 100." Not only did she reach that landmark, but also a neighbor recalled that "she played the piano for me when she was … over a hundred and I was a child." She died in June of 1902, one obituary proclaiming her a model "of all that was good in human nature, having few equals and no superiors in amiability and benevolence."[1]

A nephew visiting from Canada described Arthur clinging to his arm at Harriette's funeral, "quite gone with grief." From then on Arthur's decline was steady. A photograph taken around 1904 shows a head utterly blanched by age; he had reached that time when "though men be so strong as to come to fourscore years, yet is their strength then but labour and sorrow, so soon passeth it away and we are gone." Despite her own infirmities, Mary nursed him protectively, even shielding him from details of the Brontë Society's commemoration of the fiftieth anniversary of Charlotte's death in 1905. She informed W.T. Fields, the Society's honourary secretary that "Mr Nicholls has been very infirm and weakly for some time and we are obliged to keep him very quiet and free from the least excitement, as his heart is very weak, but, thank God, he suffers little pain, and goes out a little every day. Still, we let him see few people, nor allow even our own relations to talk very much to him. We read for him but only things of common interest. We never give him letters or anything likely to excite him or set him thinking."[2] There is an echo here of Charlotte's Mr Macarthey: anything that set poor Arthur thinking threatened to "wreak havoc in [his] physical and mental economy."

Arthur Bell Nicholls died early on Sunday, 2 December 1906. He asked for the Richmond portrait to be brought to his bedside, and the nurse who cared for him recalled that "the last words he was ever heard to utter were a whispered repetition: 'Charlotte … Charlotte …'" Predictably, the obituaries focused on the short but intense Brontë period of his life and ignored his long happy marriage with Mary. The *Times* was particularly patronizing: "the honest curate made up in devotion what he lacked in distinction; and he had won a prize in the passionate little heart – versed so deeply in love's martyrdoms and renunciations – that all the wealth and refinement and cultivation of courts and capitals might vainly have attempted to match." It would have been characteristic of Mary to accept this distorted description of her husband without a murmur, but even her humility would have been sorely tested when, many years after her death, a descendant referred to Charlotte as Arthur's "one and only love." Luckily, she would have heard a more accurate assessment of her husband in the funeral oration of the local vicar, J.J. Sherrard, whose text for the day was: "Mark the perfect man, and behold the upright, for the end of that man is peace, whose removal is like the changing of some ancient landmark."

> No one more than himself would dislike anything in the nature of a panegyric, yet I cannot help saying that no one who knew him could forbear liking the kind, true, retiring old Christian gentleman. What I admired most in him was the absence of all clericalism. He was a standing proof that a man could be a clergyman without crushing human nature under his feet. There was in him no sanctimonious profession of religion. He was quite content with just being himself. He was a man of God who did not strive nor cry, or let his voice be heard in the street. He had a great knowledge of human character, with strong likes and dislikes, and – honest man that he was – he made no attempt to hide them. How totally indifferent he was to public opinion is proved by the fact that he took no pains to correct erroneous and disparaging impressions that prevailed of his life and work in Yorkshire. In the end it was only the great pressure of his friends and the interests of truth which induced him to disclose the real facts.[3]

What would Charlotte have said had she known that her dear boy, her "Mr Macarthey" had become a cleric distinguished by the absence of all clericalism? Perhaps she would not have been surprised, given that strong streak of independence that lead him to fall in love with her in the first place.

Mary survived her husband until 1915. Two years before her death J.D. Adamson, a Canadian great-nephew studying medicine in London spent some time at the Hill House. He found his aunt "a dear old lady who spent the whole day ensconced on a sort of throne in the living room being unable to get about without help. Her benign influence pervaded the whole household and created a most pleasant atmosphere. Though I was within a year of medical graduation she treated me as though I were a school boy, almost ruining my stomach with rich food and on departure giving me a golden guinea." When Mary died the Hill House descended to her nephew, Captain Arthur Bell, then to his wife's step-sister, and finally to *her* nephew, who sold it to the Church of Ireland. For many years it functioned as the Rynagh vicarage. It is now in private hands and, as "The Hill House Hotel," advertises its Brontë connection in the Brontë Society's *Transactions*.[4] Charlotte would have reacted to this publicity with sardonic amusement; Arthur would doubtless have retreated to his study in a mood of dark gloom.

Viewed close up, most lives appear as a string of diurnally repeated actions punctuated occasionally by major events – a birth, marriage, or death, an accident, major illness, or robbery – but otherwise without apparent form. Yet when viewed from a certain distance, even the most uneventful life acquires a characteristic pattern, if only because it can now be seen as part of a larger and evolving society. The life may not acquire "meaning" or "purpose" in a religious or metaphysical sense, but it does acquire a distinctive form in which social, psychological and aesthetic elements are all at work. Conceived in this way, the life of Arthur Bell Nicholls falls into three distinct parts.

From his birth in 1818 until he took up the Haworth curacy in 1845 we know precious little about him as an individual, but quite a lot about the world that formed him: his separation from his birth-family at the age of seven, his upbringing in a lively but intellectually conservative Anglo-Irish family, and his university training for the church in Trinity College Dublin, where he acquired the uncompromising doctrinal beliefs that were later to cause him trouble with his parishioners in Haworth and with his future wife. Arthur had already been forced to leave two sets of parents, and the high church became his vicarious home, one he hoped the profane world, with all its unpredictability, could not touch.

This was the baggage, cultural and psychological, which Arthur brought to his curacy in the West Riding of Yorkshire. Here he lived through the *sturm-und-drang* second phase of his life. For someone as reserved and private as himself, to have been set down in the midst of the seething emotional life of the Brontës could only have been traumatic.

Patrick, already half blind, was spending more and more time alone in his study. Shy Emily, happiest when roaming the moors with Keeper, was not to be fathomed by an outsider. Soon Anne and Branwell came home, the latter in disgrace, apparently as the result of an affair with his employer's wife, and about to sink into addiction to dope and alcohol. As for Charlotte, 1845 was a particularly painful year. She was still under the spell of Constantin Heger, sending him letters confessing that, although she had tried to forget him she still found herself "slave to a regret, a memory, slave to a dominating and fixed idea which tyrannizes one's spirit."[5]

Arthur could have known little of this on his arrival, but he would soon pick up the village gossip from his landlord, John Brown, who was also one of Branwell's drinking partners, and as a regular visitor to the parsonage he could not help observing the daily lives of his curate's children. He was also an involuntary witness to the devastating series of tragedies which struck down one member of the family after another until only Charlotte and her father remained. During the next three and half years his feelings for Charlotte grew more intense while on her side there was at best respectful civility. His first trembling proposal came in December 1852, loosening the constraints that had previously allowed him to keep his feelings to himself. He had no idea how to handle his sentiments once they escaped and he became, as Monckton Milnes noted when he met him in January 1854, "sadly broken ... and burnt out."

Then followed the short period of marriage, for Arthur the most intensely happy months of his life. When Charlotte died, almost certainly from a complication of pregnancy, just as they were both beginning to enjoy a modicum of ordinary pleasure, Arthur must have felt – quite apart from the devastation of her loss – that the gods had marked him for their play and that to court passionate love was to invite disaster. The anti-climax of his last six years at Haworth included the loss of two other people, Sutcliffe Sowden and Patrick Brontë, to both of whom he had allowed himself a deep attachment. When his parish then rejected him it brought the agonistic phase of his life to an end.

The man who returned with Martha Brown and Patrick's dogs to Banagher would have nothing more to do with strenuous emotional life, public or private. He gave up his clerical vocation and appears to have relaxed his rigid doctrinal views. In trying to understand why he embraced high-church, Puseyite beliefs in his youth, I have conjectured that the insecurity associated with adoption, combined with the turbulence of life around him in Ireland and the rapid changes of early Victorian society would have made the Oxford movement, with its vision of the Church as a spiritual community above the temporal order and held together by ancient rituals, appear as something he could cling to. But in Haworth it became evident that however rigid Arthur's religious views made him appear, he was a deeply passionate man.

It may be that fundamental character is established in infancy and early childhood. It does not, however, follow that people never change. In fact, there were at least three Arthur Bell Nicholls: the austere clergyman expelling washerwomen from the graveyard; the private man attaching himself to a few individuals with passionate intensity; and the gentle man beloved of children, dogs and pensioners. Some combination of these qualities made Charlotte Brontë love him, and he responded after her death by remaining loyal to her difficult father, and by doing his best to emphasize her literary reputation over the world's curiosity about her private life. Although one young nephew found him "a methodistical dull bird,"[6] he was more generally remembered by the young as "Baboo Nick," dispensing sweets as he walked with children in the fields, and by adults as the peculiarly lovable man Clement Shorter thought him. To Charlotte he was "my dear boy" and, for less than a year, she was Mrs Nicholls.

Notes

CHAPTER ONE

1 William Nichol spelled his name variously as Nichol, Nicholl, Nickle and Nickles, which would suggest a limited education. Arthur Bell Nicholls' elder brother, Alan, used Nicholl; Arthur styled himself Nichols when he first entered Trinity College Dublin in 1836. Family legend has it that the 's' was added in Haworth, but on the basis of the TCD entry it would rather appear that it was the extra 'l' which was added. In 1905 he signed a first edition of *The Professor* to my grandmother, Julia Turriff Adamson, as A.B. Nicholls. Henceforth I will use "Nicholls" when any member of the family is mentioned. See Gérin, 542; Burtchaell and Sadleir, 619.

2 Anna Maria (1809), Eliza (1812), William (1813), George (1814), Alan (1816), Arthur Bell (6 January 1818 or 1819), Jane (b.?), Margaret (1821), Susan (1822), Richard (1827). Gérin, 542. Gérin gives Arthur's birth date as 1818, which is how it appears on his gravestone, but his death certificate and the application he made in 1853 to the Society for the Propagation of the Gospel, give it as 1819. See Cochrane, 149, n 3, ch.1.

3 This information appears on a typewritten slip pasted into the inner cover of J.D. Adamson's copy of Bell, F.E., *A Hundred Years of Life,* in the author's possession.

4 Gérin, 542. For what little is known of the Nicholls family see also Edgerley, 95 ff. and ABN Commonplace Book.

5 Pope Hennessy, 71.

6 Bell, H.K., 46; Trodd, 82.

7 Quane, 116.

8 Akenson, D.H., *The Church of Ireland*, 137; *The Irish Educational Experiment*, 31–6.

9 LCB, 3:276, CB to MW, 10 July 1854; Bell, F.E., 6–9; Bell, H.K., 8–9.

10 Cooke, 414–15.

11 Unless otherwise indicated, what follows concerning the Banagher Royal Free School comes from the following sources: Quane, passim; P.P. 1809, 7 (142), Report of the Commissioners of the Board of Education in Ireland, 1, Free Schools of Royal Foundation [9 July 1807]; P.P. 1834, 40 (500); P.P. 1836, 13, Report of Select Committee on Education in Ireland, Pt. 1, 1835; P.P. 1837–38, 7 (701), Report of Select Committee on Foundation Schools; P.P. 1840, 28 (427), Annual Report of the Commissioners of Education in Ireland, 1839; P.P. 1857–58, 22: 1, Report of the Royal Commission on Endowed Schools in Ireland; Minutes of Evidence, 22:2:254; P.P. 1894, 67 (308); Cooke; Martineau, *Endowed Schools of Ireland*; Wakefield, Edward.

12 Casey and Rowan, 40–1; Craig, 80–3; LCB, 3:272. Like many other Irish country houses, Cuba House fell into decay after the Civil War. When I saw it in 1978 only three walls were standing, and the long outhouse, which had once served as classrooms and dormitories, was being used by a local farmer to store and maintain his equipment.

13 P.P. 1881, 35:1:146.

14 The full complement: Alan (1822–1868), Susan (1823–1841), James (1826–1891), Arthur (1828–1891), Mary Anna (1830–1915), Joseph (1831–1891), Harriette (1833–1911), Frances (1835–1850), and William (1839–1870).

15 Quoted in Quane, 121–2.

16 Wilson, 3.

17 The college charged four levels of student fees, spread over five years: sizars, typically the sons of indigent country clergymen, paid a nominal fee of £1.1s.3d; pensioners, £42; fellow commoners, £84; noblemen, £168. See Vaughan in Holland, "Paying for the Christmas Dinner," 57, and Sagara, "From the Pistol to the Petticoat," 117.

18 Burtchaell and Sadleir, 619; LCB, 3:276, CB to MW, 10 July 1854; Gérin, 543. Both Gérin and Cochrane state that Alan also went to TCD, but his

name does not appear in *Alumni Dublinensis*; he may, of course, have entered but failed to graduate.

19 Adamson, William Agar, 47.

20 Quane, 127–8.

21 Report of Select Committee on Foundation Schools; P.P. 1840, 28.

22 Quane, 126–7.

23 McDowell and Webb, 150–61, 192.

24 For example, Cochrane, 5.

25 Crowther, 19.

26 McDowell, 15.

27 McDowell, 24.

28 *The Book of Trinity College*, 129; McDowell and Webb, 192–216.

29 Stokes; Archdeacon R.G.F. Jenkins to author, 28 April 1978; DNB (2004 edition), entry under William Maturin.

30 Ross, 119, 140.

31 Cochrane, 9.

32 Cochrane, 6–9. The Cochranes speculate that he did place such an advertisement in the *EG*, and they print three specimens from the period, but none can be identified clearly as originating from Arthur.

33 L and D, 393; Cochrane, 9; L and D give his stipend as £100.

CHAPTER TWO

1 L and D, 210–17.

2 4 August 1843, cited in Wilks, 3.

3 LCB, 1:412, CB to EN, 31 July 1845; for what happened at Thorp Green between Branwell and Lydia Robinson, see accounts of the affair in JB, Gérin, Fraser, and L and D.

4 LCB, 1:412, CB to EN, 31 July 1845.

5 LCB, 1:435–6, CB to C. Heger, 18 November 1845 (original in French).

6 LCB, 1:393, CB to Mrs Rand, 26 May 1845.

7 LCB, 1:399, CB to EN, 18 June 1845.

8 Banks, 278.

9 JB, 506.

10 LCB, 1:483, CB to EN, 10 July 1846.

11 LCB, 1:229, CB to EN, ?29 September 1840; 61, CB to EN, 19 July 1841.

12 LCB, 1:504, CB to EN, 17 November 1846; 532, CB to EN, 29 June 1847.

13 LCB, 1:547, CB to EN, 7 October 1847; 551 CB to EN, ?15 October 1847.

14 LCB, 1:544, Anne Brontë to EN, 4 October 1847.

15 The verse appeared in *Church Reform*, November 1847, and is cited in JB, 520; see also her n. 40, 934.

16 Wilks, Brian, "The State of The Haworth Churchyard," BST, 23:1:72.

17 LCB, 2: xxxvii.

18 Cited in Allott, 197–8.

19 W and S, 2, n., 294.

20 LCB, 3:248, ECG to John Forster, 23 April 1854; Edgerley, BST, 10:52:97.

21 LCB, 2:334, CB to EN, 19th 1850; 337, CB to EN, ?28 January 1850.

22 Brontë, *Shirley*, 724–5.

23 LG, 218, 195.

24 LCB, 2:671, CB to EN, ?28 July 1851.

25 Wilks, 6.

26 LCB 3:50, CB to PB, 2 June 1852.

27 LCB, 2:598, CB to EN, 4 and 5 April 1851; 599–600, CB to EN, 9 April 1851; 598, CB to EN, 4 and 5 April 1851; Edgerley, 111; Winnifrith, "Winter-Day at Haworth."

CHAPTER THREE

1 This description of Arthur's proposal to Harriette is based on a 1927 *aide mémoire* by Herbert Adamson of a conversation with his father, Alan Joseph Adamson (1857–1928), in the author's possession. Alan Joseph was a son of Harriette Bell (1833–1911).

2 JB, 300–1, 450; Cochrane, 12.

3 LCB, 3:92–3, CB to EN, 15 December 1852.

4 Ibid.

5 LCB, 3:94–5, CB to EN, 18 December 1852.

6 W and S, 4:198, Mary Taylor to EN, 19 April 1856; Virginia Woolf, *Three Guineas*, cited in LG, 276–7.

7 LCB, 3:94–5, CB to EN, 18 December 1852; BPM, ABN Commonplace Book; LCB, 2:611, CB to EN, 5 May 1851.

8 LG, 277.

9 LCB, 3:101, CB to EN 2 January 1853.

10 Ibid.

11 LCB, 3:106–7, PB to CB, 19 January 1853.

12 LCB, 3:104–5, PB to CB, January 1853 (fragment).

13 ABN to The Society for the Propagation of the Gospel, 28 January 1853, cited in JB, 716.

14 PB to W.J. Bullock, 31 January 1853, cited in JB, 717.

15 L and D, 457.

16 PB to W.J. Bullock, 31 January 1853, cited in JB, 717; L and D, 457.

17 *Keighley News* for 27 October 1923, cited in LCB, 3:358.

18 LCB, 3:243, CB to Margaret Wooler, 12 April 1854.

19 LCB, 3:129–30, CB to EN, 4 March 1853.

20 LCB, 3:148–9, CB to EN, 6 April 1853.

21 LCB, 3:149, n. 3.

22 LCB, 3:165–6, CB to EN, 16 May 1853.

23 *Leeds Intelligencer*, 28 May 1853, cited in JB, 960, n. 36; W and S, 4, n. 66.

24 LCB, 3:167, CB to EN, 19 May 1853; ABN to CKS, 18 June 1895, Brotherton Collection, Leeds University Library; LCB, 3:167, CB to EN, 19 May 1853.

25 LCB, 3:168–9, CB to EN, 27 May 1853.

26 LCB, 3:172, CB to ECG, 1 June 1853.

27 Catherine Winkworth to Emma Shaen, 8 May 1854, in Shaen, 115; Wilks, 137.

28 LCB, 2:199, ECG to John Forster, ? after September 1853; *Life*, 388.

29 LCB, 3:128, Mary Taylor to EN, 24 February 1854.

30 The first preserved letter of the renewed correspondence with Ellen is dated 1 March 1854, but a letter from Mary Hewitt to Ellen, dated 21 February, makes it clear that Ellen had heard from Charlotte earlier.

31 LCB, 3:213–14, CB to Margaret Wooler, 12 December 1853; 237, CB to EN 28 March 1854.

32 LCB 3:211, CB to Emily Shaen, 24 November 1853; 213, CB to George Smith, 10 December 1853; JB, 744.

33 LCB, 3:213, CB to Margaret Wooler, 12 December 1853.

34 LCB, 3:204, ECG to R. Monckton Milnes, 29 October 1853.

35 Richard Monckton Milnes to ECG, 30 January 1854, quoted in JB, 746.

36 C and P, 278, ECG to R. Monckton Milnes, 20 April 1854.

37 LCB, 3:239, CB to EN, 11 April 1854.

38 LCB, 3:261–2, ECG to John Forster, 17 May 1854.

39 Wilks, 138.

40 LCB, 3:239–40, CB to EN, 11 April 1854; 250, CB to GS, 25 April 1854.

41 LCB, 1:234, CB to EN, 20 November 1840. The relative was Branwell, and the young lady Mary Taylor.

42 C and P, 289, ECG to John Forster, 17 May 1854.

43 LCB, 3:240, CB to EN, 11 April 1854.

44 Ibid.

45 LCB, 3:246–7, CB to ECG, 18 April 1854; 248, ECG to John Foster, 23 April 1854; 252, CB to ECG, 26 April 1854.

46 Shaen, 112–14.

47 LCB, 3:263, CB to EN, 21 May 1854; 265, CB to EN, 27 May 1854.

48 The settlement is transcribed in Juliet Barker, "Subdued Expectations: Charlotte Brontë's Marriage Settlement," BST, 10:1:33–9.

49 JB, n. 26, 965; Fraser, *Charlotte Brontë*, 463.

50 LCB, 3:260, CB to EN, 14 May 1854; 267, CB to EN, 7 June 1854; 270 EB to EN, 16 June 1854.

51 LCB, 3:268, CB to EN, 11 June 1854.

52 LCB, 3:265, CB to EN, 27 May 1954; 270, CB to EN, 16 June 1854.

53 LCB, 3:270, CB to EN, 16 June 1854.

54 *Life*, 395.

55 Wilks, 169; LCB, 3:275, PB to EN, 7 July 1854.

CHAPTER FOUR

1 Cochrane, 55; LCB, 3:274, CB to EN, 29 June 1854; JB, 758.

2 LCB, 3:278, CB to Catherine Wooler (Margaret Wooler's younger sister), 18 July 1854.

3 Bell, F.E., 14; LCB, 3:275–6, CB to Margaret Wooler, 10 July 1854.

4 LCB, 3:278, CB to Catherine Wooler, 18 July 1854; 276 CB to MW, 10 July 1854.

5 Bell, F.E., 12–13.

6 LCB, 3:276, CB to Catherine Wooler, 10 July 1854; 278, CB to Catherine Wooler, 18 July 1854; 284–5, CB to Catherine Winkworth, 27 July 1854; ABN to George Sowden, 10 August 1854.

7 LCB, 3:287, CB to Catherine Wooler, 18 July 1853; 283–4, CB to EN, 9 August 1854; Winnifrith, *A New Life of Charlotte Brontë*, 115.

8 LCB, 3:284, CB to EN, 9 August 1854; 288, CB to EN, 7 September 1854; 290, CB to MW, 7 September 1854.

9 LCB, 3:286, CB to MW, 22 August 1854; 288, CB to EN, 7 September 1854.

10 LCB, 3:286, CB to MW, 22 August 1854.

11 LCB, 3:290, CB to MW, 19 September 1854; 306–7, CB to EN, 7 December 1854; 290, CB to MW, 19 September 1854.

12 Smith, Margaret, "New Light on Mr. Nicholls," BST, 19:3:102.

13 Peters, 384; Fraser, "A Strange Plant: Charlotte Brontë's Friendship With Mrs. Gaskell," BST, 19:8:353; LCB, 3:252, CB to GS, 25 April 1854; Ward, introduction to *Villette* (London, 1899 ed.), xxxiii, xxxv.

14 Reid, *The Memoirs of Sir Thomas Wemyss Reid*, 239–40.

15 Shorter, *The Brontës: Life and Letters* 2:366; ABN to Mrs Humphry Ward, 28 November 1899, cited in Gérin, 554.

16 L and D, 393.

17 LCB, 3:240, CB to EN, 11 April 1854; 288, 7 September 1854; 290, 19 September 1854; 293–4, CB to EN, 11 October 1854.

18 C and P, 347, ECG to GS, 4 June 1855.

19 LCB, 3:293, CB to EN, 11 October 1854; 295, CB to EN, 20 October 1854.

20 LCB, 3:296–7, CB to EN, 31 October 1854.

21 LCB, 3:297, EN to ABN, 7 November 1854; 298, CB to EN, 7 November 1854; 299 n. 3.

22 LCB, 3:287, CB to MW, 22 August 1854.

23 JB, 445.

24 LCB, 2:366, CB to EN, 19 March 1850; 354, CB to EN, 11 March 1850; Smith, Frank, 226.

25 LCB, 3:301, CB to MW, 15 November 1854; 312, CB to EN, 26 December 1854; EN to GS, 28 March [n.y. but probably 1860], File no. 2, Smith, Elder Archives, John Murray, publishers.

26 LCB, 3:304, CB to EN, 29 November 1854; 306 CB to EN, 7 December 1854.

27 LCB, 3:306, CB to EN, 7 December 1854; 318, CB to EN, 19 January 1854; 303, CB to EN, 21 November 1854.

28 Warwick, 156; LCB, 3:321, CB to Amelia Taylor, 21 January 1855.

29 LCB, 3:319, CB to EN, 19 January 1855; for the correspondence of CB to EN, Amelia Taylor, and Laetitia Wheelwright, and ABN to EN, 19 January to end of February 1855, 319–27 (319, CB to EN, 10 January 1855; 322, ABN to EN, 29 January 1855; 323, ABN to EN, 1 February

1855; 327, CB to AT, late February 1855; 325, CB to LW, 15 February 1855; 326, CB to EN, 21 February 1855; 327, CB to AT, late February 1855); *Life*, 399.

30 JB, 770.

31 LCB, 3:329, PB to EN, 30 March 1855; L and D, 452; Chadwick, 491.

32 *Life*, 400.

33 L and D, 477.

34 JB, 967, n. 96; LCB, 3:324, ABN to EN, 14 February 1855; *The Cornhill Magazine*, 1, January-June 1860; JB, 772 and 967, n. 96 in which Barker has summarized the diagnostic literature.

CHAPTER FIVE

1 *Daily News*, April 1855.

2 Hoppin, 235–6.

3 JB, 778.

4 Arnold, 283.

5 C and P, 303, ECG to Geraldine E. Jewsbury, 21 July 1854.

6 C and P, 343–4, ECG to John Greenwood, after 5 May 1855; 349, ECG to GS 18 June 1855.

7 JB, 779.

8 C and P, 124–5, ECG to Catherine Winkworth, 25 August 1850.

9 W and S, 4:189–90, EN to ABN 6 June 1855; ABN to EN, 11 June 1855.

10 W and S, 4:190 PB to ECG, 16 June 1855; 191, ABN to EN, 24 July 1855.

11 W and S, 4:190–1, PB to ECG, 16 June [misdated 16 July], and ABN to EN, 24 July 1855; C and P, 347, ECG to George Smith, 4 June 1855.

12 C and P, 363, ECG to Marianne Gaskell, 27 July 1855; 361, ECG to EN, 24 July 1855.

13 EN to GS, 19 January 1869, cited in LG, 322.

14 W and S, 4:191, ABN to EN, 24 July 1855.

15 Barker, Juliet, "Saintliness, Treason and Plot: The Writing of Mrs Gaskell's *Life of Charlotte Brontë*," BST, 21:4:101–15; C and P, 372, ECG to Margaret Wooler, 12 November 1855; 874, ECG to EN, 3 November 1855; JB, 787; Gérin, Winifred, introduction to the Folio Society edition of the *Life*, 17.

16 W and S, 4:197, ABN to EN, 24 December 1855; BST, 8:43:97, PB to ECG, 23 January 1856; W and S, 4:201–3, ECG to EN, 9 July 1856; 204–5, EN to ECG, July 1856; C and P, 393, ECG to GS, 9 July 1856.

17 C and P, 398, ECG to GS, ?25 July 1856; 409, ECG to Emily Shaen, 7 and 8 September 1856; LCB, 3:481, CB to EN, 26 August 1850.

18 I owe this to Julia Elton, Sir Abraham's great-granddaughter.

19 C and P, 400, ECG to GS, 30 July 1856; 401, ECG to Emily Shaen, 7 and 8 September, 1856; Smith, Margaret, "New Light on Mr. Nicholls," BST, 19:3:102; Smith, Margaret and Rosengarten, Herbert, xxxi; Arthur's letters to George Smith concerning *The Professor* are found in File no. 8 of the Smith, Elder Archives, John Murray, publishers.

20 C and P, 405, ECG to GS, 15 August 1856; 425, ECG to GS, 11 December 1856; 439, ECG to W.S. Williams, 19 January 1857.

21 EN to GS, 1 June (n.y. but probably 1860), File no. 2, Smith, Elder Archives, John Murray, publishers.

22 C and P, 420, ECG to GS, 15 November 1856; 422, ECG to GS, 22 November 1856; *Life*, xxvii, 371 and 392.

23 JB, 794–5; C and P, 423, ECG to GS, 6 December 1856; ABN to GS, 28 November, 1 and 3 December 1856, File no. 8, Smith, Elder Archives, John Murray, publishers.

24 C and P, 425, ECG to GS, 11 December 1856; 434, ECG to GS, 29 December 1856.

25 W and S, 4:221, PB to ECG, 2 April 1857; *Christian Remembrancer*, July 1857, reprinted in Allott, 364; ABN to GS, 2 April 1857, File no. 8, Smith Elder Archive, John Murray, publishers.

26 ABN to GS, 23 May 1857, File no. 8, Smith, Elder Archive, John Murray, publishers; *Life*, 7; W and S, 4:215, EN to ECG, 16 April 1859.

27 W and S, 4:223, William Shaen to Messrs Newton and Robinson, 26 May 1857; JB, 801, citing ABN to GS, 23 May 1867, File no. 8, Smith, Elder Archive, John Murray, publishers.

28 Most of the Cowan Bridge School correspondence is reproduced in Appendix I of W and S, 4:297–314.

29 C and P, 483, ECG to GS, 26 November 1857; *Bradford Observer*, 13 and 20 August 1857; PB to ECG, 31 August 1857, cited in JB, 804; BST, 12:63:200, PB to Dearden, 21 August 1857; L and D, 512–13.

30 Martineau, *Autobiography*, 2:355–6; LCB, 2:574, CB to James Taylor, 11 February 1851; 3:110, CB to HM, 21 January 1853; 117, HM to CB, early February, 1853, n.1; 118, CB to HM, ?February, 1853.

31 LCB, 3:111, CB to Margaret Wooler, 27 January 1853; 112, n. 6.

32 PB to ECG, 9 September 1857, cited in JB, 806; L and D, 514 has different wording.

33 The excised sections of the first and second editions, and the additions to the third edition are both included and identified in the 1971 Folio Society edition of the *Life*, edited by Winifred Gérin. The 1908 Everyman's Library edition, which I have used, follows the original, unexpurgated first and second editions of 1857.

34 This exchange between Patrick and Arthur on one side and Miss Martineau on the other is preserved in the Harriet Martineau Collection, University of Birmingham. Twelve letters survive: HM 89–98, 100 and 105.

35 LCB, 3:112, n. 6. The exchange in n. 34 continues.

36 Saunders, 142.

37 The Shakespeare Head version (W and S, 4:41), which Martineau reconstructed from memory, reads: "As for the other side of the question, which you so desire to know, I have but one thing to say; but it is not a small one. I do not like the love, either the kind or the degree of it; and its prevalence in the book, and the effect on the action of it, help to explain the passages in the reviews which you consulted me about, and seem to afford *some* foundation for the criticisms they offered." The version which Arthur sent Martineau ("MS by AB Nicholls," Birmingham University Library, Martineau Collection, reproduced in LCB, 3:117) reads: "What faults there are, I think grave: but the merits are downright wonderful – As for the faults – I do deeply regret the reasons given to suppose your mind full of the subject of one passion – love – I think there is unconscionably too much of it (giving an untrue picture of life) &, speaking with the frankness you desire, *I do not like its kind – I anticipate a renewal of the sort of objection which you mentioned to me as inexplicable to you, the first evening we met, and this time I think it will not be wholly unfounded.*" The italicized section is the part red-inked by Charlotte.

38 This may refer to the last Church of Ireland bishop of Tuam, le Poer Trench, who tried to restrict the clergy in his diocese to those who could speak Irish so that they might more effectively proselytize the peasantry.

39 C and P, 482, ECG to HM, 24 November 1857.

40 BST, 16:83:199–202, "Severe to the Point of Injustice: Two Letters by Harriet Martineau Purchased."

41 ABN to CKS, 21 January 1896, Brotherton Collection, Leeds University Library.

42 Martineau, *Autobiography*, 2:351; Smith, Margaret, "'A Warlike Correspondence': More Letters from Harriet Martineau," BST, 18:5:369.

43 ABN to GS, 23 May 1857, File no. 8, Smith, Elder Archive, John Murray, publishers; Reid, *Charlotte Brontë: A Monograph*, 194–5; Akroyd, 52–4; W and S, 4: 229, Mary Taylor to EN, 28 January 1858.

44 C and P, 496 and 577, ECG to GS, 17 March 1858 and 17 October 1859.

45 LG, 312.

46 ABN to GS, 11 and 14 October 1859, File no. 8, Smith, Elder Archive, John Murray, publishers. Alexander, 10; Neufeldt, passim; ABN to GS, 11 November 1859 (as above).

47 JB, 811.

48 L and D, 521.

49 C and P, 641–2; ECG to W.S. Williams, 20 December 1860; W and S, 4:242, Meta Gaskell to Emily Shaen, 6 November 1860.

50 W and S, 4:242.

51 C and P, 641–2, ECG to W.S. Williams, 20 December 1860; W and S, 4:241, Meta Gaskell to Emily Shaen, 6 November 1860.

52 JB, 785; ABN to GS, 25 June 1861, File no. 8, Smith, Elder Archives, John Murray, publishers; JB, 821.

53 LCB, 3:95, n. 2; *Halifax Guardian*, 10 August 1861, cited in JB, 822.

54 *Bradford Observer*, 26 September 1861.

55 For a detailed history of these confrontations see L and D, 11.

56 *Bradford Observer*, 26 September 1861; *Bradford Review*, 12 October 1861; JB, 818, 822; L and D, 519.

57 L and D, 529; JB, 821, 823.

58 L and D, 530; Hale, 128–9; Edgerley, 96; Baumber, 109.

59 Chadwick, 468–9.

60 Edgerley, 99–100; J. Copley, "An Early Visitor to Haworth," BST, 16–17:83:220.

61 Cautley; Winnifrith, "Winter-Day at Haworth."

62 JB, 823; BST, 26:1:75–78.

63 *Bradford Observer*, 26 September and 10 October 1861; *Bradford Review*, 12 October 1861.

64 JB, 823; L and D, Chapter 11, passim; Trollope, A., *John Caldigate* (1878–9, Oxford rpt. 1945), 408.

65 Hutton, Joanna, "The Sale at Haworth Parsonage on October 1st and 2nd, 1861," BST, 14:75:46–49; L and D, 535. Both state that Martha made her first visit to Banagher in 1862, but they also mention a letter from

ABN to John Greenwood, dated 25 November 1861, in which he indicates that Martha was already at Banagher.

CHAPTER SIX

1 Adamson, Philip, 56–60.
2 BST, 26:1:75–8, "Letter to Mr. Sutcliffe," 5 November 1861.
3 L and D, 530; BST, 26:1:75–8, "Letter to Mr. Sutcliffe."
4 Akenson, D.H., *The Church of Ireland: Ecclesiastical Reform and Revolution, 1800–1885*, 316–17.
5 Bell, H.K., 42–6.
6 Woolf, Leonard, 92.
7 Trodd, 40, 56–7, 101–2.
8 Bell, F.E. (15–16).
9 This account of Arthur's relationship to Martha Brown is based on his letters to her in ABN/MARTHA (5 February 1863; 7 September 1864; 14 January 1868; 17 February 1868; 23 May 1877; 8 May 1866); and on Dinsdale, Ann, "Martha Brown: Life After the Brontës," BST, 24:1:97–100.
10 ABN/MARTHA (16 January 1868; 31 May 1870; 19 July 1870); Foley, 293.
11 ABN/MARTHA (7 September 1864; 7 July 1866; 2 March 1968; 27 April 1868; 12 December 1863); L and D, 530.
12 Bell, H.K., 45; ABN/MARTHA (10 September 1877; 29 May 1878).
13 *Freeman's Journal*, 7–30 March 1920; *Irish Times*, 27–31 March 1920; Forester, 138; Coogan, 104, 188.
14 Bell, F.E., *A Hundred Years of Life*, 16.
15 Adamson, Philip, 58–9; Gallop, 298–9.
16 Bell, F.E.
17 Chadwick, 467; Gallop, 298–9; Bell, F.E., 348; F.E. Bell to Philip Adamson, 18 March 1955, in the author's possession; Sturgis; BST, 15:77:169, Report of Rosaleen A. Knight, secretary of the Irish Section of The Brontë Society, 1967.
18 Bell, H.K., 44.
19 Raymond, 374; Lane, 270–1.

CHAPTER SEVEN

1 W and S, 4:314, from *The Halifax Guardian* 8 August 1857; Bell, H.K., 43, 45; Bell, F.E., "Charlotte Brontë's Irish Honeymoon," 52.

2 EN to GS, 1 June [n.y. but probably 1860], File no. 2, Smith Elder Archives, John Murray, publishers; LCB, 1:33. In what follows I have relied heavily on the excellent account of the history of the letters in LCB 1:27–71.

3 W and S, 4:256, EN to GS, 27 February 1869.

4 W and S, 4:191, ABN to EN, 24 July 1855.

5 W and S, 4:250, Constanin Heger to EN, 7 September 1863 (translation).

6 W and S, 4:252, EN to GS, 20 February 1868; 252, GS to EN, 18 January 1869.

7 W and S, 4:254, GS to EN, 12 February 1869.

8 W and S, 4:254–5, EN to GS, 20 February 1869; 255, GS to EN, 24 February 1869.

9 W and S, 4; 256, EN to GS, 27 February 1869; 251, editors' comment.

10 Bellamy, BST, 21:7:278; LCB, 1:40; LCB, 3:94–5, CB to EN, 18 December 1852; Reid, *Memoirs of Sir Thomas Wemyss Reid*, 229–39; Reid, *Charlotte Brontë: A Monograph*, 59–62.

11 Reid, *Charlotte Brontë: A Monograph*, 179, 185.

12 W and S, 4:265, GS to EN, 10 May 1878.

13 W and S, 4:270, Biddell to EN, 27 March 1882; Turner, 154–62; Baumber; Holgate; ABN to unknown, 12 July 1898, Fales Library, New York University.

14 LCB, 1, A. Birrell to EN, 2 December 1889, 49–50.

15 Tillotson, BST, 19:1:9.

16 LCB, 1:57; Shorter, *The Brontës and Their Circle*, 28; Partington, 114; Tillotson.

17 Shorter, *The Brontës and Their Circle*, 29.

18 Bullock, ed., in Shorter *C.K.S.: An Autobiography*, xiv.

19 Shorter, "Introduction" to *Charlotte Brontë: The Four Wishes.*

20 Ibid.

21 *Yorkshire Post*, 12 September 1894.

22 This (26 April 1895) and the following quotations from Arthur's letters to Shorter are from a transcript of the originals in the Brotherton Collection, Leeds University Library.

23 LCB, 2:640, CB to PB, 17 June 1851. The bracketed description of William Morgan is from JB, 627. The ABN letters to CKS continue.

24 Shorter, *The Brontës and Their Circle*, 30; BST, 1:4:28, anon. review of C.K. Shorter, *Charlotte Brontë and Her Circle*; LCB, 1:58–9; Partington, 110; Bell, H.K.; Ratchford, 471, 478, 484.

25 Shorter, *The Brontës and Their Circle*, 476; Shorter, *The Brontës: Life and Letters*, 2, 366.

26 ABN to CKS, 17 February and 17 April 1896 in Brotherton Collection, Leeds University Library; Bell, F.E. to J.D. Adamson, n.d., in the author's possession.

27 Alexander and Sellars, 207–312; Christine Alexander, "Arthur Bell Nicholls and the Adamson Saga: New Discoveries of Brontë Memorabilia," BST, 31:194–209.

28 Bell, H.K., 43–4; Bell, F.E., "Charlotte Brontë's Irish Honeymoon," 54. For a summary of the evidence, pro and con, concerning the authenticity of the recently discovered photographs, see the exchange between Juliet Barker, Margaret Smith and Audrey Hall, BST, 22:138–44. Alexander and Sellars, 307–12, provide a full account of the history of these portraits.

EPILOGUE

1 Bell, H.K., 45; Bell, F.E., 16–17; Mary Anna Nicholls to Mary Anderson, 12 September 1901, in the author's possession; Arthur J. Bell to his mother, Emma Stokes Bell, 9 June 1902, in the author's possession; Alan J. Adamson to his mother, Harriet Bell Adamson, 30 June 1902, in the author's possession; Kathleen Landon to Marjorie Gallop, n.d., but probably 1954; newspaper [unidentified] clipping, n.d. but probably 1902, from "Our Birr correspondent", in the possession of Nigel Gallop.

2 Arthur J. Bell to Emma Stokes Bell, 9 June 1902; op. cit.; BST, 215:15:234, Mary Bell Nicholls to W.T. Field, cited in the *Yorkshire Daily Observer.*

3 Bell, H.K., 46; Sturgis; Edgerley; Lane, 271; Wroot, 16.

4 Adamson, J.D., hand-written *aide mémoire* in possession of the author; Raymond, 374; Frances E. Bell to Philip Adamson, 18 March 1955, in the author's possession.

5 JB, 472.

6 Bell, Brigadier-General Arthur H., quoted in Herbert Adamson's memorandum (1927) of a conversation with his father, A.J. Adamson, in the author's possession.

Bibliography

Adamson, Philip. *The Adamson Saga*. Edmonton, Alberta, 1961.

Adamson, William Agar. *Salmon Fishing in Canada*. London, 1860.

Akenson, D.H. *The Irish Educational Experiment*. London, 1970.

– *The Church of Ireland: Ecclesiastical Reform and Revolution, 1800–1885*. New Haven, 1971.

Akroyd, Thomas, "A Day at Haworth: A Reminiscence by The Rev. Thomas Akroyd," Brontë Society, *Transactions*, 19:1:49–54.

Alexander, Christine. *A Bibliography of the Manuscripts of Charlotte Brontë*. n.p. 1982.

– "Arthur Bell Nicholls and the Adamson Saga: New Discoveries of Brontë Memorabilia," Brontë Society, *Transactions*, 31:194–209.

– and Jane Sellars. *The Art of the Brontës*. Cambridge, 1995.

Allott, Miriam, ed. *The Brontës: the Critical Heritage*. London, 1974.

Banks, Lynne Reid. *Dark Quartet: the Story of the Brontës*. London, 1976.

Barker, Juliet. "Subdued Expectations: Charlotte Brontë's Marriage Settlement," Brontë Society, *Transactions*, 19:33–9.

– "Saintliness, Treason and Plot: The Writing of Mrs. Gaskell's Life of Charlotte Brontë," Brontë Society, *Transactions*, 21:4:101–15.

– *The Brontës*. London, 1995.

Baumber, Michael. "That 'Vandal' Wade: the Reverend John Wade and the Demolition of the Brontë Church," Brontë Society, *Transactions*, 22:109.

Bell, F.E. "Charlotte Brontë's Irish Honeymoon," *The Irish Digest*, December 1895, 52.

– *A Hundred Years of Life*, n.p. n.d. (in author's possession).

– "The Reverend Arthur Bell Nicholls," Brontë Society, *Transactions*, 15:4:348.

Bell, H.K. "Charlotte Brontë's Husband: His Later Life and Surroundings," *The Cornhill Magazine*, January 1927.

Bellamy, Joan. "Mary Taylor, Ellen Nussey and Brontë Biography," Brontë Society, *Transactions*, 21:7:278.

Blood, Sir Bindon. *Four Score Years and Ten: Sir Bindon Blood's Reminiscences*. London, 1933.

The Book of Trinity College, Dublin. Belfast, 1892.

Brontë, Charlotte. *Shirley*. Herbert Rosengarten and Margaret Smith eds. Oxford, 1979.

Brontë Society. *Transactions*. Haworth, 1895–.

Brotherton Collection, Leeds University Library. Exchange of Letters between Harriet Martineau, Patrick Brontë and Arthur Bell Nicholls. File HM 89–98, 100 and 105.

Burtchaell, G.D., and T.U. Sadleir. *Alumni Dublinenses*. Dublin, 1935.

Casey, Christine, and Alistair Rowan. *North Leinster*. London, 1993.

Cautley, C. Holmes. "Old Haworth Folk Who Knew the Brontës," *The Cornhill Magazine*, July 1910, 76–84.

Chadwick, Esther Alice. *In the Footsteps of the Brontës*. London, 1914.

Chapple, J.A.V., and Arthur Pollard, eds. *Letters of Mrs Gaskell*. Manchester, 1966.

Cochrane, Margaret and Robert. *My Dear Boy: the Life of Arthur Bell Nicholls*. Beverley, 1999.

Coogan, Tim Pat. *Michael Collins*. London, 1991.

Cooke, Thomas Lalor. *The Early History of the Town of Birr*. Dublin, 1875.

Copley, J. "An Early Visitor to Haworth," Brontë Society, *Transactions*, 16–17:83:220.

Craig, Maurice. *Classic Irish Houses of the Middle Size*. London, 1979.

Crowther, M.A. *Church Embattled: Religious Controversy in Mid-Victorian England*. Newton Abbot, 1970.

Dinsdale, Ann. "Martha Brown: Life After the Brontës," Brontë Society, *Transactions*, 24:1:97–100.

Dixon, W. Macneile, *Trinity College Dublin*. London, 1902.

Edgerley, C. Mabel. "The Rev. Arthur Bell Nicholls," Brontë Society, *Transactions*, 10:52.

Foley, T.P. "John Elliot Cairnes' Visit to Haworth Parsonage," Brontë Society, *Transactions*, 18:94:292–4.

Forester, Margery. *Michael Collins – The Lost Leader*. London, 1972.

Fraser, Rebecca. *Charlotte Brontë*. London, 1988.

– "A Strange Plant: Charlotte Brontë's Friendship with Mrs Gaskell," Brontë Society, *Transactions*, 19:8:353.

Gallop, Marjorie. "Charlotte Brontë's Husband: Sidelights from a Family Album," Brontë Society, *Transactions*, 12:64:298–9.

Gaskell, Elizabeth Cleghorn. *The Life of Charlotte Brontë*. London, 1908. rpt. 1971.

Gérin, Winifred. *Charlotte Brontë: The Evolution of Genius*. Oxford, 1967.

Great Britain: Parliamentary Papers.

Gordon, Lyndall. *Charlotte Brontë: a Passionate Life*. London, 1994.

Hale, Charles. "An American Visitor at Haworth: 1861," Brontë Society, *Transactions*, 15:77:128–9.

Healy, John. *History of the Diocese of Meath*, 2 vols. Dublin, 1908.

Holgate, Ivy. "A Pilgrim at Haworth – 1879," Brontë Society, *Transactions*, 14:71:29–37.

Holland, C.H., ed. *Trinity College Dublin and the Idea of a University*. Dublin, 1991.

Hopkins, Annette B. *The Father of the Brontës*. 1927. rpt. New York, 1968.

Hoppin, James H. *The Old Country: Its Scenery Art and People*. London, 1867.

Hutton, Joanna. "The Sale of Haworth Parsonage on October 1st and 2nd, 1861," Brontë Society, *Transactions*, 14:75:46–9.

Jones, M.G. *The Charity School Movement*. London, 1938.

Lane, Margaret. "Charlotte Brontë and Elizabeth Gaskell: the Fruitful Friendship," Brontë Society, *Transactions*, 17:89:270–1.

Lock, John, and W.T. Dixon. *A Man of Sorrow: The Life, Letters and Times of the Rev. Patrick Brontë*. London, 1965.

Martineau, Harriet. *Endowed Schools of Ireland*. London, 1859.

– *Autobiography*, 2 vols. London, 1877.

McDowell, R.B. *The Church of Ireland 1869–1969*. London, 1975.

– and D.A. Webb. *Trinity College Dublin, 1592–1952: an Academic History*. Cambridge, 1982.

Neufeldt, Victor A., ed. *The Poems of Charlotte Brontë: A New Text and Commentary*. New York, 1985.

Nicholls, Arthur Bell. 1861–1868. ABN/MARTHA. Letters to Martha Brown in Brontë Parsonage Museum.

– 1856–1867. Letters to George Smith in File No. 8, Smith, Elder Archive, John Murray, publishers.

– 1895–1902. Letters to Clement K. Shorter in Brotherton Collection, Leeds University Library.

– 1898. Letter to unknown, 12 July, in Fales Library, New York University.

– n.d. Commonplace Book in Brontë Parsonage Museum.

Nussey, Ellen. Letters to George Smith. File No. 2, Smith, Elder Archives, John Murray, publishers.

Partington, Wilfred. *Thomas J. Wise in the Original Cloth.* London, 1946.

Peters, Margot. *Unquiet Soul.* London, 1975.

Pope Hennessy, James. *Anthony Trollope.* London, 1973.

Quane, Michael. "Banagher Royal School," *North Munster Antiquarian Journal.* vol. 10:2, 1967.

Ratchford, Fannie E., ed. *Letters of Thomas J. Wise to John Henry Wrenn: A Further Enquiry into the Guilt of Certain Nineteenth-Century Forgers.* New York, 1944.

Raymond, Ernest. "Notes on Mr Nicholls and Whitcross," Brontë Society, *Transactions,* 11:60:374.

Reid, Sir Thomas Wemyss. *Charlotte Brontë: A Monograph.* London, 1877.

– *Memoirs of Sir Thomas Wemyss Reid.* Stuart J. Reid, ed. London, 1895.

Ross, Alexander. *Memoir of the Late Alexander Ross, A.M.* London, 1854.

Saunders, Valerie. *Harriet Martineau: Selected Letters.* Oxford, 1990.

Shaen, Margaret, ed. *Memorials of Two Sisters: Susannah and Catherine Winkworth.* London, 1908.

Shorter, Clement K. *Charlotte Brontë & Her Circle.* London, 1896.

– *The Brontës: Life and Letters,* 2 vols. London, 1908. rpt. New York, 1969.

– *The Brontës and Their Circle.* London 1914. rpt. New York, 1970.

– *Introduction to Charlotte Brontë: The Four Wishes.* Private edition of 20 copies. London, 1918.

– *C.K.S.: An Autobiography.* J.M. Bulloch, ed. London, 1927.

Smith, Frank. *The Life and Work of Sir James Kay-Shuttleworth.* London, 1923.

Smith, Margaret. "'A Warlike Correspondence': More Letters from Harriet Martineau," Brontë Society, *Transactions,* 18:5:396.

– ed. *The Letters of Charlotte Brontë,* vols. 1 (1829–47), 2 (1848- 51), 3(1852–55). Oxford, 1995, 2000, 2004.

– "New Light on Mr Nicholls," Brontë Society, *Transactions,* 19:3:102.

Smith, Margaret, and Herbert Rosengarten. "Introduction" to *The Professor.* Oxford, Clarendon edition, 1987.

Stokes, Gabriel. *A Report on the Case of the Rev. Arthur Smith Adamson, Against the Inhabitants of Grange Gorman.* Dublin, 1832.

Sturgis, Ethel Grace. "Charlotte Brontë's Husband," unpublished manuscript in author's possession.

Tillotson, Kathleen. "Back to the Beginning of this Century," Brontë Society, *Transactions*, 19:1:9.

Trodd, Valentine. *Midlands: Chronicles of Midland Parish.* Banagher, 1994.

Trollope, Anthony. *John Caldigate.* Oxford. rpt. 1945.

Turner, J. Horsfall. *Haworth, Past and Present.* Brighouse, 1879.

Wakefield, Edward. *An Account of Ireland.* London, 1812.

Ward, Mrs. Humphry. "Introduction" to *Villette.* London, 1899.

Warwick, David. "Squire and 'She Authors': Sir James Kay-Shuttleworth, Charlotte Brontë and Elizabeth Gaskell," Brontë Society, *Transactions*, 23:2:98.

Wilks, Brian. *Charlotte in Love: the Courtship and Marriage of Charlotte Brontë.* London, 1998.

– "The State of Haworth Churchyard: A Letter from the Rev. John Wade to the Church Commissioners 1866: 'The Abating of Fearful Nuisances'.

Wilson, T.G. *Victorian Doctor: Being the Life of Sir William Wilde.* London, 1942.

Winnifrith, Tom. *The Brontës and their Background.* London, 1973.

– *A New Life of Charlotte Brontë.* London, 1988.

– "Winter-Day at Haworth," *Chamber's Journal*, 4th ser., no. 217, 22 February 1968.

Wise, T.J., and J.A. Symington, eds. *The Lives, Friendships and Correspondence of the Brontë Family*, 4 vols. Oxford, 1933.

Woolf, Leonard, *Beginning Again.* London, 1963.

Wroot, H.E. "The Late Rev. A.B. Nicholls," Brontë Society, *Transactions*, 4:16:16.

Index